CLIMBING BACK

CLIMBING
BACK

By
Mark Wellman
and John Flinn

A Division of WRS Group, Inc.
Waco, Texas

First published in the United States of America in 1992 by WRS Publishing,
A Division of WRS Group, Inc., 701 N. New Road, Waco, Texas 76710
Design by Jean Norwood and Kenneth Turbeville

Library of Congress Cataloging-in-Publication Data

Wellman, Mark (Mark Reid), 1960–
    Climbing Back / by Mark Wellman and John Flinn.
        p.   cm.
    ISBN 0-941539-88-1 : $19.95
    1. Wellman, Mark (Mark Reid), 1960–   . 2. Mountaineers—United
States—Biography. 3. Paraplegics—United States—Biography.
4. Mountaineering—California—El Capitan. I. Flinn, John (John
Gordon), 1956–   . II. Title.
GV199.92.W4W45 1992
796.5'22'092—dc20
    [B]   92-20936
                                                                CIP

For Mike Corbett and Mark Sutherland

TABLE OF CONTENTS

ACKNOWLEDGMENTS

▼

Mark Wellman: I'd like to thank the adaptive physical education instructors at De Anza College for making me strong; John Nicholas and Tom "Smitty" Smith at West Valley College for turning me into a ranger; Paulette Irving, my best buddy in many ways, who rounded up the pictures in this book and made sure I was where I was supposed to be; and my family for their support.

John Flinn: I'm grateful to Terri Johnson and Margaret Leary, my editors at WRS Publishing, for wielding their editing pencils like surgical scalpels and not blunt instruments; Mike Corbett, for his generous time and climbing lessons; Sally Glynn, for her hospitality and persuasion; and most of all my wife, Jeri Flinn, for her love and encouragement and for being my first and best editor.

FOREWORD

When I heard the news that a paraplegic climber was
going to scale Yosemite's legendary El Capitan, I felt a
sense of real pride. As one of America's twenty million
persons with disabilities, I knew that Mark Wellman's
courageous mission would once again show the world
that *disabled* does not mean *unable*. Since then, Mark
Wellman has done much, much more to prove this
important fact of life. Whether it is his park ranger job,
or rock climbing, skiing, tennis, or writing this book,
Mark is helping us tear down the barriers that for too
long have stood in the way of persons with disabilities.

Beyond our own physical disabilities, Mark and I
have much in common, including the mountains. As a
young man, I was also deeply involved in athletics,
always trying to push myself to the limit on the football
field, on the basketball court or on the track. After some
success at the high school level, I earned a scholarship
to the University of Kansas to play basketball. It was a
dream come true. I was standing on top of the mountain.
Like Mark, I had no idea I was headed for a life-
threatening fall.

It began on December 7, 1941, with the Japanese
sneak attack on Pearl Harbor. I left college, enlisted in
the Army and eventually found myself on a troop ship
headed for Italy. In one of life's true ironies, a young
man from the plains of Kansas was about to command
a platoon of elite skiers and mountaineers, members of
the crack Tenth Mountain Division.

On April 14, 1945, during fierce combat in the rugged
mountains of northern Italy, my life changed forever. I
was hit by German machine gun and mortar fire. Left
alone on the battlefield, I drifted in and out of

consciousness for what seemed like an eternity, unable to move any of my limbs. I must say, reading Mark Wellman's gripping description of his twenty-four hours of hell on a windswept mountain ledge brought back memories about my own experience with pain, loneliness, and shattered dreams.

But none of these obstacles would stand in the way of Mark Wellman's ultimate triumph, his stunning comeback to beat the odds, and to eventually beat some of the toughest mountaineering challenges America has to offer.

I will never forget the day Mark reached the summit of El Capitan, a day when CNN helped bring this historic event to television screens around the world, including the TV in my office on Capitol Hill.

Shortly after Mark and his indispensable friend Mike Corbett finished their grueling eight-day, thirty-five-hundred-foot climb, the full U.S. Senate was voting on my resolution to commend them for "their extraordinary feat of bravery... setting an outstanding example for all Americans and persons with disabilities." The Senate isn't known for agreeing on much, but on this issue, it was unanimous.

For Mark, one challenge is never enough—two years after conquering El Capitan, he was back in Yosemite, this time pulling himself up the sheer face of the awesome Half Dome, a harrowing journey to the summit that took thirteen days. As usual, Mark made it, but only after completing thirteen days of thousands and thousands of pull-ups.

Climbing Back is a book for everyone. It is an inspirational story that will touch you, lift your spirits and convince you that the word "never" is something that doesn't apply to the truly determined and dedicated.

No doubt about it, Mark Wellman's courageous story stands tall as a role model—not just for Americans with disabilities, but for all Americans. It's a story about a man whose heart is as big as the mountains he loves.

Read about Mark Wellman and then tell someone you know: *Disabled* does not mean *unable*.

Senate Republican Leader, Bob Dole

ALONE ON THE MOUNTAIN

There was no time to linger on the summit.

Already, the sun was starting to sink low in the western sky. Night would be falling soon, and we were a long way from base camp. It was much too late in the day to be on a mountaintop, and we knew it. We had gotten a late start, we had pushed on toward the top when we should have turned back, and now we faced a nightmarish descent in the darkness.

Still, after coming this far, I had to take a moment to savor what we had accomplished. As I looked around, the whole world seemed to fall away beneath my feet. We were standing atop the highest summit in the area, which jutted up like the steeple of a magnificent granite cathedral. Above us was nothing but the California sky. It was deep blue, almost violet. To the north and south, as far as I could see, stretched the jagged granite crests of the Sierra Nevada—the mountains John Muir called "Range of Light." Dozens of summits glowed golden in the late afternoon sun. I began to pick out individual peaks I'd climbed, and each one brought back memories of past adventures.

Ever since I was a little boy, I'd been on a quest to discover the secrets these mountains held. I had grown up here, in many ways, amid the majestic pine forests, the soaring rock faces and the sparkling snowfields. The times I had spent struggling toward their summits while caressing sun-warmed granite had been the best and most intensely lived of my life.

Memories came rushing back of sweaty marches up dust-choked trails, of campsites near the shores of pristine sapphire lakes, of stiff fingers fumbling with boot laces in the pre-dawn darkness, of nimble dances up narrow granite staircases, of short-lived, glorious moments atop airy pinnacles, of triumphs over gravity and exhaustion and self-doubt.

The sight of purple shadows lengthening in the valleys below jolted me back to the present.

"Let's get out of here," said my partner, Peter Enzminger. "I'm nervous about this."

There was one last summit ritual to perform. We hunted around in the rocks until we found the metal box containing the summit register. Then we added our names to the list of those who had climbed the 13,075-foot peak called Seven Gables. We penciled in the date: August 19, 1982.

I added the message I always left in the registers: "Hey kids! It's the Wells again. Peak #48. See ya."

Seven Gables was the forty-eighth I'd climbed in the Sierra Nevada range. It would be the last I'd ever climb with my own legs.

"Which way down?" I asked.

"I don't like the route we came up," said Peter. "That ridge would take hours to descend, and I don't want to be on it after dark."

"How about if we head down the west face?" I said. "It's less direct, but the going looks a lot easier."

"Fine," said Peter. "Let's go."

I went first, hopping down from rock to rock. Usually I was the more cautious of the two of us, but for some reason I was now feeling a little cocky, almost lackadaisical. As I descended, I scanned the maze-like puzzle of ledges and chutes below for a reasonable passage through the sheer cliffs that dropped away for hundreds of feet. We were climbing without a rope because we hadn't brought one. But I moved quickly with the confidence of a mountain goat. Just twenty-two years old, I had already climbed most of the major mountains in this range.

Peter hung back. I could tell from the tentative way he was moving that he was spooked. He had every right to be. We were both exhausted after the long climb, and we had lots of dangerous terrain to cover before we'd be safely back on flat ground. Daylight was fading fast. Already we were in the shadows, and I could feel the first chill of evening.

What's more, the descent was turning out to be trickier than we'd thought. From above it had looked like an easy scramble that would have us off the steep upper mountain by dark. Now, however, ledges slanted the wrong way, vertical headwalls appeared out of nowhere, and the rock crumbled beneath our boots.

We didn't have the luxury of taking our time. We had stupidly left our flashlights behind, and we simply had to make the most of what little light was left. I pushed ahead, picking my way down a rocky gully. The rock was steep, and I should have been facing into it and carefully testing each foothold. But to save time I was facing away from the mountainside, descending it like a staircase and counting on my balance and intuition for safety.

My mind began to race ahead. I started to work out the problem of finding our way around the mountain's flank and back to base camp in the dark. I thought about how good dinner was going to taste. Even those sawdust-like, freeze-dried dinners can seem like gourmet meals after an invigorating day in the mountains. I imagined how comforting it would feel to slide into a snugly warm goose-down sleeping bag after such a long and exhausting climb.

I was thinking about everything, it seemed, except what my feet were doing.

It happened so quickly I didn't have time to be scared. One moment I was hopping onto a sloping ledge covered with loose rocks. The next I was pitching crazily forward, tumbling head over heels into a somersault. I landed on my back with a sickening cra-a-a-ack, and continued bouncing down the rocks.

"*Grab something!*" I told myself. I reached out, but it was all happening too fast. My hands glanced off the rocks as the world cartwheeled wildly around me. I flipped over again and again, cracking my shoulder and my back on the rocks.

Everything seemed to be happening in slow motion, yet at the same time too quickly for me to react. I was helpless to stop myself; I kept sliding and bouncing down the gully, shredding my skin on the rough granite.

"This is it," I said to myself. "*This is what it's like to die.*"

My head smacked into one rock outcrop; another caught me in the ribs. Then I was falling through the air, down a vertical headwall. I crashed into rocks at the bottom and kept tumbling and rolling down the steep mountainside.

I honestly don't know what stopped me. Certainly, it was nothing I did. After about a hundred feet of bouncing like a pinball down the rocky chute, my body finally came to rest on a flat ledge. If I had missed it, I probably would have kept going all the way to the bottom, another thousand feet below.

I lay there, gasping for breath. My heart pounded as if it were going to burst out of my chest. I was in a world of hurt. My clothes were shredded, my body covered with gashes and gravel. Reaching slowly behind my head, I felt something warm and damp. I pulled my hand back and found it covered with blood. When I tried to take a deep breath, a sharp, jabbing pain exploded in my chest. I felt sick to my stomach, and chills racked my body.

The pain throbbing through my chest and arms was so severe that I didn't pay much attention to what I was feeling below my waist. I drifted in and out of a foggy, almost dream-like state. I vaguely remember calling out to Peter, yelling that I was hurt. The next thing I remember, Peter was by my side, examining my limbs for fractures, pressing against my wounds to stop the bleeding, and asking me about my condition.

He gently took off one of my boots and asked me to wiggle my toes. It hurt, but I was able to do it. This was good news. It meant I didn't have spinal cord damage— or so we thought.

"Jeez, Mark, I thought you were dead for sure," he said.

"I'm hurting, man," I said. "I'm hurting bad."

Afraid to move me, Peter tried to make me as comfortable as possible on the ledge by draping a pair of pants over my legs and a sweater over my upper body. I had been wearing shorts and a light shirt when I fell, and he knew I would need protection from the shock that always follows an accident like this.

There was no way I could get the pants on over my battered legs or the sweater on over my injured upper body. So Peter carefully tucked the edges of the clothing under me. That would have to do. Near my head he laid a canteen of water, a package of M&M's and an orange.

It seemed as though Peter was with me for only five minutes, but he had spent nearly two hours tending to my injuries and preparing me for what would come next.

"Hang tight," he said. "I'm going for help. It should be here first thing tomorrow."

Suddenly he was gone and I was alone on the ledge. It was very quiet.

Now that the initial shock of the fall had worn off, I

began to shake with fear. The sky above was no longer the brilliant blue it had been earlier. It was edging into twilight, and the temperature was falling quickly. I shivered on my airy perch.

When my mind was able to cut through the pain-induced fog, I had a frightening realization of just how serious my situation was. Night would soon be upon me, and I was going to have to fight for survival, alone and badly injured, at high altitude, in temperatures that would drop to well below freezing. I was at least twenty miles from the nearest road.

There was no point in worrying about the long-term future. I had to focus all my thoughts, all my willpower, on just staying alive through the long, shivering night. Already I could feel the chill starting to invade my body, sucking out the warmth.

Getting caught outdoors at night, particularly on a mountain, must rank as one of man's most primitive fears. To be stripped naked of all your comfort, shelter and security, and to be left fully exposed to the raw and awesome power of nature, is something humans have been trying to protect themselves from since caveman days. In all my years of camping and climbing mountains, the fear of being benighted had always propelled me back to the warm security of camp before dark—even if it meant taking some chances. I guess that's what had gotten me into the trouble I was in now.

Shapeless hours passed in a sluggish haze. I pressed up next to some large rocks, hoping they would still radiate a little of their daytime heat. Unfortunately, they, too, had grown cold. Night had fallen. Overhead, stars were shining icily in the dark sky, providing light but no comfort. A breeze started to whistle slowly across the mountainside, and soon I could feel its chill fingers passing over me, under me, and even through me, robbing my body of precious warmth.

The breeze slowly gained strength, turning into a howling arctic wind. My body shivered and my teeth chattered as I tried to fight off the piercing chill. As the cold bit deeper and deeper into my core, I felt very small, very helpless, and very alone.

My only connection with humanity was the blinking lights of commercial airliners passing overhead, twenty thousand feet above me on their way to San Francisco or Denver or Chicago. Inside their warm cabins, passengers were probably snuggled up in blankets and pillows, trying to get some sleep or watching the in-flight movie. Or maybe they were picking at their airline food and squirming in their cramped seats, grumbling at their discomfort. They were the human beings nearest to me, but they provided no comfort. They were in their world and I was in mine.

Suddenly a gust of wind worked its fingers underneath the clothes Peter had draped over me. They started to flap. In my numbed state I reacted slowly, and by the time my stiff arms could try to grasp for them, they were gone into the blackness. Now the last pathetic bit of shelter I had was gone. My legs were bare to the elements, my torso covered only by a thin shirt. As the devouring and numbing cold bit deeper, I began to fear for the first time that I would not live to see the sunrise.

How would death come? Would it be sharp and painful, or would it be a gentle easing into the void? Would it be like drifting off into a deep and restful sleep, or would my soul go out kicking and screaming, scraping its fingernails as it was dragged against its will out of the present world? And what would happen after that?

I had been raised in a deeply Presbyterian household, but it had been years since I had gone to church. Now, as I felt my life beginning to slip away, and as I lay exposed before the awesome power of nature and the heavens, it was impossible not to feel religious.

I began to think about God and hoped He would

watch out for me, however things turned out. I didn't know if He kept tabs on me on a day-to-day basis, but now I drew comfort from my faith that He cared. It was all I had left, and it helped me through my agony and loneliness. Somehow, I think, it gave me the will to keep fighting.

I drifted in and out of wakefulness as the minutes crept by like hours. Time lost all its meaning, and I seemed to be trapped forever in this hellish nightmare. It wasn't just the cold. I was still wracked with pain from my injuries. The slightest movement sent jolts of agony surging through me.

Just raising the canteen to my dry lips was a painful struggle. I knew my body needed fuel to try to ward off the cold, so I fumbled for the orange and slowly brought it to my mouth. I tried to peel it, but my fingers, stiff as wood, refused to cooperate. Finally in frustration I bit off part of the peel and just smashed the orange against my face, trying to suck as much of the sweet juice as I could. Most of it just dribbled down my face.

From the waist down I felt tingling pins and needles, like when your arm or your leg goes to sleep. I wasn't able to move my legs much, but it never occurred to me that it would be a permanent thing. I was too young, and too used to being healthy, to even think about anything like that. Besides, most of my thoughts were focused on just staying alive through the long night.

My thoughts turned to my girlfriend, Nancy Jenks. We had met two years before at the store where we both worked, and we had been dating ever since. She was athletic and upbeat, a good tennis player and a good skier. I felt close to her and wished she could be there on the ledge to help me make it through the night. As the cold bit deeper, I began to wonder if I'd ever see her again.

I thought about my friends and my family and my

comfortable life back home. It all seemed so far away.

I had lived a really idyllic childhood, growing up in the quiet suburb of Palo Alto, California. It was, and still is, a progressive town in the shadow of Stanford University, about forty miles south of San Francisco. Today it's known as part of Silicon Valley, the high-technology capital of the world. Back then it was just friendly, tree-lined neighborhoods and apricot orchards.

My dad owned and ran a donut shop in another town, and later a little coffee shop not too far from our home. Those were the days when breakfast meant a couple of donuts, a cup of coffee and a cigarette. Business was pretty good for a while. My mom was a typical housewife. She did some school playground duty for a while and worked as an assistant teacher. Despite this, she had the house immaculately clean when I and my younger sister, Elaine, got home from school.

I delivered the *Palo Alto Times* on my bicycle and later worked at the newspaper plant loading bundles of papers into the trucks. In the summer I played Little League baseball. I played second base and pitcher and, while I was hardly a star, I was fairly decent. All in all, it was a real *Leave It To Beaver* childhood, hardly different from that of any boy my age in that neighborhood—except for one thing.

When I was six, I had gotten my first taste of adventure, and it had touched a nerve deep inside me that has kept tingling to this day.

My friend David's father was a pilot, and one day he invited me and my dad along on an overnight trip. We piled our camping gear into the back of a Cessna 172 airplane, taxied down the runway at Palo Alto Airport, and soon were airborne. Before long the suburbs gave way to rolling foothills and then to real mountains, alive with rugged canyons, towering cliff faces, and majestic pine trees.

These were the Santa Cruz Mountains, a small coastal range that stood between Palo Alto and the Pacific Ocean. To me, gazing wide-eyed out the window, it could have been the Yukon or the Andes—it seemed so wild. It felt as if we were in that old television show, *Sky King*.

We passed over a ridge top and swooped down into a river valley. David's father guided us slowly down over the treetops, and ahead I could see a clearing. Soon we were bouncing down a remote, backwoods airstrip, kicking up gravel and a big cloud of dust.

Stepping out of the plane, I immediately noticed that the mountain air felt cool and fresh and alive with possibilities. There were no roads here, no street lights, no telephones. The four of us were setting off into the wilderness, carrying everything we needed to survive. We unloaded all of our camping gear from the plane and stowed it in our backpacks. All I could carry was a single sleeping bag, but as far as I was concerned, I was a real outdoorsman.

I felt as if I were taking my first steps into a strange and exciting new world.

There were no man-made trails in the area, so we started forging our own way—bushwhacking through the undergrowth and looking for small game trails left by deer and other animals. Sometimes it was tough going for a little boy. The pack straps strained against my shoulders, but my tiny legs pushed hard to keep up with everyone.

We dropped down into a ravine, stepping over downed trees and hopping from rock to rock. There were ferns and pine trees and even a few redwoods. Everything seemed green and wild and full of life. We kept walking farther and farther, what seemed like miles away from the airplane, our last link to civilization.

The ravine spilled out onto a riverbank and we

finally stopped there for the night, near the river. I rolled out my sleeping bag as the others set up the rest of the camp. Filling our cooking pot from the cool rushing stream made a big impression on me. Until then I don't think I had ever tasted water that hadn't come out of a faucet.

That night, after we had finished dinner, settled into our sleeping bags and turned off our flashlights, I began to lose my appetite for our adventure.

Frankly, I was scared to be sleeping outdoors for the first time. It was getting dark, and the moon was causing spooky-looking shadows to dance and flicker around our campsite. Suddenly the woods were full of strange and frightening noises. Little crunches in the brush and the chirp of crickets can take on a menacing air when magnified by the overheated imagination of a six-year-old.

Too afraid to sleep, I spent unblinking hours staring at a dark patch of brush. I was sure bears or some other wild animals would soon emerge from it to devour me.

At some point I must have drifted off to sleep, though, because I later awoke to a wet sensation. I'd rolled down into the creek. Miserable now, I crawled up onto the riverbank and back into my sopping wet sleeping bag.

At first light I woke, again, to discover I was eyeball to eyeball with a big, slimy banana slug.

All in all, that first adventure didn't seem like a very good experience for me at the time. I was glad to get back to the airplane, back to civilization, back to my own bed. But on some level it must have affected me deeply, because as I grew older I kept going back for more.

The first real mountain I ever climbed was Mt. Lassen, the southernmost in the chain of volcanoes that forms the Cascade Range. It is 10,457 feet high and towers over everything else in that corner of northeastern California. On a clear day you can see it from a hundred miles away. Although high, there is a trail all the way to the top, which made it the perfect first summit for an eight-year-old mountaineer.

My climbing partner was my uncle, John Work Wellman, who had become a second father to me. He had been a successful chemist for Kodak and had retired when he was forty. My uncle had set up a nice life for himself in Gualala, a small town along the rugged northern California coast, about one hundred miles north of San Francisco. He studied botany, traveled, taught himself foreign languages and became a gourmet cook. Since my dad was often busy with his restaurant, Uncle John became my main ticket to wilderness adventure.

We left the parking lot long before the sun came up, using our flashlights to pick our way along the rocky trail in the darkness. The air felt cold and bracing against my cheeks. As we hiked upward, the thick pine forest gave way to a few scraggly conifers, then to grassy meadows. Using his flashlight beam to point, my uncle showed me the wildflowers that bloomed along the trail: Indian paintbrush, shooting stars, purple lupine.

Higher up we climbed above the zone of living things and entered the forbidding alpine world of ice and snow and rock. It was a revelation for me, a place that was high and wild and full of the kind of adventure and mystery I couldn't find in the suburbs. As it grew lighter, I became aware for the first time of the huge drop-off on the side of the trail, and my excitement gave way to fear. I grabbed my uncle's hand and held on tightly.

The trail grew steeper and the air got thinner, but my little eight-year-old legs kept driving me upward. At that age I don't think I was afflicted yet with summit fever, but some sort of excitement was definitely pulling me to the top.

On the windy summit I turned around slowly, eyes as wide as saucers, and tried to absorb all I was seeing. We were on top of the world, it seemed, and most of northern California was spread out below us like a map. I was full of that special exhilaration of high places.

My eyes were drawn to the one thing that challenged our supremacy: another mountain off to the north, with snowfields and glaciers that gleamed in the morning light and a summit even higher than ours. My uncle told me it was called Mt. Shasta. It scared me a little. Climbing it or any other mountain was the farthest thing from my mind, but it made a deep impression on me that I didn't completely understand at the time.

Back home in Palo Alto, I found that my daydreams were increasingly turning to these high and wild places. As I grew older my uncle began taking me on long backpacking trips. We'd drive way up into the Marble Mountains, park our car at the end of a dirt road, and disappear into the wilderness for ten days at a time. We'd rarely see another person.

These were glorious times for a ten-year-old. We'd hike all day, carrying on our backs everything we needed to sustain ourselves. I was growing bigger, getting stronger, and was proud to be able to hoist a full pack onto my back.

Often we'd strike out off the trail, blazing our own path through the woods to some remote lake or meadow. My uncle was a good teacher, and through him I learned how to navigate in the wilderness. The weird jumble of lines on a topographic map began to make sense to me, and before long I was able to match the two-dimensional squiggles to the real ridges, canyons and buttes of the back country. When I became handy with a compass, my uncle let me set our course.

Often we'd stop at a lake and pull dinner out with our fishing poles—rainbow trout, brown trout, whatever we could catch. Sometimes we'd fry them in a pan, but usually we'd just boil them. They tasted delicious that way.

We'd see deer and marmots and occasionally even a bear, and by this time I was no longer afraid of the night. When the sun went down we'd throw our sleeping bags out under the stars and lie awake for hours, picking out constellations, identifying planets and watching the shooting stars arcing across the night sky.

I began to look forward to these summer trips so much that I couldn't keep my mind on school. The teacher would be up at the chalkboard working out long-division problems, and my mind would be soaring off among the mountaintops.

School never interested me much, and most subjects were hard for me. I don't think I was dumb, but I liked to see an end result to what I was doing. I didn't see that very often in math or English. I lived for wood shop and physical education, where I felt I was achieving something.

Mostly I just counted the days until my next mountain adventure. I had become a real student of the wilderness and the skills I'd need to travel safely there. Usually I'd have my backpack all packed and ready to go three weeks before our departure date. Then I'd unpack all the gear, inspect it and pack it all back up again.

By the time I had started in high school, I began heading out into the mountains with Peter and my other friends. The mountain peaks of the Sierra Nevada range, the highest in the West, were just five hours away by car. They became our own private playground.

We'd leave the trails and head off cross-country, picking our own routes through grassy meadows, up canyons and over rocky passes. Beauty and adventure waited to be discovered around every corner: a sparkling mountain lake, a hidden glacier, a pocket meadow electrified with wildflowers. The freedom of the hills was heady stuff to a teenager, and I felt much more at home there and more sure of myself than I did back in Palo Alto.

At home I was certainly no angel—I went to parties and did my share of goofing off. But I never got into the kind of trouble a lot of kids my age did—drinking too much or driving too fast or getting busted for drugs. For me, these kinds of things just couldn't compare to the high I got every time I set foot in the mountains.

My friends and I yearned to learn every secret the mountains held. So we began climbing to their summits. We started with small peaks that yielded to a determined scramble. Soon that wasn't enough, and we began climbing bigger and bigger peaks, until we were tackling the highest mountains in the Sierra Nevada.

It became a challenge to find a safe passage through the mountain's defenses, a feasible route up through the cliff bands and ledges and ridges. We'd tiptoe across delicate footholds with a thousand feet of fresh air beneath us, and the exhilaration would make us feel more alive than we ever had before.

We craved the rarefied air of mountain summits. There were no gurus waiting for us with the secrets of life, but there was a tingling feeling of achievement and rooftop-of-the-world vistas. French alpinist Gaston Rebuffat expressed it well when he called summits "a place between heaven and earth." They were special places, off-limits to everyone but mountaineers like us.

We weren't into serious technical climbing. We were peak baggers, always looking for routes we could scramble up, unencumbered by ropes or pitons. We'd head into the mountains for ten days at a time and climb five or six peaks. Our appetite for summits was insatiable.

I wanted to know the mountains in all their moods, and I began to push out in the winter, when they were glistening under their mantle of ice and snow. One spring, several of us spent a few days crossing frozen Yosemite National Park on cross-country skis to reach the base of Mt. Lyell, the highest mountain in the park. We strapped metal-spiked crampons to our boots and picked our way up the frozen glacier to the summit with our ice axes. I remember the climb particularly well because it was so cold my boots froze solid at night. I got horrible blisters forcing the stiff leather onto my feet. It hurt something fierce for a while after I got home, but I considered that a small price to pay for the privilege of climbing Mt. Lyell in the winter.

In our senior year of high school, my friends all prepared to head off to prestigious universities. They were eager to pursue professional careers, maybe even get a master's degree. At Palo Alto High, it seemed, that's what everyone did. Peter eventually went on to work overseas for the State Department, and another friend became an engineer who helped develop the fuel for the space shuttle.

I had no such plans. I had neither the grades nor the drive to gain admission to a major college. At this stage of my life, all I cared about was learning everything there was to know about the mountains and getting better at climbing and skiing. Beyond that I didn't have any goals for my life.

My senior picture in the high-school yearbook pretty well summed up who I was at that age. It showed me posing triumphantly on the summit of 13,715-foot Mt. Abbot.

After my friends left town for Jamestown University and Reed College and the University of California, I stayed home and got a job at the local backpacking shop, a place called the Ski Hut. My parents probably wished I were getting a college education, but they seemed to understand me well enough to know that this was what I wanted.

While working at the shop, I learned new ways to experience the mountains. I took a class in white-water rafting and survived one particularly hairy incident when three of our group's four rafts capsized on the flood-swollen American River. A couple of people were hurt, and most of the group had no interest in getting back into the frothing river. They hiked, instead, for many miles along its banks.

Later, I spent one footloose summer vagabonding around Europe. Peter met me in the French Alps and we climbed several mountains, including Mont Blanc, the highest peak in Western Europe. We set off from the mountain hut not long after midnight, and climbed through the darkness. I remember gasping for breath in the thin air near the 15,775-foot summit and watching the first rays of dawn explode over much of France and Italy. It remains the highest mountain I've ever climbed.

All along I'd known, in sort of an abstract way, that danger was the flip side of the mountains' beauty. I'd certainly had my share of close calls. While climbing Mt. Abbot, we'd been spooked when handholds pulled loose without warning and rocks the size of bowling balls cascaded past us. On Mt. Lyell, one of my friends had taken a short fall and punctured his leg with a spike from one of his crampons.

But I had come through five years of mountaineering unscathed, and I was still young enough to feel invincible. My relationship with the mountains was like being head over heels in love with a beautiful and fast-living woman. People tried to warn me she was dangerous, but I never believed she would hurt *me*.

I had been wishing for it—willing it—for so long that when I finally saw it I blinked my eyes, thinking I was hallucinating. But it was there, all right: a thin band of pale blue on the horizon. Soon the eastern sky began to grow pink. My spirits began to rise. The unbearably long, cold night was finally coming to an end, and I had lived through it to see the new day. It promised to be the most beautiful sunrise of my life.

I waited for the sun to appear and flood my body with the warmth I craved, but it didn't come. The sky grew lighter, but it was colder than ever. Half an hour passed. Pre-dawn breezes sent new shivers through me. *Where was the sun? Why was it taking so long?* The hope that had welled up within me started to fade. I couldn't stand the cold much longer.

Finally, after three eternities, the first burst of orange flashed over the horizon, and I felt a tiny spark of warmth hit my cheek. Never before had anything as simple as a single ray of sunshine felt so luxurious. I stretched on my perch, feeling the warm tingle spreading slowly through my fingers, my arms, my chest, my neck and my head; but not, as I was only vaguely aware, through my legs.

I had done my part. I had stayed alive this long. Now my survival was in the hands of Peter and the rescuers he was able to summon. Immediately I began listening for the *whup-whup-whup* of the helicopter I was sure was coming to pluck me off the mountain. I began to hear that hopeful sound in the rustle of clothing, in the wind scudding across the granite, in the echo of silence on the mountain. Each time my spirits sagged. Whatever it was, I had to admit to myself, it was not the helicopter.

The entire morning passed. *Where was the helicopter? Why was it taking so long? What had happened?* I began to grow delirious with pain, and all sorts of desperate scenarios started playing out in my mind. Maybe the helicopter had crashed. Maybe they didn't have a helicopter to send up. Maybe something had happened to Peter on the way down.

Late in the morning, with the sun high overhead, I reached the point where I just couldn't stand it any more. It seemed as if the rest of the world had forgotten about me, just left me to die all alone on this Godforsaken mountain. After the shock from the fall and the cold night and the dehydration, I definitely wasn't thinking too clearly. I was getting desperate. I decided that if I was going to survive, I would have to save myself. I was going to have to crawl down the mountain, no matter how long it took, no matter how painful it was.

I slowly rolled over on my stomach and rose up on all fours. Instantly, the most intense jolt imaginable surged through my back like an electric current. I rolled over in agony as waves of pain washed over me. To this day, it's something I regret. I'm almost sure I did some additional and serious damage to my spinal cord with that stupid move. But I was feeling so desperate that I had to try.

Not long after that I became aware for the first time that I had seriously lost control of my motor functions below the waist. I didn't know what was going on, but I knew I couldn't move my legs and I knew I couldn't pee. In my addled state, I don't think it registered fully.

Where was the helicopter? Time continued to creep. I looked up to see that the sun had passed overhead and was now starting to edge over in the western sky. It was around 3:00 p.m., I estimated. I had survived, alone, for twenty-two hours since the fall. Even in my woozy state, however, I knew that if the sun set again I was finished. Already the cool afternoon breeze had started to knife through me on the ledge. There was simply no way I could survive another night out on the mountain.

What was that? Could it be? No. Don't get your hopes up again. It sure sounds like... Yes! It is! It's the helicopter! They were coming for me after all! I could hear the whooping of its rotors echoing off nearby peaks. *Where is it?* I sat up as best I could and scanned the skies for my rescuers. Finally I saw something coming up the valley. It was a California Highway Patrol helicopter, and it was flying straight toward me.

I waved my hand back and forth, desperately trying to signal the pilot. It passed right overhead, close enough that I could read all the markings on the helicopter. My heart was beating so loudly it almost drowned out the sound of the rotors. *They must have spotted me. They must have!*

Without giving any kind of signal, the helicopter turned around and headed back down the valley. I was crushed. I felt abandoned. They had to have seen me. They had to. But, I reasoned, there was no place on the steep mountainside for a helicopter to land. Maybe they were going to have to send a rescue team in on the ground, and that could take hours. I wasn't sure I had hours to spare.

As if I didn't have enough trouble, nature now struck another blow against me. All afternoon, big billowy, cumulus clouds had been building up over the Sierra crest and a cold wind had been kicking up from the north. Now the cloud bottoms were looking dark and angry. Black thunderheads seemed to fill the entire sky. The hairs on my forearms started standing up, and I could smell the storm building in the air. This was no time to be sitting like a lightning rod on an exposed mountainside, and it was certainly no time to be flying a helicopter.

But, cutting through the rustle of the wind, I could hear the unmistakable sound of another chopper—this one a little deeper than the last. As it flew closer, I could see it was having a terrible time fighting the winds. Three times it tried to hover into position, and three times the turbulence forced it away. Even under the best of conditions it was a daring maneuver. The pilot who, I later learned, was Lt. Phil Amrhein, had to get close enough without letting his rotors hit the mountain. That would mean instant death for him and his crew. In these swirling winds it required incredible skill and nerve. I wondered how much longer he would be able to hang in there.

Suddenly, on the fourth try, it was directly over me—a Huey UH-1N, like they used to fly in Vietnam. The markings said it was from Lemore Naval Air Station. A rope dropped out of the chopper's belly, and soon I could see someone rappelling down it toward me. In the gusting winds of the gathering storm, he was being blown around like a wind chime. He was wearing an orange jumpsuit, a white helmet with a visor, and reflective goggles. In my delirious state, he looked like a spaceman descending from a flying saucer. He landed near me, and soon a second rescuer was right behind him.

They introduced themselves. They were Hospital Corpsman Jim Mason, a Navy medic, and Technician Mike Potts, a crew member. They were both about my age—barely out of their teens. They seemed strong and competent and sure of themselves. They looked to me like guardian angels. After enduring the pain and fear of the last twenty-four hours by myself, just having the warmth of other human beings there to comfort me was an incredible feeling. Hope began to well up in me again.

But nature wasn't through with us yet. The thunderstorm that had been building all afternoon picked this time to break. Tongues of lightning flickered off the tops of nearby peaks and hail started to pelt us. The helicopter roared off, and was soon gone from sight.

Mike and Jim ignored the bolts of electricity crackling in the sky as they went to work on me. They tried to be gentle, but in our position it was not always possible. They lifted me onto a Stokes litter, a metal stretcher with a frame and a backboard. Despite their efforts to be careful, pain stabbed through me, and I tried as hard as I could not to cry out. Next they jabbed a needle into my arm and attached an intravenous bag filled with saline solution. As they worked, they were talking to me, trying to comfort me as much as possible.

Thunder boomed and rumbled through the dark skies as the hail continued to fall. It was a hell of a storm, and it showed no sign of letting up. Over the thunderclaps I could hear one of my rescuers talking on the radio, saying something about evacuating me with a ground crew instead of a helicopter. I heard him say we might have to spend the night where we were. I trembled on the litter, and I wondered if my ordeal would ever end.

I didn't know it at the time, but seventy-five miles away in Yosemite National Park, the alert was going out to members of the Yosemite Search and Rescue team to be ready to help out with my evacuation. Among the rescue team members was an experienced big-wall rock climber named Mike Corbett. As it turned out, he and the other rescue team members were not needed. Years later our paths would cross, and Mike would end up playing a major role in my life.

As the two Navy crew members and I cowered on the mountainside, the helicopter was ducking below the storm and touching down in a meadow three thousand feet below. There it waited for the thunder and lightning to pass. The chopper had to dump half its fuel load because it was operating at high altitude, where weight was critical. I never found out whether they dumped it in the meadow or out over the air somewhere, but I feel bad about the environmental damage it must have done.

Just when things were looking their most bleak, I finally got a break. The hail began to taper off, the lightning stopped flashing, and those angry-looking thunderheads started to drift off. The storm had passed. Not long after that, I heard the helicopter roaring up the valley once more.

This time the pilot had no trouble flying into position above us. I was tightly strapped into the litter,

smothered in warm blankets. Now my rescuers covered
my head so I couldn't see. I was glad they did, because
what happened next was one of the wildest, scariest
things that has ever happened to me.

The helicopter, hovering one hundred feet above us,
dropped a cable to the ledge. Jim quickly attached it to
my litter, then clipped himself in. There was a
tremendous jolt, and the two of us were suddenly
yanked into the sky. The helicopter banked away from
the mountain and we were swinging at the end of the
cable, with thousands and thousands of feet of fresh
air below us.

The wrenching and twisting of the litter sent shock
waves of agony through me as we were slowly winched
up into the belly of the helicopter. As soon as we were
safely inside, the chopper swooped back over the
mountain to pick up Mike the same way. Then the pilot
banked west and flew out over the Sierra Nevada,
toward Fresno in the distant Central Valley.

I began to relax. At last, I thought, my struggle was
over. No longer did I have to endure the anguish and
the uncertainty by myself. I wouldn't have to shiver
through another night out on the mountain. I was in
the hands of trained medics, and soon I would be in a
warm hospital bed. I was going to be OK, after all.

My relief didn't last long. It was obvious that
something was wrong. We were descending rapidly,
but we weren't anywhere near Fresno. We were still in
the mountains.

"What's going on?" I asked.

"We're going to have to make an emergency landing,"
said one of the crew members. "We're running kind of
low on fuel."

They had been operating on the smallest of
margins since they had dumped half their fuel load.
And all that hovering and maneuvering at thirteen
thousand feet had eaten up a lot of what was left.
Now the gauge read close to empty and the pilot was

going to have to cut short the flight.

A patch of green opened up in the forest below us, and soon we were touching down in Zumwalt Meadows in Kings Canyon National Park. But my rescuers had things under control. There was another helicopter waiting there for me, a California Highway Patrol copter like the first one that had spotted me. The medics carefully lifted my litter and carried me across the meadow to the other chopper.

This helicopter was much smaller than the twin-engine Navy aircraft and, as we lifted off, every vibration and jolt sent excruciating levels of pain through me. Every time the helicopter tilted or hit an air pocket, the litter moved and the electric current ripped through my back. I pleaded with the pilot to hold the copter as level as possible.

For the last twenty-four hours, my body had been running on adrenaline and little else. Now, as we cleared the last of the mountains and flew west toward the hospital, I felt all the pressure lifting off my shoulders. With all the struggle behind me, I was starting to feel very drowsy. My eyes grew heavy and I wanted more than anything to drift off into a long-overdue sleep.

"Mark! You've got to stay awake," said the Highway Patrol officer who was sitting next to me and holding my IV bag. "Hang in there, guy. We're almost there. You must try to stay awake. We'll be there very soon."

I must have been worse off than I thought. They were worried that, if I closed my eyes, I might never open them again. So as the helicopter churned across the Central Valley, I had to battle my overwhelming desire to slip into a deep and restful slumber.

Around dusk my ordeal finally came to an end. Our helicopter set down at Valley Medical Center in Fresno, the nearest major hospital with a heliport. There I was transferred onto a gurney and wheeled into the hospital, where a team of very concerned doctors and nurses was waiting for me. Television cameras and newspaper photographers were there, too. I was a little surprised. At the time I didn't fully appreciate what an accomplishment it was for that Navy helicopter crew to have plucked me off the mountainside.

As I was being wheeled down the gleaming white hospital corridors, an overpowering feeling of relief washed over me. My struggle to survive was finally behind me. I would live, after all.

But, as I would soon find out, the life I had known before was over.

Peter Enzminger:

I felt awful about leaving Mark alone on the mountain, especially considering the state he was in.

But I didn't feel I had any choice. I could have kept him company through the night, but it was a long day's hike out to the trailhead. If I had stayed the night, it would just have meant one day longer before he could get to a hospital.

Still, I had a lot of time to second-guess that decision. Did I do the right thing? Should I have stayed up there with him? It's a real hollow feeling to leave an injured friend alone on a mountain.

Getting down by myself wasn't easy. From the base of the peak it was still three or four miles back to base camp, and I spent a lot of time wandering around in the dark. Eventually I bumped into some other people and was able to borrow a flashlight.

Using the map, I was eventually able to find my way back to the lake where my brother and sister-in-law were camped. It must have been around 10:00 p.m. when I got there.

My brother's immediate reaction was that we had to go back up there to help Mark. Finally I convinced him that you can't climb up a mountain when it's pitch black. The thing we had to do was to head out for help at first light.

We were up at 3:30 the next morning and were off hiking within half an hour. It was rough country, and we couldn't run, but we hiked as fast as we could. It was

*twenty miles of cross-country—there were no trails—
but we managed to cover it by 10:00 a.m.*

There was a pack station at the trailhead, and we banged
on the door of a mobile home there. The people inside came
to the door, and we told them what had happened. They
called the nearest ranger station for us. It was in Bishop, a
few miles east of us in the Owen's Valley. I don't think they
even had a telephone at the pack station. They may have had
to use a radio to make the call.

Apparently there was some wrangling over who would
handle the rescue. The U.S. Forest Service ranger station in
Bishop said they couldn't handle it because it was on the
west side of the Sierra crest. That was in another ranger
district, and the other district had to take care of it.

I relayed Mark's exact position to them as best I could.
Meanwhile, I could see a bad storm was starting to move in.
By the afternoon, it was raining and hailing so hard that we
couldn't head back up to base camp to rejoin my sister-in-
law, who was still there.

That was one of the longest afternoons of my life, waiting
at the packer's station for word of the rescue. Had they
spotted him? Were they going to be able to get him off the
mountain in this storm?

I was full of anxiety, anguish and guilt. It was a trip I'd
planned—I was the one who really wanted to climb Seven
Gables—and I was feeling responsible for what had happened.
There was a lot of time to think and worry.

Later that day we finally received word that Mark was
alive, and that they had been able to fly him out. I felt utter
relief.

It was another day and a half before I could see him. My
brother and I had to hike back up to base camp to bring
down his wife and our gear. We started to make the long
drive to Fresno, but we were so exhausted that we had to
pull over by the side of the road to sleep.

The hospital notified Mark's parents about the
accident, and they were already there when I arrived.
Mark's mother was very badly shaken up. A deeply

religious person, she told me she forgave me.

I tiptoed into the intensive care unit, where Mark was. He had tubes coming out of just about every bodily orifice. I asked him if he was doing all right, and I'll never forget what he said.

"Peter," he said weakly, "at least we climbed the peak."

At the time I thought that was a bit of misplaced bravado. I still think it was excessive, but that's the kind of attitude that got him through the night.

And that's what allowed him to climb another mountain one day.

2

INTRODUCTION TO DESPAIR

Ten people in white coats hovered over me, looking very grave. One of them took my pulse; another slapped a blood-pressure cuff on my arm. Someone took out a pair of scissors and began cutting off my clothes. At the same time, doctors poked me all over my body and asked me questions.

"Can you feel anything here?"

"No."

"How about here?"

"Yeah, a little."

"And here?"

"Yes."

"IIow about over here?"

"Uh, sort of... well, no."

A nurse approached with a sinister-looking catheter.

"This is going to hurt a bit," she warned.

I looked down to see her forcing the catheter into the opening in my penis. It didn't hurt. The alarming thing was that there was absolutely no sensation at all. I couldn't believe she was touching me down there and I couldn't feel a damned thing.

"What's wrong?" I cried. "How come I can't feel you doing that?"

There was no reply. They kept working on me,

shining lights in my eyes, poking me some more and asking more questions.

"Who's your insurance company?" someone wanted to know. The question seemed to come out of right field, and I couldn't remember immediately. I had insurance, but I'd always been healthy and I'd never used it.

"I think it starts with a 'K,' " I answered.

"Kaiser?" someone said.

"Yeah, that's it, Kaiser," I said. Someone scribbled the information down on a form.

The next thing I remember, they gave me a shot of something, and I felt a big blast of adrenaline surging through me. My eyes lit up, and I was suddenly very awake, extremely conscious.

My world consisted of a white ceiling with fluorescent lights and a horde of concerned-looking people leaning over me and speaking with disembodied voices that seemed to be coming from all directions at once. They were wheeling me down the hallway toward the X-ray room.

As I tried to answer their questions, I was suddenly conscious that my throat felt painfully dry and parched. It had been many hours since I'd finished my last few sips of water up on the mountain.

"Oh, God, please can I have something to drink— some juice or some water?" I croaked. "I'm really thirsty."

"We can't give that to you right now, Mr. Wellman," someone replied.

"Please!"

"We're sorry. The answer is no."

My hospital nightmare had begun. For the next seven months I would surrender control of my entire life. What I ate, what I drank, what drugs I took, when I bathed, where and when I slept, whom I saw, when and how I went to the bathroom—it would all be in the hands of other people. Eventually I'd come to accept that it was for my own good, but initially it felt as if I'd been sentenced to prison.

They wheeled me through a couple of sets of doors and into the X-ray room. Ten sets of hands reached under me and lifted me carefully off the gurney and onto the cold slab of the light table. Underneath the breezy hospital gown, chills and goose bumps ran up my back. The X-ray machine slid into position over me, and I could hear the clicks as they fired off a number of pictures.

They showed me the X-rays, and even I could tell that things didn't look right. In the picture, two of my vertebrae were separated, displaced and crushed together, like a freight train that had been in a wreck. The fracture, they explained, involved the eleventh and twelfth thoracic vertebrae, about halfway between my neck and tailbone.

This piece of information didn't make much of an impression on me. I was still basking in the warm feeling of relief to be off the mountain and in the hands of people who would take care of me. I had no idea what it meant to have a broken back. Eventually, I figured, the swelling in my back would go down and the feeling would return in my legs.

Instead of a regular bed, they strapped me tightly into something called a Stryker frame. It looked diabolical, like something they'd used for torture during the Spanish Inquisition. It was a canvas mat stretched across a metal frame with an axle running through it lengthwise. This allowed them to turn me regularly, like a chicken roasting on a spit.

The idea was to prevent me from getting bed sores, but the whole procedure took some getting used to. I had been lying on my back for a while, counting the cracks in the ceiling, when the nurse walked into my room.

"OK," she said. "We're going to roll you now."

It was a complicated procedure because of all the tubes and hoses coming out of me. By now I had one in each nostril and a third attached to the catheter in my penis. Each of my arms had an IV in it.

The nurse undid some latches and slowly began to spin me. My world slowly rotated 180 degrees, until I was facing straight down at the floor. This was my view for the next four hours. I counted the dust balls and the cracks in the floor to pass the time until I heard footsteps. I got so I could recognize the different nurses by their shoes, which is about all you can see from that position.

"Time to roll you again," she said.

She rotated me slowly upward onto my back again, until I could go back to staring at the ceiling instead of the floor. This went on, every four hours, day and night, for the next two days.

I barely remember being wheeled into the operating room the next day; I was groggy from all the drugs they were giving me. What they performed on me, I later learned, was something called a Harrington operation.

Surgeons can fix broken bones, but they can't repair a damaged spinal cord. Once it's cut or frayed, that's it. All they can do is stabilize the vertebrae so things don't get any worse. There was no way of knowing how badly my spinal cord was damaged, if at all, until they went in and had a look.

I was knocked out with a general anesthetic, and they laid me, stomach down, on a special table with pads for my shoulders and my rib cage. The idea was that my hips would rest free and my spine would line up in its natural position. They made a long incision down my back, opening the skin to reveal my damaged backbone.

It's a very delicate operation, and at the same time it's quite violent. The surgeons had to work carefully to straighten and align my vertebrae—which takes a lot of strength—without damaging the ultra-sensitive spinal cord that snakes through them. They had to pound with a chisel to get things aligned right.

The orthopedic surgeon was almost like a carpenter, using saws and drills. He sawed part of the bone off my pelvis and grafted it onto my spine. Then the operating team inserted two metal bars, called Harrington rods, one on either side of my spine. These would serve as splints while everything healed. They're still in there.

The next day I awoke in the intensive care unit and felt as if someone had hit me in the back with a sledgehammer. The throbbing background level of pain was much worse than it had been before the operation.

Later in the day, one of the surgeons strolled into the room, examined my chart and looked up with a big smile on her face. She had some good news.

"I think you're in luck," she said. "It didn't look as if your spinal cord was severed. You might be able to walk again some day."

Of course, what my ears heard was that I'd *definitely* walk again. For the next two weeks, the only thing that kept me going was the absolute, unshakeable belief that I would recover fully. I'd been healthy and athletic my entire life, and I had no reason to think I wouldn't be that way again. It wasn't as if I had to force myself to believe I'd walk again. It's just that the alternative never occurred to me.

At the moment, though, I was far from healthy.

The following day, a physical therapist came into my room and handed me a funny-looking little device. It consisted of a clear plastic box with some balls in it, and a tube to blow into. It looked like a game you'd try at a carnival. The object was to blow hard and long enough to lift all the balls up at once. It was important, the therapist told me, to keep my lungs strong and clear of fluids after my operation. I blew as hard as I could—which wasn't very hard—and the balls barely budged off the bottom. Even that little effort made me dizzy.

I was too spaced out on drugs to care much. Every couple of hours a nurse came in and gave me a shot of morphine. They had me taking lots of pills, too, including all sorts of pain killers. Often I'd be roused out of a deep sleep so they could give me more pills or another shot. The net result was that I was oblivious to much of what was going on around me most of the time.

"Hi, Mark. How are you feeling, honey?"

Through the pain-pill haze, I could make out my parents standing over my bed. My mom's voice sounded warm and caring. If she was scared for me, it didn't show. She told me that she, my dad, my sister, and everyone at their church were all praying for me.

Someone was gently squeezing my hand. It was Nancy. She gave me a warm smile and whispered in my ear that she'd see me through this. She was there with her brother, and they'd brought me all sorts of presents to brighten up my room: some rubber dinosaurs, a pair of Groucho Marx glasses, things like that.

Nancy leaned over the bed and gave me a hug—although it wasn't easy, with all the tubes hanging out of me. Even in my groggy state, it warmed my heart to know she was by my side.

My parents rented a motel room near the hospital, and Nancy came back, too. They were by my side as often as regulations would permit, but I was pumped so full of pain killers I hardly knew they were there.

The patient in the bed next to me was an alcoholic who had suffered some sort of head injury. He had a big bandage on his head that made him look like one of the Coneheads from *Saturday Night Live*. This guy was going through the agony of alcohol withdrawal while he recovered from his injury, and he was causing a lot of trouble in the intensive care unit.

The nurses were constantly trying to tie him down to his bed. He was yelling and making a lot of noise, and once he fell all the way out of his bed. I was so groggy I hardly noticed. But to Nancy and my parents, it added to the nightmarish atmosphere of the place. They couldn't wait to get me out of there and back to a hospital close to home.

It took ten days before I was strong enough to make the trip. The nurses moved me onto a gurney and wheeled me out the side door of the hospital. After so many days of living under florescent lights, the sunshine felt odd. I was squinting into the blinding sunlight and sweltering in the one-hundred-degree August heat of the Central Valley.

An ambulance took me to the Fresno Airport, and the orderlies loaded me into an air ambulance—an airplane specially outfitted with resuscitators and all sorts of lifesaving equipment. A nurse rode next to me on the hour-long flight, which was smooth and uneventful.

We touched down at the San Carlos Airport, just up the highway from Palo Alto. I was finally back close to my hometown, but it would be many months before I could truly go home. Instead, they loaded me into another ambulance, which drove a few miles on the Bayshore Freeway to the Kaiser Hospital Trauma Center in Redwood City. This would be my home for the next seven weeks, and part of that time would be the worst of my life.

I had only been in my room a few minutes when Dr. John Smiley came walking in. He was a big bear of a man, an ex-football player with a barrel chest, and his manner was brusque. Without any preliminaries, he looked up from the chart he was holding and delivered the news in an almost offhand way.

"I'm sorry, Mark. It looks like you're never going to walk again. You're going to be a paraplegic the rest of your life."

The words took my breath away. My mind reeled as it tried to grasp what this doctor was telling me. I guess there's no easy way to say it, but the suddenness of his words, the coldness of it all, seemed almost vicious.

I didn't say anything back. There was nothing to say. A whirlwind of thoughts and emotions spun through my mind as I struggled to comprehend what I had just heard. For two weeks I had clung to the belief that I'd be able to return to a normal life. It was the only thing that had kept me alive and fighting. Now, in a few cruel words, Dr. Smiley had just stolen my entire future away from me.

From now on, I'd be a paraplegic. *A paraplegic!* I rolled the word around in my mind, with all its awful implications. I would never walk again. I would never climb another mountain. I would never ski again. I would never hike, or play tennis or ride a bicycle or paddle a kayak. I'd never stroll along the beach with my girlfriend or make love or have children. For the rest of my life, I'd be different from everyone else. I'd be less than whole.

That night my father came to visit. He walked into my room, gave me a brave smile and began to ask me how my flight had been. I cut him off and tried to tell him the news. The words, though, seemed to stick in my throat.

"They said I'm... I'm never going to walk again," I said, choking up. I suspect he already knew, but as he heard it from me and felt my pain, tears started welling up in his eyes. There was more I wanted to say, but it was no use. I buried my head on his shoulder and, for the first time since the accident, broke down and bawled my eyes out.

"OK, Mark, it's time for you to try sitting up a little," said the nurse.

For the last two weeks, I had been lying flat on my back every minute of the day. Our goal now was to tilt me up very slightly, to see if I could handle it. From now on, progress toward my recovery would be measured in the smallest possible increments. The nurse slowly tilted the upper part of my bed at an incline of about twenty degrees. Suddenly the room started spinning, and I felt dizzy and light-headed and sick to my stomach. I felt as if I were going to faint. I begged the nurse to lower me back down, which she did immediately.

Despair washed over me. I had stood on the summits of the highest mountains from the Sierra Nevada to the Alps—and now I grew faint just trying to sit up in bed.

Progress came slowly and painfully, but it came. Over the next few days, they tilted me up and down a number of times as I tried to adjust to each new position. First I was able to handle twenty degrees for a few minutes, then forty, then sixty, and so on until I was finally able to try sitting straight up at a ninety-degree angle to the bed. It wasn't much, I told myself, but at least I was getting somewhere.

Then an awful stench hit me. I looked down to see black, runny liquid squirting out. I was sloshing around in a stinking puddle of my own waste! The nurse dashed off to get an orderly to clean up the mess. I could do nothing but sit there, feeling about as low as I ever have.

The last vestige of my dignity was gone. From the bellybutton down, I could feel nothing—it was almost as if the rest of my body no longer belonged to me. I had a catheter in my penis to drain my urine, and I had no sensation that it was even there. I had no control of my bowels. My legs were just two heavy pieces of rubber that had to be lifted and moved by physical therapists. My arms had feeling, but they were so sore and stiff from the operation that they were of no use to me.

To make things worse, I came down with the flu and vomited constantly for a couple of days. I wasn't able to dash to the bathroom like a normal person, or even move my head, so it just ended up in my bed with the rest of the mess.

My legs had been extremely active before my accident, but after two weeks of lying in bed, the inactivity began to take its toll. I developed a blood clot in one of my legs. This condition is called phlebitis, and it's very serious. My leg swelled up, and the doctors had to watch me carefully because there was the possibility the clot could break off and flow to my brain or heart. That could cause a massive stroke or kill me outright. The doctors gave me some drugs to thin my blood, and after a few nerve-wracking days, the clot dissolved by itself.

Every day seemed to bring a new setback, and I lost the will to keep fighting. I was on a roller coaster of ups and downs, and the downs kept getting lower and lower. I pretty much stopped caring about my health and my appearance. I wasn't eating much—partly to prevent the mess that came out the other end—and I was losing lots of weight. I stopped shaving and let my scraggly beard grow out.

At night I sank into the blackest depression. All the things that had made me who I was as a person were gone. I had been a mountaineer, a skier, a backpacker; now I was none of those things. I was just half a person. I felt like a baby who couldn't even learn to crawl, a baby who had to have someone else change his diapers. The difference was that a real baby would grow out of that condition. I had no reason to believe I ever would.

This wasn't living, I told myself. This was hell. I looked over at the window, and the answer suddenly seemed clear. I was up on the sixth floor, about ninety feet off the deck, roughly the same distance I'd fallen in my accident. This time, though, I'd do things right and finish the job. I absolutely wanted to end my life and escape from the prison of this useless body. I even looked forward to it.

I tried to drag myself over to the window, but it was no use. I was so weak I couldn't move even a few inches out of my bed. As I sank into even greater depths of depression, I was left with the one single aspect of my life I had any control over. I raised up the remote-control button and changed the channel on the TV.

One morning, a physical therapist walked into my room with a funny-looking piece of plywood tucked under his arm. It was six inches wide and eighteen inches long. I could hardly guess what it was for; it turned out to be my first bridge toward mobility.

"This is called a transfer board," the therapist said, holding it up for me to inspect. "This is how we're going to get you out of your bed and into a wheelchair."

He went back out into the hallway and rolled in a beefed-up hospital-issue wheelchair. Its frame was thick and heavy, and its high back tilted back, almost like a La-Z-Boy recliner on wheels. Its seat was the same height as my bed. Parking the chair next to the bed, the therapist laid the transfer board between them.

Before I could move out of bed, though, they clamped me into something called a Jewett Brace. This is a metal-and-plastic device, almost a corset, to hold my back up straight and firm. I was still extremely weak, and it was crucial that I not jar my healing spinal column.

Two other therapists came into the room, and it was

quite an operation to swing my legs over and scoot my butt onto the board. There seemed to be hands everywhere, steadying me. And I needed every one of them, because I instantly felt woozy. I had absolutely no balance, and without their firm support, I would have toppled over onto the floor in no time.

With all of us working together, I slowly inched my way across the transfer board until I was in the chair. The horrible realization hit me: *I was in a wheelchair!*

It wasn't that I had grown up with a lot of bad stereotypes about the disabled. I don't think I had ever given them a single thought, one way or the other. It was just that I had been active and healthy my whole life, and now the wheelchair seemed to be a symbol of my lost freedom and mobility. From now on the chair would be my legs. That thought filled me with dread.

On that first journey out into the hallway, I was too weak to wheel myself. The physical therapist had to push me. After a couple of minutes I had to recline the back and lie down because I was getting too dizzy.

But, as difficult as that first ride was, I immediately noticed the sense of freedom it gave me. After close to three weeks of lying flat on my back in a hospital bed, the chance to go out into the hallway and see some new sights felt very liberating. A hospital corridor may not be everyone's idea of exciting scenery, but I was thrilled to see some new faces, hear some new voices and watch all the busy activity.

It took a couple of days, but I finally grew strong enough to start wheeling myself around the hallway. Those first tentative forays were like bumper car rides. I crashed into gurneys, toppled garbage cans and knocked over food trays. The steering seemed so strange, and my arms were still stiff from the operation.

It may not sound like it, but I was being super cautious. I'd heard stories of careless patients pitching forward out of their wheelchairs, and that was the last thing I wanted to do. But I was enjoying my little bit of freedom so much, pumping up and down the corridors, that I took every opportunity I could to get out of bed and into my chair.

Eventually I was spending several hours a day rolling up and down the hallways. I don't know if I was starting to get in the way, but one day a nurse led me into a room and said there was someone I really ought to meet.

"Mark Wellman," she said, "this is Mark Sutherland."

He was lying in his hospital bed, but even in that position he was quite a sight. This guy had long, flaming red hair, a ruddy pink complexion, a big bushy beard and twinkling, mischievous eyes. He was chain-smoking Raleighs, and he had an ashtray full of butts and a stack full of cigarette coupons. He was one wild-looking dude.

"How ya doing?" he asked.

Sutherland extended his hand, and I noticed his handshake was stiff and unsteady. In the entire time I've known him, it was the only thing about him that ever seemed weak.

A quadriplegic in his late twenties, he had broken his neck eleven years earlier by diving head-first off a houseboat after the tide had gone out. He had been living in a wheelchair ever since. Now he was back in the hospital to have an operation to remove a bone spur from his neck.

Sutherland didn't beat around the bush. He made it clear he didn't have much time or sympathy for anyone who sat around wallowing in self-pity.

"Life goes on," he immediately told me. "It's your choice, because there's nothing you can't get, nothing you can't do, if you choose to do it. Do you hear what I'm saying? It's all up to you. If you choose to live, you get off your ass and you live. If you choose to die, lie down. Don't get out of bed."

I had already heard this little speech from able-bodied doctors and therapists. From them it had just seemed like empty words. Now, hearing it from a guy who had been there, who had been living it, I began to feel the first signs of hope stirring in me. Maybe, I thought, there would be some kind of life for me in a wheelchair, after all.

What impressed me immediately about Sutherland was how comfortable he was with himself. He showed no trace of the awkwardness or self-consciousness I felt. There was nothing apologetic or halfway about his manner. He seemed to know just about everything about living in a wheelchair, and he was eager to share his experience with me.

My eyes drifted over to his chair, which was parked next to his bed. It was nothing like mine. My chair was a big heavy clunker, wide and slow and cumbersome, with a high back, bulky wheels and thick armrests. If mine were a car, it would have been a '64 Chevy Impala; his was an Alpha Romeo. It was nimble and sporty, with a low back, light wheels and no armrests. I could see immediately that it could go places and do things mine couldn't.

I began dropping by Sutherland's room every chance I got. They let us have beer in the hospital, and we'd pop open a couple of cans and talk late into the night. I listened, wide-eyed, as Sutherland filled my head with stories about the new world that lay ahead of me.

"Look at me. I'm an incomplete quadriplegic, and I can shoot a .44 magnum accurately, and put 'em back-to-back. I've hunted. I've fished. I've spent two weeks up along the Bear River, living under a tarp, just to see if I could do it.

"I do anything I want to do. Anything. I even drive race cars."

"What?" I didn't think I'd heard him right. "You drive *race cars*?"

"Sure," he said. "Right now I have a souped-up Dodge Challenger and a '70 Mustang notchback that I put a big block into. It's a hot car."

"But how?"

"Driving's no problem," he said. "You just have to hook up some hand controls. You run bars from the gas pedal and brake up to the steering column, and you work them with knobs."

"Sounds complicated," I said.

"Nah, it's easy. It only costs a couple hundred bucks, and you can do it to any car with an automatic transmission. You'll see."

During those late-night bull sessions with Sutherland, the idea that impressed me the most was that you could be in a wheelchair and still be cool.

He told me about a friend of his, a paraplegic who was a fairly good wheelchair racer. There was a whole world of wheelchair athletes out there, he said, playing basketball, playing tennis, racing marathons, skiing.

Mark was a born storyteller, and I never grew tired of listening to him spin tales of all the women he'd dated, all the hell he'd raised, all the adventures he'd had in his wheelchair. Now he was settled down, living in a mobile home in California's Gold Rush country. He was married to a disabled woman named Susie, and he had a fulfilling, self-sufficient life. He took college classes, counseled people like me and worked as an activist for disabled rights. Before that, though, he'd had more than his share of wild times in his chair.

"I was taught how to get on and off a bed by a cute little therapist from West Virginia," he told me one night. "She got up on the bed and she said 'If you can get me, you can have me!' "

"Get outta here!"

"I swear it happened," he said. "She wasn't lying, either."

My eyes were wide as saucers and my jaw just about hit the floor.

"Another time—again, this was before I was

married—me and a friend were rooming together. We were both quads. A girl about nineteen years old came by to visit her grandmother—she was in a real nice miniskirt.

"Me and my friend made a bet who could get a date with her first. The bet was my money versus the use of his car. Well, before the afternoon was over, I was getting the keys from him. She and I struck up a real good relationship. For my birthday, she gave me a picture of herself that my wife has since burned. You see, she was a nude model."

Locker-room talk like this might seem kind of crude to some people, but at the time it boosted my spirits more than all the pep talks from the able-bodied therapists put together. That night, for the first time, I began to allow myself to think that women could be attracted to a guy in a wheelchair.

Sutherland passed on lots of practical information about taking care of myself, too. The doctors and therapists spent time on this, but it was different hearing it from another guy in a chair. Sutherland knew what was really important, and he knew how to make me pay attention.

"Watch your butt," he said one day. We were talking about pressure sores—a constant worry for people in wheelchairs. You spend so much time sitting in the same position, and you can't feel anything down there. You have to be constantly vigilant that you don't get little sores that turn into something much more serious.

"I once had a friend who had a sore," Sutherland said, "and he let it get infected to the point where it got into his bloodstream and he ended up dying."

That's all I needed to hear. It impressed me enough that I became extra careful and checked myself several times a day. Over the years, I've gotten my share of small sores, but I've always caught them before they could become a major problem.

Sutherland also warned me not to listen to everything

the doctors and rehabilitation people told me about choosing a wheelchair. He said they'd recommend something sensible and clunky, like a chair that could be folded up to fit in a car trunk. He told me I'd eventually be happier in a sports chair like his, which would allow me to be much more mobile.

"Why don't you try mine out?" he said. "Hop in and give it a spin."

I dragged myself out of my chair and into his. Immediately I noticed how light and maneuverable it was. I could dart in and out between the beds and turn corners on a dime, but I was having trouble keeping my back upright in the short backrest. I was still wearing the Jewett Brace, and I was a little unsteady.

At that moment, a nurse walked into the room, gave me a stern glance, and ordered me out of Sutherland's chair immediately. I wasn't ready yet for such a sporty chair, but I made up my mind that as soon as I was, I'd get one—no matter how much it cost.

It was Sutherland who introduced me to the term I like to use to describe people in wheelchairs. Back then, activists were just starting to come up with new names for people like us. Over the years the term in vogue has gone from "lame" to "crippled" to "handicapped" to "disabled" to some of the new politically correct labels like "physically challenged," "differently abled" and "handi-capable."

The people who think up these terms mean well, but in the end these things are just words, nothing more. Words can't help us walk again, and I don't think they can put compassion in the heart of a bigot.

The term I like to use, the one Sutherland taught me, is "gimp."

Some activists don't like that word because it's been used derogatorily in the past. However, among my friends, being called a gimp is a badge of honor. It's a word we use among ourselves with pride.

Sometimes, when my able-bodied friends would come visiting in the evening, I could hardly wait for them to leave so I could wheel down to Sutherland's room and learn more about my new life. I was just setting out on a lifelong journey into a new and strange world, and Sutherland was my guide and mentor. Because of his encouragement, this new world no longer seemed so bleak. He was opening my mind to possibilities I'd never considered.

Ten weeks after my accident, I was finally ready to take my first trip outside the hospital. Nancy and her sister were going to take me out to dinner at a steakhouse across the street from the hospital.

As the evening approached, I was filled with mixed emotions. Part of me wanted more than anything to get out of the sterile environment of the hospital and take the first steps back into the everyday world outside its doors. But part of me was scared, too. It would be my first time out in public as a gimp, and I didn't know how I or anyone else would react. I wanted to be comfortable and self-assured, but I didn't know if I could pull it off.

It was a disaster. I wheeled across the busy street and negotiated the entranceway without too many problems, but as soon as we entered the restaurant I felt self-conscious. I felt like an invalid; I felt awkward. Immediately, I wanted to spin around and roll back to the hospital, but I forced myself to go through with it.

The hostess led the way, and I wheeled myself slowly and carefully through the restaurant, taking elaborate care not to bump clumsily into the tables. Someone moved a chair away from our table, and I wheeled up and took my place.

We ordered our dinners, and even that seemed weird. Giving your order to a waitress is the most normal thing in the world—usually no one even thinks twice about it—but now I felt strange and self-conscious. I wondered what the waitress was thinking. Was she forcing herself to be extra polite, was she speaking more slowly and enunciating more clearly, just because I was in a wheelchair?

All around the restaurant, I thought, the other diners were staring at me—taking quick peeks over the tops of their menus or stealing glances as they walked to the salad bar. I wanted to hide.

Nancy and her sister tried to make conversation. All of us wanted this to be a normal, relaxed dinner out in a restaurant, but it wasn't working. I felt too uncomfortable. I ate my dinner as quickly as I could, then asked them to take me back. It was a bad scene, and I couldn't wait to get back to the hospital, where I was just one of the many gimps.

It was two weeks before I got up the nerve to venture out of the hospital again. This time, I thought, things would be different. I was invited to a potluck dinner party at the home of a friend in the town of Woodside, a few miles away in the hills above Palo Alto. A bunch of my old co-workers from the Ski Hut would be there, people I'd known for years before my accident. I'd be surrounded by friends in a warm, comfortable, supportive atmosphere, away from the staring eyes of strangers.

I took extra care in shaving, washing up and dressing. I removed my catheter and put in a plug so I wouldn't have to worry about a urine bag hanging off my leg. When Nancy came to pick me up, I was waiting excitedly on the curb.

Right from the start, though, things started to go wrong. It was the first time I'd tried to get into a normal car, and it turned out to be a lot tougher than I'd imagined. Nancy helped lay down the transfer board between my wheelchair and the car seat, and I felt awkward as she assisted me in sliding into the car. I still had no balance, and was always on the verge of toppling over at any moment. Nancy got me settled in my seat, closed the door, walked around the car and got into the driver's seat. I felt pretty useless.

We had to repeat the process all over again when we got to the party. As I slid into my wheelchair, I realized I'd have to start looking at every detail of the world through new eyes. The driveway was made out of gravel, and it proved to be murder to roll through in my chair. I had to have Nancy help push me.

As we came up the driveway, I could hear people talking and laughing inside the house. Then, at the front door we were confronted by a six-inch high curved step. In the past I'd bounded right up this step lots of times without ever giving it a second thought. Now it might as well have been the Great Wall of China. There was no way I could get my chair up it and through the front door.

I wheeled around the house to the back door, which, thankfully, was wider and had a much shorter step. Moving through the house, though, I kept banging into furniture and doorways. I was painfully conscious that my hospital chair was wide and ungainly, about as easy to maneuver as a semi-trailer.

As I wheeled around the party, saying hello to my old friends, I was keenly aware that I didn't have the grace I had had when standing on my legs. Being in a wheelchair ensures that people are always looking down at you. I'm five-foot-nine-inches tall, and all my life I'd been used to looking across or slightly down at most people. Now I found myself craning my neck to look up at everyone. It added to my self-consciousness.

Despite everything, I was having a great time. I was in good humor, and it felt great to be back with my old friends, swapping stories about climbing, skiing and kayaking. Everyone wanted to hear about my accident and the dramatic rescue; it had made the news back in the Bay Area. I was catching up on all the gossip from the store and hearing about people I hadn't seen in a while. I was really enjoying myself, laughing with my buddies for the first time since my accident.

Then I caught a whiff of something awful and familiar. Damn! I'd had an accident. Black, runny waste was starting to drip into my pants. It was my worst nightmare, and it couldn't have come at a worst time. Mortified by embarrassment, I quickly wheeled away, hoping no one else had noticed the odor. Looking around the room, I caught Nancy's eyes and motioned for her to come quickly.

"We've got to go," I whispered. "Let's get out of here—fast."

Nancy understood immediately and helped me make my way out the back door, hastily saying goodbye to everyone. As I slid over the transfer board onto the car seat, I could tell that my pants were soiled all the way through. It was humiliating.

The stench was all over Nancy's car, and as we sped back to the hospital in silence, I felt about as low as a dog that couldn't be housebroken.

Ever since I'd arrived in Redwood City, I'd been hearing stories about an amazing place called Vallejo. It would be the next and most important stop on my journey back to the real world, sort of a technical college or finishing school for gimps. Vallejo was the place where I'd learn the skills to begin building for myself the kind of life Sutherland had.

I was eager to get there, but some problems with my insurance kept me in Redwood City for three extra weeks. I grew impatient, but finally the day came. An ambulance took me on a ninety-minute ride north to the Kaiser Vallejo Rehabilitation Center. It was, and is, a modern-looking complex on a windy hilltop overlooking the northern reaches of San Francisco Bay.

The first guy I met there was a cheerful Vietnam vet in his forties.

"Wanna see a wheelie?" he asked.

Before I could answer, he leaned back, lifted his front wheels off the ground and spun around 360 degrees.

"How the hell did you do that?" I asked.

"It's easy," he said. "You'll learn soon enough."

And I did.

Later that day I wheeled myself into the rehab gym. It was a bright and cheery place—a spacious, airy room with polished hardwood floors, mirrors along the walls, parallel bars and lots of natural light flooding in from skylights. It looked like a big dance studio, but instead of being filled with dancers, it was full of gimps in and out of their chairs.

In one corner, quadriplegics and stroke victims were sprawled out on foam mats up on tables, where physical therapists were helping them roll from side to side, working on balance and isolating muscle groups.

In another corner, a young paraplegic wearing metal leg braces was red in the face and grunting as he used his arms to drag himself, upright, the length of the parallel gates. Two therapists stood by ready to catch him if necessary.

Along one of the walls, gimps in their chairs were working out with weights, grunting as they pumped up their upper bodies.

Along the other wall, there was another group of people in chairs who were not moving around much. These people, many of them white-haired, sat motionless, arms hanging limp by their sides, faces frozen in blank expressions. They were victims of strokes and severe head injuries, and the tremendous struggles they faced in their recoveries made my own seem like a piece of cake. I was reminded of that old saying about the man who always complained he had no shoes, until he met a man who had no feet.

On the other hand, some patients with mild strokes were able to walk, and I couldn't help but envy them.

There were forty beds at Vallejo, and, I later learned, a tragically high number of them were filled by people who had messed up their lives under exactly the same circumstances: they had been drinking and driving and not wearing a seat belt.

A nurse showed me to what would be my home for most of the next two months. It was a spacious, four-bed hospital room, with a toilet in one adjoining chamber and a shower in another. It looked comfortable enough and well set up for a gimp who was still fumbling his way around in a chair. But, I soon learned, the best part of all was my roommate assignment. I'd be bunking with Mark Sutherland.

We'd have one more roommate, Chris DeFazio. A quadriplegic, he had recently broken his neck while jumping off a relative's roof into a shallow swimming pool. As he tried to recover from his injury, he was having some tough times back home. His wife divorced him and took custody of their three-year-old daughter. (They had been having some marital problems before his accident, and this just compounded things.) So now Chris found himself fighting to make a new life for himself in a wheelchair at the same time that he was being forced to rebuild his personal life.

The three of us fed off each other. When one of us was down, the other two pumped him back up. The more serious things got, the lighter we tried to keep the atmosphere in our room. We'd crack jokes about catheters and bowels that seemed to have an agenda of their own, and this made the reality easier to bear.

Soon we all settled into a routine. The lights came on each morning at 6:30 a.m., waking me from deep sleep. A nurse walked into our room with three trays covered with aluminum foil—our breakfasts.

"Good morning, guys," she said. "Rise and shine for a new day."

The breakfasts were always the same: eggs and sausage and toast. It was as tempting as airline food, and by the third day, I'd completely lost my appetite for it. But I knew I had a long day of hard physical work ahead of me, so I forced myself to finish it.

While Sutherland and I ate, the nurse lifted Chris into a device that looks like what you'd use to hoist an engine out of a car. Then, with him swaying there buck naked, she wheeled him into the shower.

We took turns eating and bathing. When it came my turn, I was able to wheel myself into the shower and transfer myself onto the plastic shower seat by myself. Using a shower head on a long nozzle, I could easily clean myself.

Getting dressed was easier now, too. The occupational-therapy people had given me a tool, a long stick with a trigger at one end and a clamp at the other. Using the stick, I was able to grab my pants and pull them up over my legs. After two months of depending on others to dress me, it felt good to finally be able to do it myself.

Another nurse entered the room with a small paper cup for each of us. These were our pill cups, and they contained all the various pills we had to take: for me it was a blood thinner and a laxative. By 9:00 a.m. we were wheeling into the physical therapy room for our first session. I rolled up to a mat where five other patients were working with a physical therapist. For the next hour, we practiced getting off the ground into our chairs, using our arms and whatever other muscles we could still use. Then the therapists held our feet as we did sit-ups to strengthen our abdominal muscles.

My back was still wracked with pain from my operation, and for the first few days, I grimaced and complained as I did my exercises. I got absolutely no sympathy at all—not from the therapists, not from the other patients. They just ignored me. At first this made me feel even worse, but it didn't take long for me to realize they were doing it for my own good.

One of the first things we worked on was popping a wheelie, as the Vietnam vet I had met my first day had done. Learning to do one, it turned out, was part of the official curriculum at Vallejo. Popping a wheelie looks cool, but it's not just for show. It's one of the tricks for getting over curbs where they don't have curb cuts— which is still most places. To teach you, they run straps down from the ceiling, which you attach to your chair as a safety line. That way you can practice your wheelies without worrying about tipping over backwards.

Within a week I was rolling down the hall with my front wheels in the air, grinning like an idiot.

One physical therapist who really took an interest in me was Chuck Hanson. He acted as my personal fitness coach, and it was his ability to squeeze every last drop of effort out of me that really paid off in the long run. Chuck was a compact, muscular guy in his early thirties, short, with sandy blond hair and a mustache. He was from the East Coast, but he looked like a real California surfer dude.

"Drive your hips!" he yelled. "Drive your hips!"

I had metal braces on my legs, and I was out of my chair, struggling to walk the length of the parallel bars, using only my arms for support. It was excruciatingly hard work, and I was red in the face and sweating.

With an intense look on his face, Chuck was walking along right next to me, ready to catch me. He was staring me right in the eye the whole time.

"Keep it going! Come on—I know you're stronger than that. Keep it going!"

I was straining so hard I felt as if veins were popping out of my head, but I managed to drag myself twenty feet to the end of the bar. Chuck was there with a big smile and a new nickname for me. I had been swaybacked before my accident, and he noticed that the changes in my physique made my little butt stick out even further.

"Way to go, Monkey Butt," he said. "I knew you could do it."

Walking the bars was one of the hardest things I did in rehab, but eventually it paid off. The muscles it built allowed me to get up stairs by holding onto the railing and dragging my legs up. With crutches, I was eventually able to walk, but it has never proven very practical. It's a slow, tiring and clumsy way to get around. It's much easier and more graceful in a chair.

Chuck became a real friend to me. He'd invite me over to his house for dinner, and sometimes he'd drop by my room with a pitcher of margaritas and we'd talk late into the night. All of the therapists showed a deep level of personal interest in me, but none more than Chuck.

When Chuck finished with me in therapy, it was Bert Carlson's turn. Bert was the oldest therapist at Vallejo—he must have been in his sixties—and he didn't have the modern training that some of his younger colleagues had had. What he lacked in advanced training, however, he made up for in experience. He had been working with the disabled since World War II, and he didn't need a college degree to tell him what worked and what didn't. A short, muscular guy with a greying flattop, Bert taught me some of the most valuable things I learned about getting around in the everyday world. He had an old car body that had been chopped in half, and I spent hours practicing getting into the driver's seat and pulling the wheelchair in behind me. Bert designed all sorts of exercises to build the muscles I'd need for these essential skills. He had pulleys for building certain muscle groups and something called "rickshaw lifts" for others. The latter entailed pushing down with your shoulders and arms against a bar, which enabled you to lift yourself out of your chair seat.

"Get the lead out!" he'd always say. Bert was definitely old-school, with a military disposition, and he never let us forget that it was costing eighteen thousand dollars a month to keep us in rehab. This wasn't summer camp, he always reminded us. Still, behind the gruff exterior, he cared about his patients. Bert was always willing to stay behind and work a little longer with anyone who needed it. We spent a couple of hours each day in occupational therapy, which was really a course in learning how to live and function in the real world. It's amazing how difficult things can be until you make a few modifications here and there. Then they're no sweat.

Take cooking, for example. A regular kitchen is murder in a chair. It's not just that the sink and stove top are at eye level. The problem is that you can't even get close enough to use them. At Vallejo they had a kitchen modified for the disabled. It was fairly simple to remove the cabinet doors from below the sink and stove top, so you could wheel up close and get your legs in under there. A tilted mirror above the stove let you keep an eye on your dinner while it cooked. Most of the other cabinet doors had been removed as well, because it's difficult to open and close them in a chair.

With these simple changes, we could be as handy in the kitchen as anyone. And after a couple of months of eating hospital food, we jumped at the chance to buy fresh ingredients and cook up our own potluck dinners. We'd invite the therapists and some of our friends in and have a little party.

At the end of the day we'd wheel back to our room, physically exhausted. Then it was time for TV, TV dinners, and a few beers. Sutherland, Chris and I talked constantly, and the brotherhood we formed provided a psychological rehabilitation that was every bit as important as the physical one.

One day the staff brought us into the auditorium,

turned down the lights and showed us something that had us riveted to the screen. It was a gimp sex film, as graphic as a porno movie but more sensitive. It was about a quadriplegic and his girlfriend out on a date. They go grocery shopping, buy a bottle of wine and go back to an apartment. They're having dinner, drinking wine, and in the next scene they're in bed—and it was explicit. He had an awfully wild tongue. We looked at each other in disbelief. For a gimp to want to do this in a movie was pretty incredible.

Sex is a big topic with the disabled, just as it is with everyone. We're no different—as I've already said, we have our share of locker-room discussions. Able-bodied people have a hard time understanding, but the disabled can and do have active and satisfying sex lives. It's hard to generalize, because it's different for everybody. But, as the saying goes, your biggest sex organ is your brain—and the disabled have very active brains!

I can only speak about the topic from the man's point of view. But I'm sure most of what I say applies to women, too, although some of the technical details might be a little different.

Even for the guys who have no feeling or physical functions below the belt, it's possible to have great sex. If you've ever seen the movie *Coming Home*, maybe you remember the steamy love scenes between Jon Voight and Jane Fonda. When you're paralyzed from the waist down, you tend to be in less of a hurry and focus more on touching, caressing and the more sensual side of a physical relationship.

In January, five months after my accident, Sutherland, Chris DeFazio and I left Vallejo and moved back to our homes for a month. It was just a trial period to work the bugs out of home living. Physically it wasn't too hard for me. My dad put a ramp up to the back door and got a plastic shower seat for me. I was able to get around the house without much trouble. The hard part was having nothing to do and nowhere to go, just sitting in the house all day watching *Donahue* and soap operas on TV. I quickly learned there was more to rehabilitation than just being able to get up over a curb in my chair. I was going to have to become more than just a "wheelchair potato" in front of the tube.

At the end of the month, each of us moved back to Vallejo for four more weeks of "tuning up." As an indication of how much my life had changed, I was happy to leave home and return to the rehab center to be with my new buddies. There was still work to do, skills to learn and muscles to build, but much of the most important work went on inside my head. I felt I still needed to draw more strength and inspiration from the other guys.

Now, during our late-night beer sessions, our talk focused less on the present and more on the future. We'd learned all we could about the mechanics of living in a wheelchair; now the rest was up to us. Each of us was filled with mixed and confused emotions. We felt a sense of anticipation and excitement about returning to the real world. But at the same time we were more than a little scared to be leaving the protective and nurturing environment of Vallejo.

For me in particular, the future was a frightening question mark. Sutherland and DeFazio had careers to return to; I had nothing. I was no longer a mountaineer or a skier or a hiker. Deep inside I kept alive the hope that some day, somehow, I could return to the mountains. First, I would have to build a whole new life for myself.

Mark Sutherland:
There's always been a tradition of pairing up newly injured people with those of us who have been in chairs for a while. It's almost like being welcomed into a special

brotherhood. It's a way for us to pass on some of the things we've learned. I've never yet met anyone in a chair who wasn't willing to spend time working with a new person.

No one can talk to a wheelchair user any better than another wheelchair user. The first time I had any counseling of any sort, it was from an able-bodied person. I told her where to step off in a real short time. She didn't understand and she didn't know.

Back when I met Mark, it was a really informal system. If you were lucky, there would be someone around to show you the ropes. If not, you were out of luck. Now it's more formalized. Hospitals and rehab centers bring in peer counselors to talk to the new patients. Unfortunately, there often aren't enough to fill the need.

When I met Mark, he immediately impressed me with his spirit. I could tell he was going to make it because he wasn't crying over spilled milk. Every one of us wallows in self-pity at one point or another—for some it's sooner; others, later—but Mark seemed to move past this stage faster than most. He must have felt these things inside, but he seemed as if he'd already made up his mind to go out and have a life.

I can remember the exact moment I knew Mark was going to make it. Late one night, after hours and hours of talking, he looked me right in the eye and told me he was going to go back out and climb another mountain. I don't know that too many other people would have believed him, but I did. It's because I knew nothing was impossible.

Right off the bat, Mark attacked the weight room with a vengeance. He was the hardest worker in the place, and it was obvious he was setting higher goals for himself. I knew he was in a lot of pain, but he just worked right through it.

The time we spent together, both in Redwood City and in Vallejo, was really important to both of us. Weird things happen when you try to recover from a big accident, and it's easy to lose your dignity. The camaraderie helps you realize you're not the only person going through this. You can get your dignity back—or at least a percentage of it—from the other guys and gals. Rehabilitation is only partially about the physical part. There's also the mental and the social part, and that's where your buddies come in.

The hardest part comes when you have to leave that sheltered, close-knit fraternity and go out into the real world. They try to tell you the rehab center is like the real world, but it's not. The real world has curbs you can't get over, doors you can't get open and hills you have to go over.

Mark never seemed worried about climbing those hills. In fact, I could tell he was looking forward to it.

3

CHANGING COURSE

Clank! The stack of lead weights slammed to the bottom of the bench press machine. Lying on my back, I blew out a sharp breath, grunted and forced the metal bar up again until my straining arms were fully extended. Then I quickly let the stack back down. *Clank!*

Jeff Forman moved the metal key a notch lower, adding another ten pounds of lead. Now there were 150 pounds on the stack. I groaned and slowly raised the bar. *Clank!* Again. *Clank!* Forman lowered the key another notch. One hundred sixty pounds. Rivulets of sweat ran down my face. I strained, let out an animal grunt and lifted the iron stack. *Clank!* Another one. *Clank!*

Forman moved the key. One hundred seventy pounds.

Red in the face, forearms shaking, I shoved up the bar and let it drop. *Clank!* I noticed that a crowd had gathered to watch and yell good-natured insults at me.

"C'mon Mark, you gimp! Move it! Give me another one!"

Forman called this little game "burnouts," and the name was certainly apt. Starting with sixty pounds of weight on the stack, the idea was to keep increasing the load by ten-pound increments, doing two repetitions at each level, until I was lifting the entire stack—180 pounds. Then I'd have to move back down the stack until I was back at sixty pounds.

Clank! I finished the workout and dropped the stack of weights for the last time. Drained, I slid out from under the bar. Now it was payback time. Forman took his place under the bar and I prepared to move the key down the stack of weights, notch by notch.

"Let's go, Forman," I said with a tired smile. "Let's see some effort, you wimp!"

Jeff Forman, a gregarious former rugby player, had become my unofficial personal trainer, motivator and friend. For an able-bodied person, he really seemed to understand what was going on in the minds of gimps. He had undertaken the task of helping me transform my body into that of the ideal wheelchair athlete. I couldn't help the fact that, from the waist down, I looked like Olive Oyl. But from the waist up, I *wanted* to look like Schwarzenegger.

By a stroke of luck, one of the nation's top physical education programs for disabled people is located at De Anza Community College in Cupertino, just a few miles from my home. I had taken a couple of classes at De Anza before my accident, and I remembered seeing far more people in wheelchairs than you'd expect to find on a typical college campus.

In January 1983, a couple of weeks after I left Vallejo, my father drove me down to De Anza to sign up for classes. I still didn't have any idea what I wanted to do with my life, but the college looked like an ideal place to start searching for an answer. Whatever I ended up doing, I knew it was going to require me to be physically strong. This looked like the perfect place to build myself up.

As I wheeled through the bustling campus, I immediately noticed things I'd overlooked in my able-bodied days. Just about every building that needed one had a wheelchair ramp, and not just one of those short, steep ones, either. These were long, gradual inclines you could wheel up without getting red in the face. The entrances to the library, cafeteria and student center were equipped with automatic doors, like those you'd find at a supermarket. Even the picnic tables had cutaway sections that allowed you to roll right up and join other students for lunch.

I wheeled into the viewing area above the huge swimming pool complex. About a dozen empty wheelchairs were parked on the deck while their owners swam laps in the pool. Around the corner was the adaptive physical education gymnasium. I rolled over to the doorway and peered inside. It looked a lot like the gym at Vallejo, with a hardwood floor, mats, weight machines and mirrors. Busily working out were men and women with just about every disability you could imagine: spinal cord injuries, multiple sclerosis, cerebral palsy, head injuries, strokes, amputations and blindness. They represented just a small fraction of the five hundred disabled people enrolled at De Anza.

A man in a blue warm-up suit walked up and introduced himself. He had bright, intense eyes and he spoke with a thick Massachusetts accent. He said he was Jeff Forman, one of the leaders of the adaptive physical education program. He told me he was going to work with me to design a custom program, according to my physical condition and goals.

"So tell me, Mark," he said. "What exactly are your plans?"

Ever since the day Dr. Smiley had told me I'd never walk again, my goal had remained the same. I wanted to prove him wrong. Most people just smiled indulgently when I told them that. I imagine they thought I was tilting at windmills. But I instantly felt comfortable with Forman, and I decided I could confide in him.

"I want to walk again," I said.

He didn't blink.

"You're going to have to keep working hard and chipping away at it, and realize the goal is not going to happen right away," he told me. "You're going to have to climb one stair at a time. You're going to have soreness, you're going to have frustration. But you will see progress."

Forman looked me right in the eye.

"We're going to make you a stud," he said. "We're going to have your arms bulging out. Every muscle you have left, we're going to bring them up to their maximum. We're going to pump them up."

With Forman exhorting me, I attacked the gym as if my life depended on it. And, in some ways, I guess it did.

I was up early every morning and out waiting in front of my house when the van from De Anza pulled up. It was generous of the college to provide door-to-door transportation, but riding in that van was always the worst part of my day. I hated the sound of the motorized lift, and I chafed at having my chair strapped down for the drive to Cupertino. This made me feel like an invalid, and I think it made me work even harder to become self-sufficient as soon as possible.

In the morning, I'd work out with Forman or one of the other teachers. I'd attend classes in stretching, balance and strength training. I kept pushing myself, working harder and harder each day. Eventually I was able to do two hundred push-ups and one hundred sit-ups in one session. Then I'd attach a twenty-five-pound weight to my waist, support myself by my arms from parallel bars, and do "dips" to strengthen my arms and shoulders. After that I'd practice dragging myself up and down stairs, holding onto the railing and hauling my chair behind me.

Then I'd hop in my chair and wheel over to the swimming pool. I loved swimming, because it got me out of my wheelchair and allowed me to stretch out. At first they used a machine called a Hoyer lift to transfer me into the water. It looked like something you'd use on a boat in dry dock. Later I learned to enter the pool by myself, using the handrails and steps.

A Styrofoam pad between my legs helped keep me afloat, and hand paddles gave me more resistance and strengthened my arms. It was twenty-five yards across the pool, and I worked up to doing seventy-two laps— a full mile. Then I'd put on my leg braces and walk about one hundred yards around the perimeter of the pool.

After a couple of months I began to see results. The muscles in my upper body were growing large and powerful, and my endurance was increasing. One day I went into the physiology lab so they could test my level of physical fitness. I'd undergone the same tests before my accident, and I was curious to see how I compared. They dipped me into a tank to measure my body fat, and they hooked my wheelchair up to a treadmill-like device to test my cardiovascular levels. The results showed that I was in as good a shape as, if not better than, I had ever been as an able-bodied person.

That winter, when snow started falling in the Sierra Nevada, I began to get the familiar skier's itch. I convinced the De Anza student union and college ski club to put up the money to buy an Arroya sit-ski. At the time it was the most advanced model on the market, but compared to what's available now, it was rather primitive. It looked like a sawed-off kayak with ski runners on the base, and it worked more like a toboggan than a ski.

Nancy and I drove up to the Dodge Ridge Ski Area, along with Susan Michalski, a disabled ski instructor. I felt a tinge of excitement to be returning to the mountains for a little taste of adventure. But the feeling soon evaporated amid all the hassles.

Just getting me into the ski lift was a major operation.

The operator had to stop the lift as several other people strained to boost me and the sit-ski up into the chair. I had to hook my safety strap tightly around the chair because of the very real possibility that I could tumble out of the seat on my way up the mountain. At the top, the whole procedure had to be reversed.

Heading down the bunny slope, I was tethered to Susan, who skied fifteen feet behind me and controlled my progress. It was necessary, but I felt as dependent as a baby being wheeled around in a stroller. Skiing for me had always been about the joy and freedom of movement, and this had nothing to do with that.

Later I got the hang of it well enough to ski by myself, but I still felt awkward. The experience was more akin to sledding than skiing. I realized I was at the mercy of the ski designers. I heard rumors they were working on more advanced models that performed like real skis, and I couldn't wait to get my hands on one.

Wheeling by the De Anza tennis courts one day, I noticed that the people knocking balls back and forth across the net were all in wheelchairs. Watching them play, I realized wheelchair tennis was the same as able-bodied tennis in every respect, except that you got two bounces.

Immediately I wanted to wheel out onto the courts and join them. I'd been a good tennis player in high school, and I figured it wouldn't be too hard to make the transition to playing in a wheelchair. I already had the strokes, I already knew the strategy, and I already had the court sense.

None of that prepared me for the first time I picked up a racket and parked myself behind the back line. As the first ball floated over the net toward me, I turned my chair and started trying to move into position. It wasn't easy. My right hand had to hold onto my racket and spin my wheel rim at the same time. By the time

I could move a few feet to my right, the ball had already sailed past me and hit the back fence.

I didn't do much better on the second ball. It bounced right over my head.

Trying not to let my frustration show, I realized this wasn't going to be as easy as I thought. I was going to have to learn a whole new game. But I've always been competitive, and I knew it was as hard for all the other gimps as it was for me. And I was determined to be one of the best.

I began to spend long hours out on the courts, practicing with other gimps, with able-bodied people, even with a machine that fired balls at me. I'd be out there two or three hours every day, working to improve my anticipation and the fluidness of my movements. I knew I'd have to hit the gym even harder to develop the upper body power I'd need to cover the court more quickly.

Eventually I began to see improvement. I found myself ranging from side to side on the court, chasing down just about any ball my opponent could hit. My serve developed into a formidable weapon, and I won lots of points with clean aces.

The competition pumped me up like nothing I'd experienced in a long time. I played all-out. My fingers got chewed up from getting caught in the spokes. I'd lunge at balls and go flying out of my chair, cutting my knees on the court. Once I was concentrating so hard on trying to win my match that I didn't notice a nasty blister forming at the base of my tailbone.

All that was part of the game. I wanted to be good, wanted to get some respect from the other players, and a skinned knee or a blister was a small price to pay. My first few tournaments ended quickly, with losses in the first round. After a year of hard practice, however, I found myself moving up into the middle of the pack.

The wheelchair tennis circuit was divided into categories, from the "D" level to the open division. I started as a "D" and rapidly moved up, skipping by the "Cs" and ending up in the "B" division. In the mid-1980s, the sport was just starting to become highly competitive.

I began traveling to tournaments up and down the West Coast, playing everywhere from San Jose to Seattle. In September 1985 the circuit took me to Fresno, the site of my hospital stay three years earlier. It was every bit as sweltering as I'd remembered.

In the blistering heat, I played one of my best matches ever. My opponent blew me off the court at first, taking the first set 6-1. Then I dug in and began rallying back, point by point. I fought off a couple of match points in the second set and went on to win it in a tie-breaker. Both of us were dripping with sweat and physically drained, but with the match tied at one set apiece, we had to go out on the court and play again.

Heat waves were shimmering up from the court as I served to begin the final set. It quickly became a battle of wills, with neither of us giving an inch. The score went to 6-6. It was gut-check time, and I absolutely refused to surrender. In the tie-breaker I hit a couple of serves my opponent had trouble handling, and I pulled out the victory.

Shaking his hand at the net afterwards, I felt dizzy and ready to collapse. But the match had filled me with self-confidence. I realized that all those hours of hard work in the gym had paid off. Within the competitive world of wheelchair sports, I was now more of an accomplished athlete than I ever had been as an able-bodied person.

I went on to do well at the nationals in Irvine the following week. I didn't win the tournament, but I emerged as the sixth-ranked "B" wheelchair tennis player in the nation.

One day, back in the gym at De Anza, I noticed a funny tingling at the top of my thighs. At first I thought

I was imagining things, but then I felt it again. *Could it really be happening?* I fought the urge to let my excitement get too high.

Slowly, over the course of several months, I definitely began to notice sensation returning to parts of my body that had been numb since the accident. First I regained a little bit of feeling in my waist area. Over a period of months, it spread down to the tops of my legs, and kept growing until I had partial sensation down to mid-thigh. The damage to my spinal cord had only been partial, and now some of my nerves were finding ways to rewire themselves and come back on-line.

All that time on the weight machines had built up the quadricep muscles in my thighs, and I found I could actually move my legs a little. One blessed day I even discovered that some sensation had returned to my penis. I still had to use a catheter for urinating, but I found I could once again function sexually, at least more or less normally.

For a short time, I dared to hope I would regain complete use of my entire body. I knew it was a long shot, but in my weaker moments I allowed myself to daydream of once again climbing mountains, running through wildflower-dotted meadows and giving up my wheelchair forever.

More time passed, and the sensation stopped spreading. The doctors examined me and told me I'd regained all the feeling I was ever going to. It took me a few days to get over it, but I realized I had no choice but to work even harder to create a life for myself in my wheelchair.

Around this time, my relationship with Nancy came to an end. The final straw came during a wedding for one of the physical therapists from Vallejo. I lost my temper over something stupid and blew up at her and that was pretty much it. We had been moving in different directions for quite some time. Nancy was focused on her career and eager to move ahead in the business world. She had graduated from San Jose State University and had taken a promising marketing job with Levi Strauss & Company.

I still had no direction in my life other than wanting to work out and get stronger. I didn't look much past the next workout. Nancy had stood by my side through the worst times of my recovery, but we just weren't meant to spend the rest of our lives together.

Some people probably thought we broke up because I was in a wheelchair, but that wasn't true. It was a small part of it, but nothing more. My relationships with Nancy and the women I've known since have been as complex as those of any other guy. There are all sorts of reasons why relationships blossom and fade between two people, and gimps who blame every love affair gone sour on their wheelchairs are deceiving themselves.

I've met lots of women since my accident, and if anything, being in a wheelchair has brought me good fortune. Physically, I'm not threatening to anyone. I think some women are even impressed by the fact that I've striven so hard to be independent and able to care for myself in any situation. It's a person's attitude toward life that is important, not whether they're in a wheelchair or not.

I think my breakup with Nancy helped me realize it was time to look for a direction for my life. I was now twenty-four years old, and I knew I didn't want to spend the rest of my life lifting weights, swimming laps and swatting a tennis ball.

I needed to go out and find a career in the real world. It's something I had been avoiding for years, since long before my accident. I still didn't know what I wanted to be when I grew up, but I knew I was running out of time to find out. The prospect was scary. I didn't have many skills, I didn't have a college education and I didn't have any interest in the nine-to-five office jobs that are suited to a guy in a wheelchair. And I knew I couldn't live forever on the seven hundred dollars a month I was getting from social security.

One day I went to see Shirley Negrin, a counselor with the State Department of Rehabilitation. I'd first met Shirley while I was in the hospital in Redwood City, and we'd spoken a few times in the two years since then. Once, she had given me some tests to discover my aptitude and interests in different fields.

This time, when I wheeled into Shirley's small office, I felt there was more riding on our conversation. I knew I was going to have to start making some decisions about my future.

"Have you thought much about what you want to do for a living?" she asked.

"No, not really," I admitted.

"What about becoming a park ranger?"

My mind raced. I loved the thought of being back in the outdoors, living among the mountains and trees, but I'd never given any thought to working as a ranger. There just seemed to be too many obstacles to overcome. I imagined the job entailed too many things that couldn't be done in a chair.

"Uh, well... I'd love to, but I don't see how I could," I said. "I mean, don't you have to be able to hike on trails and get around in the back country and things like that?"

"Not necessarily," she said. "Why don't we go talk to a ranger and find out?"

A couple of days later Shirley and I drove up to Fort Funston in San Francisco, which is part of the Golden Gate National Recreation Area. Located on the headlands at the entrance to San Francisco Bay, it's popular with city people who want to escape the hustle and bustle and noise of downtown San Francisco for a few hours. Shirley introduced me to Frank Dean, one of the rangers. He gave us a tour of the park and told us about the duties of his job. Much of it was administrative work, studies and public speaking.

"Being a ranger doesn't necessarily mean you spend all your time hiking around the back country," Frank told me. "There are a lot of other jobs that rangers do, and I think you could probably do most of them in your wheelchair."

I was all ears.

"As a matter of fact," he continued, "we're looking for a volunteer right here, someone to help out with some of the gardening projects. Are you interested?"

"Sure," I said, jumping at the chance.

Frank took me over to the nursery and introduced me to another ranger named Jim Milestone. He was involved in a monumental effort to remove all the exotic shrubbery from around World War II gunnery emplacements. Ice plant dominated the area, and he was slowly replacing it with native species like dune grass. It was a huge job for one person, and Jim didn't have much of a budget to do it.

"Welcome aboard," he told me. "I sure could use some help."

He gave me a uniform to wear. For the next three months I spent several hours a week in the greenhouse, watering the plants and transplanting dune grass into little cylinders called leech tubes.

It wasn't a really important job, but it got me outside working, and it opened my eyes to a lot of possibilities. I began to realize that Shirley was right—I could be a park ranger in my chair. I knew it was the career I wanted.

Working at the Golden Gate National Recreation Area had one other huge benefit: it helped me get my own van. I met with the California Department of Rehabilitation people, and we agreed that if I was going to go to school and work, I'd need my own vehicle. They bought me a green Ford van and set about making modifications to it. They wanted to install a mechanical lift and ramp to get my wheelchair inside the cargo door, but I think I surprised them by telling them I didn't want one. I knew I was strong enough to do it myself.

A specialty shop installed a padded plywood platform that allowed me to lie down in the back of the van. This was important, because I needed to get out of my chair several times a day and stretch out to avoid pressure sores. With a little practice, I became pretty good at getting in and out by myself. I'd open the cargo door, hoist myself into a sitting position on the plywood platform, and then lean back, using my body weight to help lift the chair up into the van. Then I'd boost myself up between the two front seats, slide around into the driver's seat and be ready to go.

While waiting for the modifications to be made on my van, I took an hour-long driving lesson from the state rehabilitation people, practicing in a modified Cadillac. On the left side of the steering column were the hand controls, just as Mark Sutherland had described them. Two metal bars extended up from the gas and brake pedals to a little control panel. I worked the knobs with my left hand and steered with my right. There was a toggle switch on the hand-control panel for the high beams, and a button for the horn. A little plastic handle on the control panel set the parking brake. We drove around a parking lot and a couple of back streets, and it didn't take me long to get the hang of it.

When my van was finally ready, I couldn't wait to hop in and hit the open road. I immediately pulled out into fast-moving traffic on Highway 101, and it was exhilarating to rediscover that long-lost feeling of freedom. It was the same kind of liberation I had felt when I was sixteen and got my first driver's license—only much, much more intense. Until you've had your mobility taken away from you, there's no way you can appreciate how much it means.

Now there could be no putting it off: If I wanted to be a park ranger, the next step was to go back to school. The idea made me a little nervous, because it meant leaving the protected environment of De Anza and moving into a program where everyone but me would be able-bodied. I hadn't cracked open a textbook in close to four years, and the thought of sitting in a classroom for hours at a time filled me with dread.

The nearest park-management program was at West Valley College in Saratoga, several miles south of De Anza. As I wheeled myself through the campus on the first day of classes, a notebook on my lap and pens in my shirt pockets, much of my nervousness disappeared. The physical strength and grace I had developed from wheelchair sports made me feel confident and self-assured. I wasn't exactly the "Big Man on Campus," but I was no longer that awkward invalid who had wheeled into the restaurant three years earlier.

I found the right classroom, rolled in, moved a chair away from a table and parked there. If my classmates thought it was strange for a guy in a wheelchair to be studying to be a park ranger, they never let on. From that first day, the instructor, Tom "Smitty" Smith, treated me just like all his able-bodied students. He demanded as much out of me as he did out of anyone, and I wouldn't have had it any other way. I wasn't there for sympathy or charity. I was there to become a park ranger.

Before long I had a huge stack of textbooks covering all sorts of subjects: conservation, land management, horticulture, biology, interpretation, wildlife, law enforcement, search and rescue, emergency medicine and park design.

I stayed up late at night, eagerly poring through them. In class, I paid attention and raised my hand frequently to answer questions. I was studying harder than I ever had in high school because the subjects now meant something to me. They were my ticket to my future.

I was now focused and driven in a way I had never been before. My days of just drifting through life had abruptly ended during that fall up on the mountain. My hard years of rehabilitation had taught me the importance of setting myself a goal and striving toward it. I had worked extremely hard just to be able to return to the able-bodied world, and I wasn't about to' stop there.

Our education didn't just take place in the classroom. A couple of times a week we'd drive up into the nearby hills to Sanborn County Park for some hands-on training. This was hard, sweaty stuff. We'd clear brush, build trails, pound nails and pour cement.

When we built trails, I grabbed a pick and pitched right in with the crew. It took a little experimenting to find the proper technique, but I soon found I could swing the tool effectively from my chair. My arms were so strong from all those pull-ups and "burnout" drills that I could send the rocks and dirt flying.

I crashed through the brush in my chair, helping to lay out the route for a new path at Sanborn. Sometimes I'd get caught in a rut or stopped by a rock, but my classmates never seemed to mind giving me a quick boost. Over several months, our class helped build a long trail connecting two regional parks in the foothills.

One of the classes in the program was mountaineering. Rangers need to know the principles of mountain climbing so they can participate in rescues, whether they're in the field or the radio dispatch office. I signed up for it not because I had any immediate plans to start climbing again, but because it was a required course.

To learn the basics of rock climbing, we all drove a couple of hours down to Pinnacles National Monument, a wonderland of weird volcanic rock formations jutting up out of the chaparral above Salinas. With a bit of a struggle, I rolled my wheelchair about a mile up the rocky trail to the crag where we stopped to hold class. I felt a pang of nostalgia as the instructors uncoiled brightly colored nylon ropes.

It was here, for the first and only time in the course, that I was left behind. I helped some of the students adjust their harnesses and check their knots, but when they started picking their way up handholds and footholds, I had to watch from the ground. I tried not to let my disappointment show. Occasionally I shouted up words of encouragement, but mostly I sat in silence, remembering those long-ago days of freedom and adventure.

If nothing else, I think my presence served as a reminder of what can happen during a single moment of carelessness in the mountains. I hoped it was a lesson my classmates learned well.

My disappointment at being left out during the rock-climbing class didn't last long. Our next outing was to be three days of snow camping in the Sierra Nevada, and I would be going along as a full participant.

As we passed the last town of the foothills and drove up into the mountains, I could feel the excitement building in me. The February sky was a bright blue, the air was crisp and cold, and the peaks were all gleaming brightly with snow. For the first time since my accident, I would be returning to the true wilderness. Also, it would be my first extended vacation from my wheelchair in four years.

But I was full of doubts, too. Would I be able to negotiate the rugged terrain in my sit-ski? Would the cold prove to be too much for my feet and legs? Would the effort of transporting myself through the snow, setting up camp and cooking meals prove to be such a hassle that it would steal away the joy? Would I be a burden to the other people in my class?

We drove as far as the road was plowed and parked our cars near the Bear Valley Ski Resort. As everyone pulled overstuffed backpacks out of car trunks and unloaded cross-country skis from ski racks, I looked around at the other members of the group. We were a mixed bunch. There were some experienced mountaineers, people who had climbed difficult peaks and made arduous winter crossings of this entire mountain range. For them, this trip would be a walk in the park. At the other extreme, we had some beginners who had never spent a night in a sleeping bag or carried a backpack on their shoulders. They had a struggle ahead of them. I fit in somewhere in between. I had as much experience as anyone, but in my awkward sit-ski, I might as well have been a beginner.

At first we skied along the unplowed road, heading deeper into the mountains. Here the path was downhill, and I had little trouble moving across the hard-packed snow. I had some short ski poles that I pushed myself with. It was hard work, but I was able to keep up with the group. I would have liked to have been able to carry my own gear, but in this set-up it was impossible. Some of the more experienced skiers carried my stuff, as well as that of some of the beginners.

It felt as if spring was just around the corner. The high country was already starting to shed its winter coat, and shrubs and bushes were emerging from the snow. Trees were shaking off their heavy loads, and occasionally a glop would land next to the trail or smack an unsuspecting skier on the head. This was always good for a laugh.

We turned off the unplowed road, and suddenly things got much more difficult for me. Now we had to forge our own path up and across a ridge eight hundred feet above us. Immediately I discovered that my sit-ski was not built for going uphill. I strained with my poles until I was out of breath, gaining very little progress for the effort.

Luckily we had planned for this. The group had brought along a climbing rope, some nylon webbing and even a little hand-operated winch. It became a real team effort. Sometimes I would attach my ski to a piece of webbing that ran around the waist of one of the experienced people. At other times, the instructor, John Nicholas, would have the whole class line up along the slope and pull me up with the rope.

We traversed past the shore of frozen Duck Lake and set up camp on a hill overlooking the lake. I felt a warm spark of pleasure as I performed my old backpacking rituals: unpacking and pitching my A-frame tent, pulling my goose-down sleeping bag from its stuff sack and fluffing it up, firing up my little Svea 123 backpacking stove to boil water for tea. These little camp chores didn't mean much in themselves, but in their familiarity I felt a strong connection to a hundred other nights spent in the wilderness. It was like a reunion with a dear old friend I thought I'd lost forever.

The next day we all pitched in to dig snow caves and construct igloos. Some people slept in them, but I decided my tent was a more appealing place to spend the night. I cooked dinner for part of the group, and from the way the pot emptied out, I'd say my special back-country spaghetti recipe was a big hit.

That night, as I lay cocooned in my warm sleeping bag, I couldn't stop smiling. Everything was turning out even better than I'd dared to hope. Despite the need for a little help in places, skiing had proven to be a wonderful way to travel in the wilderness, granting me access to places I could never reach in my wheelchair. My legs and feet stayed toasty warm with extra socks and long underwear. I didn't feel like a burden to the group; everyone treated this as a team effort and a learning experience.

But the most important thing was that I was finally back out in the mountains.

Smitty helped me get my first paying ranger's job. He worked as a seasonal ranger in Yosemite National Park, and heard about a summer position that would be perfect for me. I immediately called up Dale Barnett, the Yosemite ranger who was doing the hiring. We talked about the job, and I told him about my experience as a mountaineer, my desire to become a ranger and the program I was completing at West Valley College.

"I know I can do this job," I told him, trying to muster up all the confidence I could. "I really want to work in Yosemite, and I can start any time."

He paused for a moment, then said: "You know, Mark, you seem qualified, and I think you're a good candidate. I'd like to hire you, but I just can't. The employee housing just isn't set up for a disabled person. I'm sorry."

I couldn't believe what I was hearing. I wanted this job. I needed this job. But I had run head-first into the obstacles disabled people face every day, the kind I would face every day for the rest of my life—unless I found a way to get past them. This was a turning point. If I let him turn me down for this job because I was disabled, it might kill my confidence and momentum to build a new, independent life for myself. I had to persuade him to give me an opportunity.

"How about if I come up there and make my own decision about whether I can live in your employee housing?"

There were a few moments of silence at the other end of the line as Barnett thought it over. I hoped he couldn't hear my heart pounding.

"Fair enough," he said. "Come on up and let's give it a shot."

Barnett was right. As we pulled into Camp Mather, I could see that the housing certainly wasn't set up for

a person in a wheelchair. I was to live in a tent–cabin—
a cement platform with canvas walls and roof—in the
woods near the Hetch Hetchy Reservoir.

The bathroom was fifty yards away, and the showers
were really primitive. If you wanted hot water, you
had to build a fire under the water heater and wait for
it to warm up. But the hardest thing about Camp
Mather was trying to maneuver my wheelchair through
the dirt and thick carpet of pine needles. My wheels
kept slipping and skidding. I knew living here would
be tough, but I was hungry for the job.

"It's no problem for me," I told Barnett. "I can live
here."

"Fine," he said. "You've got the job."

The first time I put on my Yosemite ranger's uniform,
I was filled with a pride I hadn't felt in years. I spent
a long time checking myself out in the mirror, making
sure my nameplate was straight, adjusting my Smokey
the Bear hat. Finally I was back out in society, holding
down a job and earning my own money again. I was
making only six dollars an hour, but after almost four
years of receiving disability and social security checks,
that first real paycheck went a long way toward
restoring my self-respect.

Not that my job was glamorous. My assignment was
to staff the kiosk at the Big Oak Flat entrance station.
All day long I'd collect the three-dollar entrance fee
from motorists, hand them their maps and give them
directions to the various sights in the park.

Together with some other rangers, I made a couple
of quick modifications in the kiosk to allow me to work
there. We put in a ramp up to the door and a plywood
covering over the well where the rangers usually stand.
That way I could reach the cash register from my chair.
Most of the time, though, I stood up with my leg
braces, holding onto the window sill. If I was sitting in
my chair when they drove up, they just saw the top of

my head, and it must have looked to them like I was a midget. I doubt if any of the visitors at the entrance station ever knew I was disabled. Nobody every said anything.

It wasn't really my idea of being a ranger, taking people's money and choking on car fumes all summer. But it was a start. I had a real job, I was working in one of the premier national parks in the world, and that was all that counted at the moment.

On my days off I'd hop in my van and drive the twenty miles down to Yosemite Valley. During my mountaineering days I'd kept my distance from the valley, which gets about three-fourths of all visitors to the park. With the hordes of Winnebago warriors and Instamatic-toting tourists, it can resemble the Disneyland of the High Sierra. The tourists are drawn by the name-brand sights of Yosemite—Half Dome, El Capitan, Yosemite Falls—and also by the gift shops, restaurants, bars and other city comforts. I had always avoided the valley and headed for the solitude of high and wild places.

Now I saw Yosemite Valley in a different light. It was flat and designed to enable visitors to get around easily. Now I realized that its miles of roads, hard-packed trails and paved bike paths made it one of the most wheelchair-accessible of any national park.

I spent hours wheeling my chair along the paths, crunching over pine needles and inhaling the sweet mountain air. It didn't take much, I discovered, to escape the masses of people in the valley. Most of them never seemed to want to venture onto even the easiest trails. I'd roll myself along the path to one of my favorite spots and spend the afternoon drinking in the breathtaking scenery.

Sometimes I'd drive up to Tenaya Lake in Yosemite's high country, and go for a swim in its chilly, snow-fed waters. I'd wheel my chair slowly down into the lake, until the water level just about came up to its seat cushion. With my flotation pads I could swim around the lake, and it always felt great to get out of the chair and stretch a bit. I'd pull myself up onto a sandy beach and feel the warm sun on my chest as I watched the sunlight and clouds play on the jagged granite mountains above me.

It wasn't the same as climbing those mountains, but it was a long way from the hospital bed where I had spent those nights of black despair and hopelessness. I felt at home here, and I couldn't have been happier. I was starting a new life for myself among the mountains.

A couple of weeks after I started work, my living conditions improved tremendously. Some firefighters I knew called the park's housing supervisor, and he found me an empty trailer in an employee housing area called Hodgdon Meadow. We called it Hog Town. They built a ramp up to the door and I moved in. I had to admit it was much more comfortable than my tent–cabin.

It was about a mile from the entrance kiosk, and every morning I'd put on my green and grey ranger's uniform and wheel myself up a long hill to work. It was a good workout for me, and all the other park employees seemed to get a kick out of seeing the gimp ranger rolling to work. They'd wave to me as I went past, but it was hard to wave back—I needed both hands on my wheels!

Later that summer I got to leave the kiosk from time to time to do other jobs. One of them entailed driving the ranger truck to the six campgrounds along the Tioga Pass Road to collect camping fees. I had some portable hand controls, and it took me only a few minutes to bolt them onto the steering column of the ranger truck. I'd make my rounds to the campgrounds, extracting all the pay envelopes from the deposit boxes. Then I'd drive back to the Big Oak Flat ranger station, count all the money and fill out the proper forms.

Maybe it wasn't the most exciting way to spend the day, but that's part of the job of being a ranger. Besides, it was fun to get out of the entrance kiosk for a couple of hours. By the end of the summer I think I had erased all the doubts in the minds of the Park Service—and in my own—about my ability to perform the job of a park ranger from my wheelchair. I still couldn't get into the back country much, but, as I discovered, there were plenty of jobs that didn't require it. My bosses must have been happy with the work I was doing, because they invited me to come back the following summer.

That next season I worked as an interpretive ranger, answering the public's questions and spreading the word about Yosemite's natural history. My first assignment was the visitors' center, the first stop for most tourists who arrive in Yosemite Valley. I worked behind a counter, and if people didn't see my wheelchair parked nearby, there was no way for them to know I was disabled.

I was excited at helping to educate the public about the park, and I spent long hours boning up on the flora, fauna, geology, weather, history and activities. I knew the height of every waterfall, the characteristics of every pine tree, the footprint patterns of every animal. I knew the customs of the Native Americans who first settled in the valley, what they ate and who they traded with. So when the first visitor walked up to the counter, I was totally prepared.

"Can you answer a question?" he asked.

"Sure. What would you like to know?"

"Where can I get an ice cream cone around here?"

Nor did the next visitor tap into my rich fund of knowledge.

"Where is the bathroom?" she asked. "Oh, and do you sell T-shirts here?"

One of the strangest questions came from the man who wanted to know where the geysers were. I had to try to keep a straight face as I told him they were one thousand miles away—in Yellowstone National Park.

Luckily the visitors weren't all like that. Many of them had only a short time to spend in the park, and they wanted advice on what to see and do. I was never at a loss for suggestions. First-time backpackers would ask about certain trails or procedures for keeping their food away from hungry bears, and there were people who wanted to know about the trees or the raccoons. Others wanted to see the rest of the park, and I was happy to give them information about the groves of ancient redwood trees or the sights in the high country. It never ceased to amaze us how many people would walk up to the counter, tell us they had only two hours to spend in Yosemite and ask for suggestions. My favorite response came from one of the older rangers.

"Do you see that meadow out there across the road?" he'd say. "If I had only two hours to spend in Yosemite, I'd go out there, sit down—and cry."

Sometimes I'd get to hop on my bicycle and roam around the valley to talk to visitors and answer their questions. I had something called a "row cycle," a bicycle I could operate by rowing a hand-crank mechanism. It had three gears, and I could move quite fast on it. It was a wild-looking bicycle, and it always attracted attention. It was a fun way to break the ice with visitors. We'd start talking about the bicycle, and then maybe they'd ask about the different kinds of wildlife or ask where the other half of Half Dome went. I really enjoyed the days I got to work outside like that.

Living was getting easier, too. They moved me into a cozy little cabin in Yosemite Valley, right next to the administration building. It already had a ramp going up to the front door, built for the previous occupant, who had also been disabled. The cabin wasn't completely accessible—I couldn't get my chair into the bathroom, for example—but by holding onto things, I could walk myself around. All in all, it was a pretty comfortable place. There was plenty of room outside to park my growing collection of toys. Eventually I accumulated two sports wheelchairs, two kinds of downhill skis, some cross-country skis and a bicycle. I would end up living in that cabin for most of the next four years.

As the years went by, I took on new and different jobs. Once I spent the whole night manning a road blockade in my wheelchair, stopping traffic because of a wildfire in the park. On several other big fires I worked as a radio dispatcher, relaying commands among battalions and helping coordinate the firefighting effort.

One of my favorite jobs was to give campfire talks and evening slide programs. I'd wheel up in front of the crowd, and all eyes would be on me, all ears tuned in to what I was saying. It was a natural high to have an audience hanging on my every word. One of the standard talks I gave was about climbing. I'd show a short film and then demonstrate some of the equipment that an able-bodied climber would use.

Once, when I was out on roving duty in my chair, I was the first ranger on the scene of a grisly accident. A Japanese girl had taken a rental bicycle up to Lower Yosemite Falls. On the way back down the steep path, she had had trouble figuring out the coaster brakes and had lost control. Going faster and faster, she missed the sharp turn at the bottom of the hill and crashed into the boulders along the river. Someone came running to get me, and when I got there the girl had a compound fracture of her arm—the broken bone was poking out through her skin. She was nearly hysterical and going into shock. I radioed the park medics and comforted the girl until they got there. It took them only about two minutes to arrive, and I'm sure we were both relieved.

Initially, though, it was my job to take control of the situation, and I'm proud to say no one asked for a "real" ranger. In fact, no one ever said anything like that in my presence during the four years I worked in Yosemite. It happened to plenty of women rangers, though. I think I was spared that kind of discrimination because of the way I carried myself in my chair. My upper body was bulging with muscles, and I still retained a lot of self-confidence from being a wheelchair athlete. I think people picked up on that.

Every day I seemed to notice more visitors in wheelchairs. I guess word had gotten out that Yosemite was an accessible place, at least compared to other national parks, and people in wheelchairs would come from all over the world.

One of the things I wanted to do was to make it even easier for disabled people to enjoy the place. I took on the job of access coordinator, and advised the Park Service and the Yosemite Park and Curry Company, the concessionaire, about the need for wheelchair ramps and curb cuts. We worked on a wheelchair-accessible trail via a stone causeway from the nature center at Happy Isles to two islands in the Merced River. The Park Service wanted to pave the trail with asphalt, but I pushed for something more natural. I won, and they're using a decomposed granite that's been tamped down. People in wheelchairs don't always need to be on pavement. In a place like Yosemite, I think they like to have a little more contact with nature.

With every passing winter, I spent more and more time skiing up at Badger Pass, the small downhill ski resort in Yosemite. I was finally getting to be a pretty good skier with my sit-ski. I could negotiate every run at the resort with no trouble at all. Eventually the Park Service let me spend one day a week there, performing first aid and occasionally working as a ski patrolman up on the mountain.

In the winter of 1988–89, I worked with the Curry Company to develop a program for disabled skiers.

The concessionaire bought a few sit-skis, some outrigger poles for use by amputees, and some bibs and leashes for blind skiers. One of the things we had to do was train the ski patrol to be able to evacuate disabled skiers from the chairlift in the event of a breakdown.

The program continues today, and it's given me great satisfaction. I can still remember the time I spotted a young boy in a wheelchair on the deck of the ski lodge. He watched wistfully as the rest of his family had fun out on the slopes. You should have seen his face as I came schussing up to the deck in my sit-ski, sending out a spray of snow as I stopped right in front of him.

"Want to learn to ski?" I asked the boy.

"Yeah! But, um... how?"

"C'mon. We can show you."

If I ever had any doubts about the value of our disabled ski program, the look of absolute joy on the boy's face dispelled them immediately. Over the years, lots of people with spinal cord injuries, amputations and blindness have had that same look of joy as they experienced the thrill of skiing for the first time at Badger Pass.

In the summer, I kept pushing myself to see as much of the park as was humanly possible in a wheelchair. Once I wheeled all the way up to the base of Vernal Falls, which was quite an undertaking. It's one of the most popular hikes in Yosemite, a short but very steep mile and a half. The first part is quite flat and I did fine, although I got a few puzzled looks from the other hikers. Then the trail started climbing sharply. I grew red in the face and my arms strained to roll my wheels uphill against the pull of gravity. At the same time, I had to fight to keep from rolling backward and losing the progress I'd gained.

The trail climbed along the frothy Merced River, which was tumbling down in huge cascades on its way to Yosemite Valley. There are some great views along this stretch, but I couldn't see them. A rock wall, built to keep hikers from falling into the icy river, extended up to my eye level. I was also straining too much to enjoy the scenery.

Much of the trail bed had been blasted out of solid granite; other sections had been paved long ago to make it easier for the mule trains that supply camps in the high country. In places the rock was too rough or the old pavement too broken up to allow me to pass. I had to get out of my chair and crawl past these sections on the warm granite while a friend carried my wheelchair.

Finally, after a little over a mile, the trail dropped steeply down to a wide wooden bridge at the base of Vernal Falls. I parked myself there, exhausted, and let the cool mist wafting down from the falls refresh me. Vernal Falls is one of the shortest in Yosemite, but it's also one of the prettiest. It's wide and powerful, thundering into a deep emerald pool as its roar echoes off the enclosing granite cliffs. As I caught my breath, I watched a rainbow dancing through the spray. It was a beautiful place to be, but I knew there had to be a better way for me to enjoy the splendor of Yosemite.

I soon found one when I bought a kayak. Once I was in the water, I was as mobile as any able-bodied kayaker. It gave me an incredible feeling of freedom.

Springtime was my favorite time to paddle the Merced River. Yosemite was quiet without the summer crowds. There was often still a dusting of snow atop Half Dome and some of the other high points of the valley rim, and the river would be running high, fast and chilly with all the melted snow. Best of all were the waterfalls. Many of the finest ones appear for only a few weeks in the spring and early summer, plunging thousands of feet from the rim to the valley floor in a single breathtaking leap.

One kayak trip I made stands out in my memory. I

could hear the mules braying as we drove up to Clark's Bridge, near the stables. As a friend lifted our two kayaks out of my van, I rolled my chair down to the riverbank.

Pushing out into the current, I immediately began to get a new perspective on Yosemite. The sights, sounds and sensations were so much different from those I'd get from the roads and trails that crisscross the valley floor. I paddled my kayak around in a slow circle, craning my neck up to watch the changing light on the impossibly high granite walls that rose nearly a mile above me.

Cascading down from Glacier Point was a rushing staircase waterfall I'd never noticed before. Another thin ribbon of water was dancing over the cliff known as Royal Arches, the drops scattering into the wind before they even hit the valley floor.

Swimming across the river in front of me were six ducklings, pedaling their webbed feet furiously so as to keep up with their mother. In a back eddy, an aloof Great Blue Heron glided back and forth. Up in a Ponderosa pine tree, I caught sight of two majestic Peregrine falcons waiting to swoop down on an unsuspecting Stellar blue jay.

I let the current silently carry me along as I leaned back and watched the continuing spectacle of Yosemite's granite cliffs drift by above the treetops. Yosemite Falls roared down from the rim in a massive plume. Clouds floated across the sky, sending their shadows scudding up and down the granite walls. Along the banks, spring wildflowers framed the edges of lush green meadows. The river spun me around slowly until my eyes fell on Half Dome, standing like a proud parent over the eastern end of the valley.

I heard a noise and swung around to see a buck with a huge rack of antlers dashing across a shallow section of the river. Further downstream, I caught sight of a beautiful black bear and her two cubs standing, alert on the riverbank, watching me glide by.

At Superintendent's Bridge there's a little rapid, and we stopped to play in it, zipping through the whitewater chute and circling back in the eddy to do it again.

The immense glacier-polished monolith of El Capitan drifted into view above us, dominating everything in its shadow. It was beginning to glow golden in the late afternoon sun. My favorite waterfall, Horsetail Falls, was glistening on its long journey down from the summit.

I lay back in my kayak and studied the soaring granite wall, so colossal it beggared my imagination. The interplay of sunlight and shadow revealed a vast expanse of elegant towers, flying buttresses, scooped-out bays and deep fractures. One entire face was covered by a huge section of black rock that looked remarkably like a map of North America. Over the rippling sounds of the river, I could make out the tink-tink-tink of a climber hammering a piton into a crack, thousands of feet up on the cliff face. Squinting, I could barely make out a speck of red perched halfway up a long series of cracks. Even with my mountaineering experience, the rarefied world of the big-wall climber seemed so strange, so alien to me.

I wondered what life was like for them up there, alone in their vertical world.

Jeff Forman:

Mark was my favorite student of all time. He never took a back seat to anyone, and he wasn't content to just sit back and collect social security. Mark really wanted to make something of his life.

Of all the hundreds of disabled people who have passed through our program at De Anza, Mark stood out from the crowd. He represented our ideal. He was there to get stronger and improve every day, and everyone took notice—not just the other disabled people, but the staff as well.

Some disabled people eventually settle into a s
"learned helplessness." They allow other people to
for them, and they lose the motivation to be fully inde
Here we see them lying back on the mats, saying to
"OK, exercise me now."

From the start, it was clear Mark wouldn't settle
He was incredibly motivated. When he hit the
machines, he went at it so hard that he got everyone in
His motivation was contagious. If Mark's program
for forty push-ups, he'd do fifty. If his program cal
fifty laps in the pool, he'd do sixty. Then I'd see him
the track, doing lap after lap in his chair. I'm not sur
he knew exactly what he wanted out of life at the tim
it was clear to everybody that he wanted to be someb

Not long after Mark arrived here, I wrote in his
"Work him as hard as you can."

In 1987, when Mark left and I closed his file, I wrote:
is constantly working out and improving. He is
inspiration to us all."

4

EL CAP BECKONS

At sunset they come shuffling wearily back into the campground, their shoulders draped with iron and steel, their bodies clanking like medieval knights. Weather-beaten and stubbly, their faces tell of risks taken, of fears vanquished, of hard victories won.

Beneath their tattered clothing and dog-tired muscles, there is a weird manic energy pulsating. It is as if every single one of their nerve endings is tingling. As they drop their heavy racks of pitons and carabiners onto a picnic table and carefully sling their coiled climbing ropes over a tree branch, they seem to be grinning like dope fiends. Yet they are under the influence of nothing heavier than the adrenaline jangle that comes from having spent the day matching their skills and wills against the soaring granite walls of Yosemite.

Soon they are joined by more climbers, straggling into camp in twos and threes. Packs are dropped, and all heads turn to watch one guy pantomiming the crux moves of his climb, recreating his vertical dance steps for the crowd. He and everyone else talk excitedly in a language that is absolutely impenetrable to outsiders.

"So I'm jamming up to the crux, and the crack is bottoming and way greasy..."

"Kenny bagged some serious flight time today, took a couple of screamers off that expanding flake."

"...and I'm trying to lieback the book, but the rope drag is just *heinous*."

"If he can just nail that dyno sequence tomorrow, he'll have the redpoint..."

Still wired with adrenaline, several of them move over to the fifteen-foot-high granite boulder in the center of the campground. One side affords an easy scramble to the top, but that's not what interests them. They take turns trying to struggle up the side that's overhanging and seemingly as smooth and polished as a mirror. Using the finesse of a ballet dancer and the brute strength of a weight lifter, their fingers search out holds the size of pennies; their toes find nubbins as small as pencil erasers.

The climbers take turns trying to slither up the boulder like lizards, looking for loopholes in the law of gravity. But, one by one, they come crashing back to earth, landing on their feet with a thud and a laugh.

Watching them at a distance from my wheelchair, I feel an almost physical yearning to join them, to touch the stone again, to sense the fresh air beneath my toes. I know it's crazy. Climbing took my legs away from me. But, as I sit here, I find myself once again feeling the strange attraction that motivates climbers to risk everything for those glorious moments high above the everyday world. I long to struggle toward a summit again, to feel the thrill that comes from living on the edge in a high and wild place. I envy these guys, and I want to join them.

Every spring, the impossibly steep granite walls of Yosemite attract some of the very best climbers in the world: the big Himalayan expedition boys from Britain; cigarette-puffing Italians, fresh from some hideous north face in the Alps; Japanese climbers, wiry and tough; penniless Poles, short on gear and long on nerve; the French, with their punk haircuts and earrings; gruff Austrians; good-natured New Zealanders.

For four months of the year, their home is a dusty, run-down campground officially known as Sunnyside, but which they always call by its original name, Camp Four. Ostensibly, they share the place with tourists. However, it doesn't take a detective to tell the two groups apart. The tourists sleep in heavy canvas tents from Sears Roebuck; the climbers own state-of-the-art nylon models that would look right at home at Everest Base Camp. Some of these tents, no doubt, have actually been there.

These climbers are mostly dropouts from society, footloose vagabonds who have left behind jobs, possessions and girlfriends to follow the climbing season around the world. They are a scruffy bunch, and at one time they were not particularly welcome in Yosemite. These days, though, their worst offense tends to be "canning"—removing cans and bottles from the garbage cans to collect the deposits.

Over the years they have become a popular fixture of the scene, and most tourists and Park Service employees enjoy peering through binoculars and telescopes to follow their painstaking progress up the cliffs. Tourists, in fact, seem to be in awe of the climbers. If they spot one walking across the parking lot with a rope and a rack of hardware over his shoulder, they'll stop him to ask about everything from how they hammer pitons to—and this is the biggest mystery— how they go to the bathroom up there.

To an outsider, they may all seem to be cut from the same cloth, but within their private world there are well-defined groups whose memberships rarely overlap. Some are sport climbers, dedicated to short but outrageously difficult routes. It's not unusual for them to spend weeks working out the exacting sequence of moves needed to ascend one one-hundred-foot section of rock. With their Lycra tights and chalk-covered hands, they resemble gymnasts more than mountaineers. The best of them have whippet-thin physiques, but pound for pound, they're some of the strongest athletes in the world. They like to impress the tourists by cranking off one-finger pull-ups.

Another group are the weekend warriors, Californians mostly, who hold down nine-to-five jobs and commute to Yosemite every Friday night, pulling into Camp Four long after everyone else has gone to sleep. They have the newest and best equipment, because they're the only ones who can afford it. They climb as hard as they can for two days, maybe giving themselves a good scare once or twice, and are back at their desks by Monday morning.

Then there are the big-wall climbers, a breed apart from everyone else. Their faces are permanently baked from the sun, their hands blackened from the graphite powder on carabiners. These are the real "hard men" of Yosemite. (There are lots of female sport climbers, but very few women take up big-wall climbing.) They'll spend a week at a time forcing their route up the biggest, smoothest, most seriously vertical rock faces Yosemite has to offer: Sentinel Rock, Washington Column, the Leaning Tower, Half Dome and the biggest wall of them all, El Capitan.

These are the climbers who hammer pitons all day until their arms go numb, subsist on a few crumbs and a sip of water, and rock themselves to sleep in creaky hammocks swaying thousands of feet above the tops of the pine trees. When people think of the typical Yosemite climber, these are the people they are thinking of.

Within this breed, there is one climber who stands above the rest. For many climbers, an ascent of El Capitan is the achievement of a lifetime. By 1987, this man had climbed it an astonishing forty-one times— more than twice as many as anyone else. He had climbed it at least once in every month of the year, and had reached the summit by twenty-five different routes. His name is Mike Corbett, but around Yosemite Valley, he is known as "Mr. El Cap."

The first men to struggle up El Capitan had taken forty days, spread out over eighteen months, to reach the top. These days, most experienced climbers require at least three or four days for the ascent. Mr. El Cap had done it in a single day—in the winter, no less.

A real climbing bum, he had dropped out of city life and moved to Yosemite when he was barely out of high school to chase after adventure on the sheer granite walls. Corbett has been more or less a permanent resident of the park for the last seventeen years, living year-round out of his tent in Camp Four. Recently he has been working in the Yosemite Medical Clinic a couple of days a week as a janitor, which qualified him for a major increase in his standard of living—a cramped basement apartment. As much as any climber in Yosemite, Corbett is a living embodiment of Eric Beck's classic observation: "At either end of the social spectrum there lies a leisure class."

I had been hearing all the stories about Corbett for several months before I finally met the guy. One day I was wheeling myself out of the gym after a workout with Gwen Schneider, who was a nurse at the clinic and also Mike's girlfriend. There, leaning up against a tree, was an unassuming figure in jeans and an old sweatshirt. A Camel cigarette dangled from his lip.

I'd been around climbers enough to know they generally weren't chisel-jawed, macho characters like Clint Eastwood in the *Eiger Sanction*. But Mike Corbett, the king of big-wall climbing in Yosemite, was such a quiet and ordinary-looking guy that I might have mistaken him for a Winnebago-driving tourist from Bakersfield.

We chatted briefly, and in his conversation he was equally modest. There was none of the bragging and posturing that you sometimes get from much less accomplished climbers. In fact, there was only one thing that gave him away as a climber: his bulging, Popeye-sized forearms. From the elbows to the fingertips, Corbett was probably as strong as anyone in Yosemite.

Mike and Gwen said goodbye, and, although I continued to bump into him around Yosemite over the next few months, we never did more than exchange pleasantries. We never seemed to have much to talk about. I thought it odd that Mike never once brought up climbing, the overwhelming passion of his life.

Mike Corbett:

I didn't want to talk about climbing because I knew that's what took Mark's legs. It was really awkward. If he had hurt himself in a motorcycle crash, I sure wouldn't have been calling him up raving about the new motorcycle I just got. It was the same way with climbing. I didn't want to patronize him, and it was just something I didn't feel good about discussing with him.

I felt uncomfortable around Mark. Gwen kept telling me what a nice guy he was, and how I should get to know him better, but I resisted. Around this time I got to know another disabled person, Shirley Sargeant. A woman in her sixties, she's an historian and author of thirty books about Yosemite. Shirley wheeled around Yosemite Valley in an electric wheelchair called a Roadrunner. She would come into the medical clinic for physical therapy a couple of times a week, and it was my job to recharge her chair's batteries. As I chatted with her, I realized she was as full of life as any of us. The more I dealt with Shirley, the more comfortable I became around disabled people, and the easier it became to get to know Mark.

Our first little breakthrough came during the Winter Club dance in December 1987. Held in the Camp Curry Pavilion, it's a dinner dance to benefit the local ski club. It's the social event of the winter season, and just about everybody who lives and works in Yosemite goes to it.

At one point in the evening, Mark and I found ourselves together. I had had a few beers, and I think Mark had, also. As usual, I felt a little awkward to be with him. We chatted a little about nothing in particular. There was a long pause, and then Mark looked down at his motionless legs. Then he looked me right in the eye.

"You know this happened climbing, don't you?" he said.

"I do know that," I replied.

It wasn't much, but I think that little exchange broke the ice between us.

The idea started growing slowly in my head. After a couple of seasons of staring up at the beautiful granite monuments of Yosemite, I started thinking seriously about trying to climb again. I didn't know how I would do it, I didn't even know if it was possible, but I knew I wanted to find out.

If I'd learned one thing since my accident, it was that a lot of sweat, determination and positive thinking would allow me to accomplish things that might have seemed impossible. I had built a nice life for myself as a ranger, but I yearned to throw myself into something big and uncertain, with no turning back. I wanted to face new adversity and challenge, and to live and breathe with it every day until I overcame it.

As far as I knew, no paraplegic had even tried to scale any of the big walls in Yosemite, and to me that made the idea nearly irresistible. How many things are there in life that you can be the first to do?

For some reason, despite what had happened to me, I wasn't afraid of another accident. I think I was too dazzled by the dream of being up on the rock again to worry about it.

I knew I would need the right partner. Choosing a climbing partner is always serious business, because it requires an extraordinary level of trust you don't find anywhere else. Roped together on a vertical rock face, you literally hold each other's lives in your hands. In my case, finding the right partner would be even more critical. I would need someone who was a top-level climber, who was methodical and safe, and who was willing to work tirelessly with me to overcome all the hurdles.

I broached the subject to two excellent Yosemite climbers, Pat Teague and Kevin Brown. To my delight, neither of them laughed at the idea. They both thought it was possible, and each of them said they'd like to try it with me. But nothing ever came of our talks.

One day in January 1989, the mailman delivered the latest issue of *Sports and Spokes* magazine. It's the monthly bible for wheelchair athletes, covering all the basketball tournaments, marathons and ski races. I did a double take as I pulled this issue out of my mailbox. On its cover was a dramatic photograph of a woman in a wheelchair being lowered down a steep cliff on a rope, almost as if she were rappelling.

It had been taken on a river-rafting trip in Australia. The group had had to stop and portage its raft around a short waterfall. On the way, the woman—a Washington, D.C., park ranger—was lowered down a vertical headwall on two ropes, one tied around her waist, the other around her chair.

I was so excited I couldn't sit still. I just had to show this picture to someone. I put the magazine in my lap and wheeled out of my cabin, down the ramp and out into the road next to the park administration building.

A truck was just getting ready to back out of a parking space across the street. I recognized the driver—it was Corbett. I wheeled up next to his window and held up the magazine.

"Mike—check this out," I said.

"Wow," he said. "This is tricky." Corbett paused for a second, as if he were chewing over something in his mind, then looked at me and said: "Are you interested in doing any of this stuff again?"

"Oh, yeah," I told him. "I've already talked about it with a couple of guys."

"There must be a way to figure something out," Mike said. "We should get together and see if we can rig it up. There's got to be a way. I just know there's got to be a way."

Corbett had to finish his mail rounds, so he handed me back the magazine and drove off. The issue might have died there, but the next night I bumped into him in the Mountain Room Bar. The place is legendary in the history of climbing in Yosemite. Some of the most spectacular and ambitious ascents in the national park's history have been planned on cocktail napkins there, over a few beers by the big picture windows. Of course, some of the most outrageously bold climbs never got past the cocktail-napkin stage.

The spirit of the place must have gotten into Corbett. We were talking about climbing in general terms, and about how I might approach it, when his eyes got wide and he looked at me and said: "Climb El Cap with me!"

"Sure," I said, before even thinking it through. "I'd love to."

We were both instantly mesmerized by the idea. We would be pioneering new territory, a whole new sport, almost. There were no examples to follow, so we would have to invent every technique, every piece of equipment, every training exercise ourselves. As the night wore on, we were oblivious to everyone else in the room. We talked excitedly about the different ways I might be able to climb, what sorts of problems we'd need to solve, what kind of gear we'd need, what life would be like up there on the massive rock face.

Right from the start, we had a fairly good idea how we'd pull it off. Normally, on a big wall like El Capitan, the first climber ascends the rock by inserting pitons and other devices into the cracks and climbing up them with two little stirrups called *étriers*. After 150 feet or so he stops and anchors the rope, which the second climber climbs up with two ascending devices called Jumars. These slide up a rope but bite hard when pulled down, working like a ratchet that allows a climber virtually to walk right up the rope. Climbers normally attach stirrups to them so their legs do most of the work. But if Corbett did all the lead climbing, we figured, it might just be possible for me to pull myself up the rope using only the Jumars and my arms.

I took a sip of my Heineken, looked Corbett in the eye and told him: "You know, we're going to have to do this climb with four arms and two legs." This would become our slogan.

We were mentally about halfway up the monolithic face of El Capitan when we looked up and realized it was last call. They were putting the chairs up on the tables in the bar.

Corbett and I went back to my cabin, where we stayed up until 4:00 a.m., continuing to hatch our scheme. We even set a blast-off date: April 19. It was only three months away.

Mike Corbett:

I liked the challenge of engineering a way up El Capitan with Mark. I almost think I had gotten a little bored with El Cap. I'd climbed it so many times that every time I walked up to the base of it, I knew I could make it to the top. Now, I think, I was feeling a little cocky. Not only could I climb El Cap, I could climb it with a guy who can't walk.

It was about ten days before we were ready for our first practice. We agreed that we would try things out first in a tree. I didn't want to attract any attention, so I found a big black oak that was back off the road, out of sight of tourists and other climbers. Mark was able to wheel his chair through the snow to the base of the tree.

It took me a couple of tries, but I was able to toss one end of my climbing rope over a big branch about fifteen feet off the ground. I anchored the other end to another tree and tugged on it to make sure it was secure. Then I clipped the two Jumars into the rope and jugged a few feet up the rope, using only my arms. It was incredibly strenuous, but it was possible.

"Hey, I think you can do this," I told Mark.

Next it was Mark's turn. He parked his wheelchair underneath the rope and grabbed onto the Jumars, one hand on each ascending device. Grunting, panting and red in the face, he slid one up the rope, then the other, hauling his body up a little higher with each movement. It took him about fifteen minutes of hard work, but he climbed the rope all the way to the tree branch. I lowered him back down into his chair.

Technically it was a success, but we both could see it was really hard for Mark. The system just wasn't very efficient. If he had to pull himself thirty-six hundred feet up El Capitan this way, he'd never make it. We spent the rest of the afternoon tinkering with the system, hooking one Jumar onto his waist harness and having him pull with both hands on the other. It got a little easier for Mark, although we both knew we'd have to improve the system tremendously before we could tackle El Capitan.

Still, by the end of the day we were both more enthusiastic than ever. We had no hard evidence, but I think we both had a feeling we were going to be able to pull this off.

We were back out there the next day. A friend named Lee Stevens dropped by. He was an experienced cave explorer, and he brought along all sorts of devices he thought might be helpful to us. Lee fumbled inside his pack and produced a Gibbs ascender, a rival brand to the Jumar. I knew they were popular with ice climbers and cavers because they worked well on icy and muddy ropes. But big-wall climbers hardly ever used them.

I was kind of stubborn about things like this, but I was intrigued because I'd heard stories about how easily cavers were able to walk up ropes. So for once I didn't let my stubbornness overrule a good idea.

Lee hooked up his Gibbs ascender to Mark's waist harness, and we clipped a Jumar into the rope for his hands. The difference was remarkable. Mark was able to zip all the way *up to the tree branch with half the effort.*

He came down and went right back up again. We did this several times, because we needed to know if he could climb up 150 feet of rope without a big rest. That's what he'd have to do time after time on El Capitan.

Climbing up the rope was a real thrill for me. It was only fifteen feet up to the tree branch, but I knew it was the first step in a journey that would lead us to the summit of El Capitan.

Swinging around on the rope, I felt light and mobile and free from the confines of my chair. It dawned on me that once we were up in the vertical world, all the normal rules of mobility and gravity were void. Once I mastered the art of ascending the rope like an inchworm, I would be almost as mobile as any other big-wall climber. The January air was cold and invigorating, and my mind was filled with all the exciting possibilities.

Still, I had to admit that climbing up the rope was much tougher than I'd expected. That first time took just about all the strength I had, and it was hard to see how I'd be able to keep doing that all the way up El Capitan. The second day was a little easier after we hooked up the Gibbs ascender, but as I pulled myself up the rope time after time, another problem developed.

The motion was awkward and put a tremendous strain on my joints, and I could feel a bad case of tennis elbow developing in both my arms. By the end of the practice session, my elbows were stiff and painful. Trying not to get discouraged, I thought about the problem for a minute. In the gym I was able to crank off pull-ups all afternoon with no strain on my elbows, and that gave me an idea.

"Mike, do you think we could hook a pull-up bar onto the Jumar?"

"I don't see why not," he said.

That had the promise of solving one problem, but

there was another large one lurking on the horizon. It was one thing to be climbing a rope hanging free from a tree branch; it was quite another to be climbing one on the side of a jagged rock face. My legs, with little feeling and almost no muscle or fat to protect them, would suffer a terrible beating. It wouldn't take much for the abrasion to tear open cuts and sores, and for me that would be very serious. Pressure sores from sitting in a wheelchair all day would be nothing compared to the skin injuries I could get from thrashing against the granite.

The more I thought about it, the more I worried. For me, the possible damage to my legs was the single biggest fear I had of climbing El Capitan. We had to find a way to protect them, or the climb would remain a dream that never came true.

Mike Corbett:

On February 2, I borrowed Mark's van and drove down to Fresno on a shopping expedition. It was a wild drive. I had never owned a car, and had never driven very much. And when I hopped into the driver's seat of Mark's van, it was obvious it was no normal car. It had hand controls.

"You'll figure it out," Mark had told me as he tossed me the keys. "Everyone does."

I went careening down the mountain roads, feeling my way along with the hand controls. At the town of Fish Camp I stopped for gas. When I started the engine up, the accelerator stuck and the engine revved up high, creating a big scene. Climbing thousands of feet up a rock wall doesn't bother me, but driving that van had me spooked.

Anyone following me would have gone crazy trying to figure out the purpose of my shopping expedition. In Fresno I first pulled into an army surplus store called Tent City and loaded up on two yards of canvas, some foam pads, flat nylon webbing, tubular nylon webbing, thin nylon taffeta and waxed thread.

My next stop was National Hardware. There I bought

thirteen inches of half-inch-thick threaded bar, washers, nuts and a bunch of bungee cords. My last stop was a sporting-goods store, where I picked up some mountain-bike handlebar grips.

I drove back to Yosemite and went to work. I set up a little workshop in my basement apartment. I threaded the metal bar through a carabiner hole in one of the Jumar ascenders, locking it in place with rubber gaskets, washers and nuts. Then I fitted a bicycle grip on each side.

I was really proud of my creation, and I couldn't wait to show it to Mark. I ran over to his cabin and found the lights off and the door locked. However, I was able to follow the tracks of his wheelchair through the snow to the employee cafe, where I found him eating dinner. I pulled all the parts out of a big bag and assembled them again so Mark could see how it all worked. A big smile crossed his face. I think we both knew that this was the device that was going to get us up El Capitan.

Soon we were back over at the tree trying it out. It was the breakthrough we were hoping for. Mark could pull himself up in a natural motion and change the positions of his hands on the bar from time to time to relieve the stress. With a little practice and some tinkering with the equipment, he was able to raise himself six inches with each pull-up. It wasn't much, but we figured if he did enough pull-ups, he would eventually get to the top.

It's probably a good thing we didn't do the math at the time, or we would have learned that climbing El Capitan was going to require Mark to do more than seven thousand pull-ups.

One evening I wheeled around to the medical clinic to see how Corbett was doing. I reached down and rapped on the window of his basement apartment, and he came around to the door to let me in. By holding onto rocks on the side, I was able to lower myself down the stairs. Mike grabbed my chair and brought it inside for me. On a table he had laid out the beginnings of the answer to my other big problem. There were big pieces of canvas and padding stitched roughly together to make what we would later call "rock chaps." These would protect my legs from all the abuse they would take on the hard granite. Corbett was in the process of incorporating a climbing harness into the design, so it would be all one piece.

They were just a prototype, and we knew they'd need work, but I couldn't wait to try them on.

"I don't know, Mike," I said, once I had them on. "I think maybe I'll need more padding on the hips."

"How's the fit in the thighs?"

"It feels OK, but they seem like they could ride up on me."

Meanwhile, in Arizona, a friend of Mike's, John Middendorf, was working on another design for the rock chaps at his outdoor-equipment company, which was called A-5. They arrived in the mail one day, but I could tell immediately that they weren't what I needed. They had all the padding on the front, and I thought I'd probably need more on the sides. Also, they were made out of cotton, and didn't seem like they'd hold up to the kind of rough treatment I intended to give them.

By the first week in March, Corbett had his version of the chaps ready to test out. He had been working constantly to improve them. He'd sew late into the night with his Speedi Stitcher when he needed to be at work by 5:30 a.m. the next day. By now the chaps had sprouted some leather patches, more padding and an integral climbing harness.

Finally they were evolved to the point where we were ready to try them out on the rock. On March 5, Corbett and I loaded up everything in a big pack and headed back over to the Church Bowl area of Yosemite Valley. This time I wheeled past the familiar oak tree and went right up to the cold granite wall.

The cliff was absolutely vertical and polished, split

only by one thin crack. We had already decided that for my kind of climbing, the steeper and smoother the rock was, the better. As I watched from my chair, Corbett fitted a little metal wedge into the crack, clipped on a carabiner, attached an étrier and stood up in the top step. Then he reached higher, slotted in another wedge and repeated the whole process. The wedges, called nuts or hexentrics or stoppers, work like pitons, but can be placed without a hammer and cause less damage to the rock.

I'd never seen Mike climb before, and I was immediately impressed with how effortless it seemed for him. There was no wasted motion, no scraping of feet, no heavy panting. It was just *wedge-clip-step, wedge-clip-step*, until he was fifty feet off the ground. Then he anchored the rope to two expansion bolts already in the rock and rappelled back down, removing his wedges and carabiners as he went.

"OK, Mark," he said, turning to me. "It's your turn now."

I wheeled over until my chair was right next to the rock. I slid into both pairs of rock chaps—first the pair A-5 made, then, on top of them, the pair Corbett had stitched. Wearing both, my legs felt heavy and awkward, almost as if I were wearing a cast.

Then I clipped my pull-up device and the Gibbs ascender into the rope. I took a deep breath. This was a big moment for me. It had been seven years since my accident, and this would be my first time back on the rock. And it wasn't as if I was simply picking up where I left off. This little climb was far steeper than anything I'd tried in my able-bodied days—and it was nothing compared to what El Capitan was going to be like.

I wrapped both hands around the pull-up bar and heaved myself up out of the chair. After the Gibbs ascender on my waist took my weight, I slid the pull-up bar a little higher and raised myself again. Mike was right next to me, climbing up a separate rope.

"How does it feel?" he asked.

"It's weird," I told him. "I'm a little scared. After getting hurt on the rock, this just feels a little strange."

Three feet off the ground, I knew it wasn't working right. Immediately I discovered that my body wanted to turn sideways to the rock. Able-bodied climbers always face into the rock, and, assuming I'd climb that way too, we'd designed the chaps with most of the padding on the front. But with my legs raised into almost a sitting position in the chaps, it was much more natural to face sideways, switching sides every so often. This meant we were going to have to redesign the rock chaps, moving most of the padding to my hips and the sides of my legs.

My elbows were also taking quite a beating. I lowered myself back into my chair, switched my knee pads onto my elbows and borrowed some pads from Mike to put on my hips. Then I raised the pull-up bar and tried again.

This time it felt a little better. With Corbett next to me, I kept yanking myself up and sliding the bar higher and higher until I was a long way off the ground. I knew I was almost as high as a five-story building, but I forced myself not to look down. My breathing was getting faster, my heart was pounding harder. I snatched a peek down to see my chair, directly below me and looking very tiny. A feeling of exhilaration swept over me. I was climbing again!

When I reached the bolts, Corbett gently lowered me on the rope until I was back in my wheelchair. As Mike walked and I wheeled back through the trees toward the road, we both felt satisfied. The rock chaps were going to take a lot of work and the system of ascenders would need some fine tuning, but the system definitely worked. If I could get up fifty feet of rock, I figured I could get up the thirty-six-hundred-foot face of El Capitan.

Mike continued to spend nearly every night working

on chaps, adding some padding here, a leather patch there, some reinforced stitching somewhere else. Sometimes he'd poke his finger with the Speedi Stitcher, and it would hurt for days. By the time he was finished, he probably put in two hundred hours on the chaps. He was very proud of his work, and rightly so.

One day Corbett dropped by my cabin with something else on his mind.

"Hey," he said, "do you want to go over to El Cap to look at our route?"

I'd never gotten an up-close view of the thing, and it sounded like a good idea. I think Corbett wanted to psych me up, but in retrospect it may not have been the wisest thing to do.

With Corbett giving me a push now and then, I was able to wheel my chair through the dirt and scrub about halfway from the road to the base of El Capitan. Then we hit the bottom of a big rock field that climbed up to the foot of the wall. I parked my chair there and grabbed the seat cushion.

"Hop aboard," said Corbett, as he turned his back to me and leaned forward slightly.

For a little guy, Corbett is awfully powerful. He carried me piggyback, hopping up from rock to rock, for one hundred yards at a time. When he needed a rest, I leaned up against a rock or sat down on my seat cushion.

As we got closer and closer, the giant monolithic face of El Capitan kept rearing up higher and higher. I couldn't believe how massive it was. I'd been driving past it for years, and I knew objectively that it was the biggest piece of exposed granite in the world, rising some thirty-six hundred feet above Yosemite Valley. However, those guidebook facts didn't prepare me for what I saw. Until I got almost close enough to rub my nose against it, I never appreciated just how enormous it was.

It was a dizzying vertical expanse, towering so

immensely above us that it almost blotted out the sky. Granite buttresses and exfoliation flakes that appeared insignificant from the road now towered hundreds of feet above us, making me feel as tiny as an insect.

From time to time in Yosemite you hear about climbers who spend months preparing to climb El Capitan. They gather up all the necessary pitons and carabiners and ropes, buy all their food, fill all their water bottles, attend all their send-off parties. Then they hike up to this very spot and feel their nerve drain away. Overwhelmed by the incomprehensible scale of the rock, they turn round and try to forget they ever wanted to climb El Capitan.

Of course, I knew this wouldn't happen with Corbett. He just wanted to point out some of the features on the route and give me a feeling for the size of what we were up against. He was showing me the various cracks and ledges that connected to form our route, but most of what he said went right past me. I craned my neck and stared upward, transfixed by the awesome power of the stone.

As Corbett piggybacked me down the rock field, I felt a sense of desire and boldness surging through me. I wanted more than anything else to conquer El Capitan. With Mike as a partner, I knew I had a good shot at it. I felt psyched up and ready to go.

As I got back to my chair, I noticed that my palms felt clammy against the wheel rims.

Mike Corbett:

From the start we both knew the personal stakes were high for both of us. If Mark got killed or injured, I was definitely going to take the blame. People were going to look at me as someone recklessly trying to pull off a publicity stunt by taking a paraplegic up El Capitan.

On the other hand, if I got hurt or killed, Mark was going to be judged rather harshly, too. He'd be the guy in the wheelchair who talked the El Cap expert into risking everything to take him up. No matter who was at fault, we'd both end up being judged harshly by the community if anything happened.

Someone else might have tried to keep this a secret, but right from the start I was shooting my mouth off about what we planned to do. I knew it was going to be a big event, a part of Yosemite history, and I wanted people to know about it. There was another reason, too. If everyone knew in advance that we were setting out to climb El Cap, it would be tough to back out. I've always thought that if you toot your horn about something, it puts pressure on you and forces you to try your best to pull it off.

One of the very first things I did was write to Tom Brokaw at NBC News. I knew he liked to do a little climbing in his spare time, and I figured that if anyone in the media would give us some support, it would be him.

In mid-February I was working at the medical clinic when I got a phone call. The voice at the other end of the line said, "Tom got your letter." It was Brokaw's secretary at NBC News, and she told me they wanted to film as much of the climb as they could. A film crew would be coming out soon to shoot some interviews with us.

I also contacted the Fresno Bee, *and they sent a reporter and photographer up to meet us. Also coming to Yosemite was Jay Mather, a prize-winning photographer from their sister paper,* The Sacramento Bee. *I placed a call to the Associated Press, and they made an appointment to send up a reporter and photographer, too.*

We were shooting our mouths off to everyone who would listen, and I figured that there was no way we could back down now. We were committed, but Mark was always more reluctant than I was to talk to reporters. I figured that he was just more modest, but there was another reason for it, too.

I didn't want my mom to hear about the climb from a newspaper or a friend. I wanted to talk to her about it myself. It was going to be difficult—I knew that. My dad was sick, and she didn't need another thing to worry about. So I called her and, as gently as possible, told her I was planning to go up El Capitan.

"Up the backside, on the trail, right?" she said. "I think that's marvelous..."

"No, Mom," I interrupted. "I'm planning to climb the vertical face."

There was silence at the other end of the line. I could tell my mom was trying hard not to cry.

"I've read stories about that," she said, her voice breaking. "I think you're crazy. That's a dangerous idea. Climbing took your legs, and now you're talking about going back up there? I don't want you to do it, Mark."

I told her we'd talk more about it later and said goodbye. I was twenty-nine years old and didn't need anybody to make decisions for me. I was starting to have serious second thoughts myself, and with my dad sick and my mom freaking out, it was hard to summon up the boldness I'd need to see this project through.

On a stormy night in mid-March, I telephoned Corbett. "I'm sorry, Mike, but I can't climb El Capitan with you," I told him. "I'm going to bow out of this gracefully."

"You can bow out, but I don't think it's going to be very graceful," Corbett replied. "We've shot our mouths off to everyone. What's the problem?"

"I'm really scared of this thing," I told him. "I lie here at night and it seems like too much. Part of me really wants to do it, but my parents are bummed. My accident put my mom through hell, but she was always there for me when I needed her. I just don't know if I could put her through it again."

"Maybe we can still do it," said Corbett. I could hear the disappointment in his voice. He was trying to salvage our dream. "Let's just think about it for a while."

We left it at that. The following week, I was going

home for Easter vacation, and there would be plenty of time to talk it over with my mom.

Mike Corbett:

I was devastated when Mark backed out. The idea of climbing El Capitan with him had been the consuming passion of my life for the last two months. It had filled my every waking thought. At night I'd lie awake working out logistics, solving problems and imagining what it would be like to make it all come true. We'd told the world we were going to climb El Capitan, and now I was feeling like a braggart with a big mouth.

During those six days Mark spent at home with his folks, I was a nervous wreck. I stayed near the telephone, waiting for the call that would tell me the climb was back on. The call never came, and as the days went by, I grew more and more impatient. Finally, on the sixth day, I couldn't stand it any more. I had to know. I picked up the phone and called Mark's parents' house. His mom answered and said Mark wasn't there. She said he'd left for Yosemite, and asked if she could take a message. I told her no, I'd call him in Yosemite. I didn't want her to know who I was.

That day I kept phoning Mark's place and dropping by on foot. I paced back and forth in front of the cabin. What could be taking him so long? Finally, after an eternity, he pulled up in his van.

"Well?" I asked.

"I want to do it," he said. "I just don't want to do it on April 19, like we planned. I'm going to need a little more time."

As it turned out, Mark never did reach an understanding with his parents. He didn't really discuss it with them. He was committed to the climb, and that's all that mattered to me. As the days passed, though, I could never pin Mark down on a date. I started putting pressure on him. At one point I even threatened to back out of the climb if he didn't commit himself.

"I've put in a lot of work on this," I told Mark. "At least

tell me when. If it's a year from now, that may be too late, but maybe six months would be OK."

"Fine," he said. "How about September?" That was almost six months away, but it would have to do. In the meantime, I had two weeks of vacation coming at the end of April, the time I'd originally blocked out to climb El Cap with Mark. I decided to climb it anyway. If Mark wasn't ready to do it then, I'd go with Gwen.

On April 12-14, Gwen and I climbed about nine hundred feet up to a little flat spot called Heart Ledge, anchoring a series of ropes in place so we could come back a few days later and do the entire climb. I knew I was just going through the motions; my heart just wasn't in it. I was really committed to climbing with Mark. I told Gwen, and she understood.

The next day I dropped by Mark's cabin and asked him if he wanted to go up to Heart Ledge with me and spend the night. All the ropes were in place, I told him. All he'd have to do is the pull-ups. It would be a perfect dress rehearsal for our climb.

As I pulled myself up the rope, six inches at a time, it didn't take long before I could look out over the treetops and see the awesome panorama of Yosemite exploding all around me. Half Dome, Cathedral Rock, Glacier Point—I had a new perspective on all the famous landmarks from my airy position.

Below me the cars were just dots, the people too small to see. The snowmelt-swollen Merced River was just a tiny blue ribbon meandering past the base of El Capitan. All the practice and training was paying off. Corbett and I had done dozens of practice climbs, and I had spent long hours in the gym, cranking off pull-ups with a forty-five-pound weight tied around my waist.

By now I was used to having lots and lots of fresh air beneath my toes, but as I inched my way higher, the exposure started to get spooky. A chill wind whistled across the massive expanse of rock. Now even the treetops below me looked tiny.

My shoulders and arms started to flame, but I kept cranking my pull-ups. After about three hundred feet the angle increased from near-vertical to dead-vertical, and things got easier. I wasn't scraping against the rock so much. The rock chaps Corbett had put so much work into were protecting my legs beautifully.

After doing pull-ups for close to four hours (with a lot of rests!), I finally reached the top of the rope and pulled myself onto Heart Ledge. It is about as big as a picnic table and, as I would learn later, it is about as comfortable as ledges get on El Capitan. Corbett came up right behind me with sleeping bags, food, water and everything else we'd need to spend the night. Then, not long after arriving, he turned around and started rappelling back down. He had a meeting to attend, and he promised to be back later that evening.

As soon as Mike left, it was incredibly quiet up on the ledge. All I could hear was the wind scudding across the granite. From my perch high above Yosemite Valley, I could look down on all the familiar landmarks laid out below me like a road map.

The sun-warmed granite felt toasty and inviting. I was all alone so I thought, "What the heck?" I stripped off all my clothes and let the sun toast my body, which was naked except for the rope tied securely around my waist. For the next four hours I lay there, watching thin clouds drift across the sky and observing the interplay of light and shadow on the glacier-polished peaks of the High Sierra. As the sun dropped lower into the western sky, the huge granite formation called Cathedral Rock, directly across the valley from me, began to glow pink and orange.

I propped myself up on a rock to watch the sunset. A warm tingle of satisfaction welled up inside me as I realized I was once again experiencing the beauty and adventure I had feared my accident had taken away from me forever.

Corbett was back, shortly before dark, with dinner: salami, bagels, Beanie Weenies and Gatorade. We ate silently as the last of the evening's light flickered out on Yosemite. Soon I was inside my sleeping bag, watching the shooting stars arcing across the lively night sky. Directly above me loomed more than half a mile of El Capitan, a massive presence more felt than seen.

I don't think I ever drifted off to sleep that night. I lay awake, watching the constellations ticking off time on the celestial clock, and thought about how far I'd come in the years since my accident. I'd built a new life for myself, one filled with adventure on a scale I could never have imagined. And, I knew for sure, even bigger adventures were just around the corner.

This little shakedown cruise erased all the lingering doubts for both of us. In the morning, as we prepared to rappel back down to Yosemite Valley, I felt sad that we weren't continuing to the top. I told Corbett, and it seemed to perk him up.

Mike Corbett:

We were incredibly lucky we postponed the big climb. The day after Mark and I rappelled down from Heart Ledge, a late-season storm blew into Yosemite and dumped a foot of snow on top of El Capitan. It would have been miserable at best, and possibly life-threatening, for us to have been up there.

Still, I was so antsy I just couldn't wait until September, and I suspected Mark felt the same way. I was the first one to broach the subject. I asked Mark if he'd mind moving up the date, and to my delight he agreed to it. We decided sixty days was enough notice, and we circled the date of July 19 on the calendar.

El Capitan

**YOSEMITE NATIONAL PARK
CALIFORNIA**

1. Mammoth Terrace
2. Night 2
3. Chimney in which Mike Corbett got stuck
4. Night 3 – Grey Ledge
5. Night 4
6. Shield Roof
7. Night 5
8. Groove Pitch
9. Night 6
10. Night 7 – Chickenhead Ledge

BURSTING THROUGH BARRIERS

The bright red rope stretched up and up and up, disappearing into the blue California sky. I craned my neck and strained my eyes, but I couldn't see the top of it. The nylon cord, as thick as my index finger, would be my lifeline and umbilical cord for the next week. Anchored to a rock at the foot of the wall, it also marked the start of the journey that would end—if all went well—on the top of El Capitan, more than half a mile directly above me.

Mike Corbett bent down and lowered me gently onto a smooth rock. It was 8:00 a.m. and cool, but already we had felt a hint of the strength sapping heat that lay ahead. Even as Corbett was piggybacking me the quarter-mile up the scree slope from the road, his T-shirt had become drenched with sweat.

Both of us were itching to take that first step off the ground. After six months of dreaming and scheming and practicing, after all the preoccupied days and sleepless nights, after dozens of ascents of oak trees and thousands of pull-ups in the gym, after all the last-minute emergencies, we couldn't wait to begin our adventure.

Too excited to sleep, I had spent the night tossing and turning, checking the clock every fifteen minutes.

At 5:30 a.m. it was still dark outside, but I couldn't stand it any more. I rolled out of bed and into my wheelchair, and started getting ready. Mike had already cached most of our climbing gear and personal supplies on a ledge partway up El Capitan, so it was just a matter of getting dressed and asking myself for the thousandth time if I'd forgotten anything.

I wheeled over to my closet and rummaged around in the back until I found what I was looking for: the boots that had been on my feet when I had had my accident on Seven Gables, seven years earlier. They hadn't had much wear and tear since then, and I liked the symbolism of wearing them on my return to climbing.

Around 7:30 a.m. there was a knock on my door. It was Corbett and Dave Riggs, a producer from NBC.

"Ready to do it?" asked Mike.

"You bet," I said.

We all piled into Dave's rental car. I had popped the wheels off my chair and tossed it in the back. The campers in Yosemite Valley were just staggering out of their tents to make their morning coffee as we drove west along the Merced River. Inside the car, nobody said much; we were all locked deep in private thought.

A couple of miles from my cabin there's a spot where the road makes a bend. The trees open up a bit to reveal the immense monolith of El Capitan, rearing up to fill one's entire field of vision. Looking out the truck window, I couldn't even see the summit.

"Good heavens!" I said to myself. "Am I really going up that thing?" Just ahead at the turnout, there was an unusual number of vehicles for that early in the morning. As we climbed out of Dave's car, I realized they belonged to reporters, all of whom were waiting to talk to us. I gulped. The thought of standing up in front of the television cameras like some conquering hero filled me with dread. I hadn't done anything yet. Mike was so confident in his abilities up on the rock

that he liked to talk to the press. But for me, talking to
TV cameras was scarier than climbing El Capitan.

Microphones were thrust forward. Half a dozen
journalists gathered around us and began asking
questions.

"How do you feel right now?"

"Are you nervous?"

"How long is this going to take you?"

"Why are you doing this?"

"Are you out to prove a point?"

"Where are you going to sleep up there?"

"How are you going to go to the bathroom?"

"What if something goes wrong?"

"How do you feel?"

"Are you scared?"

As I started wheeling across the meadow toward the
base of the wall, a cluster of photographers and
television cameramen walked backward in front of me,
jostling each other for position. They got pretty
physical, like NBA forwards wrestling for a rebound.

"Quiet, please!" someone barked. "National TV!"

I couldn't take any more. I turned to the nearest guy,
a photographer from the *Fresno Bee*, scowled at him
and said, "Back off. Give me some room!"

That seemed to help a little. But as Mike piggybacked
me up the talus slopes to the beginning of the climb,
they still followed. When we reached the ropes dangling
down the face, I worked as quickly as I could to slide
into my rock chaps and attach my pull-up bar and the
other mechanical ascending devices.

I checked and rechecked every strap, every buckle
and every safety gate to make sure they were all hooked
correctly. Then, as the shutters of four or five cameras
crackled like a herd of crickets, I raised the pull-up bar
and took my first step off the ground.

At last, the journey had begun. Only 6,999 more
chin-ups to go.

Pumped up with adrenaline, I covered the first fifty

feet in record time. I couldn't wait to get out of earshot
of everyone else so I could be alone with my thoughts.
It was a relief to be finally coming to grips with the
climb itself. Now there would be no time for second
thoughts or self-doubt. We would be too busy.

As I inched my way up the rope, gaining half a foot
with each pull-up, Corbett stayed on the ground and
continued talking to reporters. Finally, after another
hour, everyone seemed to have their notebooks filled
up, so Mike attached his own Jumars to the rope and
started up. When he was thirty feet off the ground, a
well-coiffed woman from a television station in Fresno
came running up the talus. She was late and she was
furious. Even from my position, a couple of hundred
feet up, I could hear her cursing.

The woman raised her microphone toward Corbett
and shouted, "Any last words?"

"Yep," said Mike. "Bye!"

Mike Corbett:

*Our first day would be an easy one. Gwen and I had
already spent some time climbing the first one thousand feet
of the route and anchoring ropes in place. This would allow
us to get almost a third of the way up El Capitan by the first
night, which would be a real boost for our psyches. At one
time, big-wall climbers considered this to be "cheating," but
now it's quite a common thing to do. I guessed it would save
us at least two days, maybe more.*

*El Capitan might look like a forbidding blank wall from
the ground, but there are hundreds of cracks and ledges that
serve as pathways for climbers who know how to use them.
There's hardly an inch of granite that hasn't been climbed.
There are now about fifty different routes to the top. Some
are harder than others, but none are easy.*

*The one we picked is called "The Shield," and it was such
an obvious choice that we agreed on it that first night in the
bar. It's one of the smoothest, steepest, most direct routes up
El Capitan—although it's only about average in overall*

difficulty. For Mark, the key thing was that it was almost all straight up. Some routes zigzag with lots of traverses, and our rope-climbing system wasn't built to travel that way. It had been designed to go up, not sideways or down. I'd climbed The Shield route twice before—once taking just over a day—and I knew it was a safe route that offered us the best chance of getting to the top.

The worst part of climbing a big wall like El Capitan is hauling all your supplies behind you. Imagine trying to dance while dragging a couple of steamer trunks around the dance floor. We were bringing along about 225 pounds of gear, most of it stuffed into two big haul bags that looked like oversized versions of a boxer's punching bag. The overflow filled two backpacks.

We had brought four ropes, forty-five pitons, a couple of hammers, 175 carabiners, twenty-five camming devices, twenty wired stoppers, sixty short nylon slings and a kit— never used—that allowed us to drill bolts directly into the rock. Much of this hardware—thirty-nine pounds in all, the equivalent of a small child—was slung over my shoulders when I climbed.

We each had a sleeping bag, rain jacket and pants, pile jacket, polypropylene underwear, wool hat and gloves, headlamp and a cot-like device for sleeping that is called a "Portaledge."

Our pantry included canned pineapple, peaches and fruit cocktail; hard salami; cheese; bagels; sour balls; lemon drops; breakfast bars; Pepperidge Farm cookies; Fig Newtons; Gatorade and a personal favorite of mine, a canned mixture of baked beans and hot-dog slices called Beanie Weenies. One item that was a bust was canned beef stew. We ate everything cold, right out of the can, and we quickly learned that canned beef stew will not tempt even the heartiest appetite if you don't heat it to melt that gel.

Our heaviest single item—and the most precious—was water. We would be traveling through a sun-baked vertical desert, and the only liquid available would be what we carried with us. We had plastic bottles that carried a total of twelve gallons—about three quarts a day for each of us if the climb took seven days. The water alone weighed close to one hundred pounds.

Hauling all these supplies up the rock face had less to do with climbing than engineering. I would arrange pitons, pulleys and Jumars to create a sort of ratcheting winch system. Between my body weight and Mark's arm strength, we'd manage to lift the loads behind us. It was a slow and sweaty wrestling match.

Earlier, Gwen and I had hauled everything up to our first night's destination—a fairly large ledge called Mammoth Terrace.

I didn't catch up to Mark until two rope-lengths below Mammoth Terrace. An able-bodied climber in good shape can make the trip in several hours; it took Mark about four and a half. Not bad, considering he was using only his arms.

A drop of sweat trickled down my forehead and stung me in the eye. Already it was hot, and it promised to get hotter. Hardly anybody climbs El Capitan in the middle of the summer—for good reason. The glacier-polished granite acts as a big reflecting oven, and as a climber, you feel like an ant scaling the side of a cast-iron skillet. But I didn't want to be in anyone's way, and I didn't want anybody else in our way. I knew that in July we could have the place pretty much to ourselves. Besides, both Mark and I had experienced our worst moments as climbers in the cold. For us, heat was the lesser evil.

Mammoth Terrace is about the size of three picnic tables laid end to end, and it's about as comfortable a place as you'll find on a big wall. When we finally pulled ourselves onto it, Mark's shoulders were burning from all the chin-ups—he'd done close to two thousand that day. I was pooped myself. There were still three or four hours of daylight left, but we were too drained to do anything except sit on the ledge and count the minutes until the sun dropped behind the ridge to the west. The rock beneath us felt warm to the touch, but if we sat perfectly still, we didn't sweat too much. Neither of us even wanted to *think about trying to eat until it cooled off.*

Before nightfall we had visitors on the ledge: an NBC cameraman and three climbing friends—Murray Barnett, John Dossi and Steve Rathbun. The four of them dropped by for a little bon voyage party. As celebrations go, it was rather sedate. They popped open a bottle of beer, but neither Mark nor I felt like having any of it. We were focused on the two thousand feet of flint-hard granite that towered above us.

The next day, we knew, the real work would begin.

The first light of dawn woke me out of a deep sleep. I stretched luxuriously in my sleeping bag, rolled over on my side, opened my eyes—and suddenly remembered where I was. Peering over the side of my Portaledge, I could see nothing but fresh air between me and the floor of Yosemite Valley, a thousand feet below.

I checked the knot on my harness; it was good and tight. I had slept with the harness around my chest and a length of nylon webbing around my waist, tied to the rope on a very short leash. The rope was anchored to a piton hammered securely into a crack above my head. This was no place to go sleepwalking.

Sleeping in the Portaledge was surprisingly comfortable. It's basically a big, super-strong cot suspended from above by a length of nylon webbing attached to each corner. Once I learned to trust the various pitons, bolts and camming devices that held it to the wall, I could relax and stretch out. I slept as well as I did at home—maybe even better, because I was so tired from the day's climbing. Every once in a while, though, I'd awaken with that falling sensation you sometimes get in your dreams. It's bad enough when that happens at home, but on El Capitan it really put my heart in my throat.

Directly below me, sleeping on the granite ledge, was Corbett. I peered over and looked for signs of life, but Mike was still dozing. He liked his sleep, and he needed it. He had a big day ahead of him.

I lay back in my sleeping bag and watched the light of the new day begin to silhouette the peaks of the High Sierra. Overhead, a wispy cloud glowed pink. Across from us, the first rays of sunshine ignited the summit of Cathedral Rock into a bright orange glow.

A whooshing sound startled me. I sat up to see a pair of swifts zipping by. The sudden movement made my Portaledge sway, sending a wave of terror through me for a microsecond.

Already it was starting to warm up, so I slid out of my goose-down sleeping bag. I was naked except for the harnesses. Reaching over, I carefully untied the short plastic leg braces that were attached to the webbing supports of the Portaledge.

Everything we weren't using was tied down securely or stuffed into one of the haul bags. Otherwise, a careless elbow could easily send some necessity plunging into the void below. Living in the vertical world, I was learning, required a whole new set of rules. In the everyday horizontal world, gravity is your friend. It keeps your feet on the ground, where they belong, and it makes sure all of your possessions stay where you put them. But in the vertical world, gravity is a thief ready to steal your things, an assassin always waiting for its chance to strike.

Once I'd attached my leg braces, I reached for the nylon stuff sack that had served as my pillow. It, too, was tied to the Portaledge frame. Out of it I pulled socks, underwear, a tank top and pants. As I dressed, I tried not to make any sudden movements that would start my platform swaying again.

I caught a whiff of tobacco smoke and looked down to see Mike lying on his back, puffing on his morning cigarette—the first of many he'd smoke that day. I fumbled around in the haul bag until I found a can of pineapple chunks, opened it with a Swiss Army knife and slowly ate half. Then I handed the rest down to Mike. That was breakfast.

As I struggled into a special butt cushion called a J-Protector and then into my rock chaps, Corbett was arranging all his pitons, camming devices, wired stoppers, carabiners and nylon slings on a big sling around his shoulder. Every piece of gear had to be in exactly the right order so he wouldn't waste valuable energy searching for it while hanging precariously from tiny holds.

When Mike had packed away his sleeping bag and his warm clothing, we were finally ready to start the day's climbing. Standing up on the ledge, he once more checked the knots on the two 165-foot ropes tied to his seat harness. One was a stretchy climbing rope, designed to stop a falling climber gently. The other was a stiffer static line, better for chin-ups and hauling our supplies.

I grabbed the climbing rope and clipped it through an aluminum belay device attached to my harness. This allowed me to pay the rope out as Mike climbed, and to lock it tight if he fell. When two climbers rope up together, it's a symbolic and very real bonding—the strongest in any sport. You are literally handing your life over to your partner.

"On belay?" asked Corbett.

"Belay on," I replied.

Mike had an uncanny ability to eye a crack and know the exact size of the piton or camming device he needed. Less experienced climbers waste time and energy trying first one size and then another, but Mike always got it right the first time. He slid a thin "knife-blade" piton into the crack and tapped it with his hammer, gently at first, then harder and harder. The piton rang like a bell, the pitch getting higher with each whack of his hammer. That's the reassuring sound of a good, solid piton.

After snapping a carabiner onto the piton, Mike

clipped the climbing rope through it, attached his two nylon stirrups (étriers), and climbed up to the top step. Then he reached as high as he could and slipped another piton into the crack to repeat the whole process.

Soon Corbett was fifty feet above my head. The rope, which had been sliding through my belay device in regular spurts, suddenly stopped. I could sense that Mike was in a tough spot. A rope is more than a lifeline between two climbers—it's also a telegraph line that provides information. By reading the tugs and vibes that came down the nylon cord, I could tell whether Mike was confident or hesitant.

"How's it going up there, buddy?" I yelled up.

"It's kind of hairy right here," Corbett called down. "Watch me."

"You got it," I said, keeping a sweaty hand firm on the rope.

Mike, as usual, climbed past the obstacle without trouble, and soon the rope was snaking out again at a brisk pace. After an hour and a half, only about ten feet of rope were left at my end. Suddenly the rope stopped sliding out again, and Corbett's distant voice came drifting down the rock.

"OK, Mark, I'm up. Off belay!"

"Belay off!" I yelled back.

A few minutes later Corbett came sliding down the static rope. Sitting on my Portaledge, he helped me hook up my pull-up bar, the other two ascenders and all the bungee cords that connected everything. I checked every knot and connection one more time.

"See you at the top," I said.

"Right."

I raised the bar, pulled myself up and gained six inches. Another chin-up, another six inches. After all the tension of guarding the rope for Corbett, it felt good to finally be moving. By now the sun had struck the face of El Capitan and the rock was warm to the touch. Sweat dripped down my face. I faced sideways, my left hip and elbow pad scraping against the rough granite. Another chin-up, another six inches.

After about seventy-five chin-ups, I took a short breather. Folklore has it that a climber should never look down, but I couldn't resist. Yikes! I was so high off the ground and so alone in the middle of this huge expanse of vertical rock that it would have seemed funny if it hadn't been so terrifying. (For me, the most challenging moves on El Capitan were the moves that played out inside my head, the ones that allowed me to control my fear while clinging to a single strand of rope a thousand feet off the deck.)

Fear had a wonderful way of recharging my pumped-up arms. I slid the bar up and attacked the rope above me with new vigor. Twenty minutes and three hundred chin-ups after leaving my Portaledge, I reached the end of the rope.

As I climbed, Corbett jumared up the other rope with a pack on his back. As he ascended, he tapped each piton out of the crack and clipped it back onto his shoulder sling. He would need to use them again and again up higher.

At the high point, Corbett attached his mechanical ascending devices to the anchor pitons to make an ingenious hauling system. By using his body weight as a counterbalance and my arms for a boost, we were able to raise one of the two haul bags up to our position. Wrestling with the beast was an exhausting and thirsty business, and it left us both drained. Then Mike had to rappel back down, tie the second haul bag to the rope, jumar up again with the other pack on his back and repeat the whole winching sequence.

In this fashion, we figured, Corbett would end up climbing El Capitan three times before we were done!

Mike Corbett:
On the third day the route led up through a "chimney," a vertical crevice wide enough to fit my entire body inside.

I scurried up it with no problems, but then I got a bright idea I'd later regret.

To save time, I decided to carry a pack on my back and attach one of the haul bags to my waist as I climbed the chimney a second time to remove the pitons. I had barely started when my progress came to a sudden halt. With the bulky pack on my back, my shoulders were too wide to squeeze up the crack. I wiggled, grunted and cursed under my breath, but it was no use. I was stuck.

I twisted my body and leaned sideways to try to break free. Suddenly I felt a crushing weight on my chest. The ninety-pound haul bag was pinning me tighter into the rock, squeezing the air out of my lungs. I was taking short, shallow breaths, trying to stay calm—and failing.

A flood of high-decibel profanities went flying up towards Mark. Some of them were aimed at him. None of this was his fault, of course, but he was the only one around.

"I wish there was something I could do to help you," he yelled down. "But there's nothing I can do. Try to stay calm and think this thing through."

Thrashing around inside the chimney, knuckles bloodied, I was more frustrated than frightened. I felt completely helpless. It was like trying to wrestle with a one-hundred-pound suitcase inside a phone booth. The haul bag was pressing against my solar plexus, increasing my sense of panic.

Finally, after what seemed like about half an hour of wiggling, scraping and gasping for breath, I worked my way loose and popped out of the chimney. When I reached Grey Ledge, where Mark was waiting for me, I was still shaking.

"We're quitting early today," I told him. "I'm frazzled. I need a break."

For days we had been staring up at the intimidating crux of the climb—an overhang jutting out twenty-five feet from the wall. It was called the Shield Roof, and it was the stuff of nightmares. We knew we were going to have to climb up the underside of it, clinging upside down like spiders, with almost half a mile of nothingness beneath us.

The roof had been weighing heavily on our minds since Mammoth Terrace, and several times a day one of us would crane our neck up at it, shake our head and say, "I can't wait until we're over that thing."

It wasn't just that the climbing would be scary and the exposure sickening. The Shield Roof also marked the point of no return. Once we surmounted the overhang, retreat would be all but impossible. Our rappel ropes would be left dangling out in space, twenty-five feet away from the wall. We would have no choice but to continue to the summit. And if we ran into trouble above the point of no return—a sudden storm, a fall, an injury—well, neither one of us wanted to think about it. The Shield Roof was the psychological as well as the physical crux of our climb.

We spent the fourth day inching closer and closer to it. Corbett tried to act calm and self-assured, but I could see the strain beginning to show on his face. His worry lines were caked with dried sweat, and in his eyes I could see a reflection of my own concern. Late in the afternoon Mike angled up and left above me, following a series of shallow cracks and dubious-looking flakes until he could reach up and touch the underside of the roof. He anchored his ropes right there and started back down to the belay anchors where I was waiting. The next day we would have the roof for breakfast.

Even below the roof El Capitan arches out slightly, and as Corbett rappelled down he was swinging out over the dizzying void. I had to pull him back into the wall with my end of the rope. It looked like a wild ride, but I knew it was nothing compared to what awaited us the next morning.

We passed a restless night in our Portaledges, impatient for morning to arrive so we could come to grips with the roof. Dawn brought gusting winds that rattled our little sleeping platforms—and our nerves. Up and moving early, we worked quickly to climb the ropes back up to the previous day's high point.

I could just about bump my head on the underside of the roof. Mike checked his gear sling one more time, checked the knot on his harness and looked me in the eye. He felt nervous, and he was trying not to let it show.

"Ready to do it?" I asked.

"Guess so," was his reply.

Corbett leaned back and clipped a carabiner into the first in a line of bolts that had been drilled into the rock by the first ascent party. Mike is only about five-foot-seven, and it was obvious that whoever drilled the bolts was a lot taller. Dangling in the top steps of his étriers, Corbett had to make some long stretches to clip the bolts.

A couple of times he had to trust his weight to old, rotting nylon slings left in place by previous climbers. As Mike moved farther out over the abyss, the howling wind blew him sideways and whipped the free rope violently. He had to wait for the gusts to die down before committing himself to his next long and delicate reach.

Mike disappeared over the lip of the overhang, and soon the rope was inching out at a steady pace. Communication was impossible because of the wind and the overhang, but I could tell he had passed the hard part. Now he was back on terrain that was merely dead vertical. Finally the climbing rope stopped paying out, and a few minutes later Corbett came sliding down past the roof on the free rope.

Once again I had to reel him back into the wall. When Mike reached me, there was no mistaking the look of relief on his face. He had forged the route past the Shield Roof; now it was my turn. The tension was almost more than I could stand.

"Lower me out," I told him nervously. "Get me out of here. I can't wait until this thing is over."

The plan was for Corbett to slowly let his end of the rope out until I had swung away from the wall and was dangling beneath the lip of the overhang. As I pendulumed out over bottomless space, the wind caught me and whipped me around like a paper lantern. My heart felt as if it would burst through my T-shirt.

Over the roar of the wind, I thought I could hear something else, but I couldn't make out what it was.

"Listen," yelled Corbett. "Do you hear anything?"

"Yeah," I replied. "What is it?"

"It's people on the ground! They're cheering for you!"

He was right. Nineteen hundred feet below us, people were watching and shouting encouragement. It amazed me that their voices could reach us over such a distance, but I could clearly hear them shouting things like, "Go for it, Mark!" The idea that friends and even strangers were down there rooting for us sent a warm burst of confidence surging through me. Knowing I was not alone took away the anxiety.

But this was clearly no place to bask in applause. I was now swinging out over kingdom come, hanging by a single thread—albeit a very strong one. The rush of wind came barreling along the expansive granite face, and suddenly I was being buffeted around and blown sideways.

It was time to get out of there. I grabbed the pull-up bar and cranked myself up. With adrenaline surging through me, I zipped up the rope in no time at all. Soon I was past the lip of the overhang and back on the sun-warmed granite wall. I reached the cluster of pitons that anchored the top of the rope and stopped, but my heart continued to pound.

We had conquered the Shield Roof. Now there could be no turning back. Our only way home lay over the summit of El Capitan, still almost a thousand feet above our heads.

Mike Corbett:

You'd think it would be frightening to pass the point of no return, but the opposite was true. Psychologically, it was as if a weight had been lifted off our shoulders. Now we were committed to the top; there could be no more doubt or indecision. Once the bridge was burned behind us, once we had no choice but to move ahead, the picture became clear and focused.

Not that we were ready to celebrate, though. That evening, as we erected our Portaledges and prepared to bed down for the night, Mark was edgy and irritated. It was the first time I'd ever seen him like that. He was visibly agitated with me—about the climb, the rock chaps, everything. He just couldn't wait to get the chaps off his legs; I assumed he was mad at me for not making them more comfortable.

I had a few words for Mark, too. I wouldn't hesitate to yell at him when the rope got tangled or when he was idle while there was plenty of work to do. I had to remind myself that living on the side of a vertical rock wall was second nature for me, but a bewildering new experience for him. I was as hard on Mark as I was on any of my climbing partners; I didn't cut him any slack just because he was a paraplegic. One reason for my testiness, I think, was that I felt uneasy about what lay ahead the next morning. The Shield Roof certainly wasn't the end of the hard climbing. The next one hundred feet consisted of a thin, shallow crack that regularly spits out pitons, camming devices—anything you try to stuff into it.

It was called the Groove Pitch and, technically speaking, it was even trickier than the roof. This was where a friend of mine had suffered a big-wall climber's worst nightmare. He was almost to the top of the crack, gingerly stepping onto a piton, when it suddenly popped out. Then the next one popped, and then the one after that and the one after that. As he plunged down the rock face, every single piece of his hardware pulled out of the crack. Climbers call this a "zipper fall." They're always terrifying and often injurious. Luckily, the wall is so sheer there that my friend didn't crash into anything on the way down. The belay rope finally caught him, but not before he had fallen seventy-five feet.

After all that worrying, climbing the Groove Pitch the next morning was almost anticlimactic. I cruised right up it without trouble, finding lots of pitons and other gear already in the crack. I used a few tricks of my own to make placements in marginal spots. Soon I was rappelling back down to set up the bags for hauling.

"That wasn't so bad, was it?" asked Mark, as I bounded down the rope. I think he could see the relief on my face.

There was one more significant incident that day. I was hammering away at a piton in a crack above the Groove Pitch when I felt a little jab in my left eye. My eye started watering, and I had to stop hammering for a minute. I assumed a tiny chip of granite had dinged me. That evening, a serious look came over Mark's face as he looked at me.

"What's that in your eye?" he asked.

"Uh, it's just dust or something."

"No, man, there's something in your eye. I can see it."

I rubbed my eye and said, "No, it's just dust. It's no big deal."

I was wrong. It was far more serious than that. A sliver of steel from the piton had lodged in my cornea. I shrugged it off at the time—there was really nothing I could do about it—but later it would prove to have serious consequences.

That night, though, I was too upbeat to dwell on it. Both Mark and I were in festive moods. We had climbed the hardest rock that El Capitan could throw at us on this route, and we knew it would take something extraordinary to stop us now.

That evening I was lounging on my Portaledge, waiting for Corbett to hand me down a bagel, when I heard a whoosh that sounded like a far-off jet. Startled, I looked out to see a Peregrine falcon swooping right past us.

The majestic bird had his eyes locked on his dinner: a horrified swift that was trying every evasive maneuver in the book. It was no use. Yellow talons spread wide, the falcon moved in for the kill. I cringed for the luckless swift, but felt privileged to see the magnificent hunting bird in action.

Amazingly, El Capitan is home to all sorts of wildlife. The Peregrine falcon, a rare and endangered species of raptor, likes to build airy nests on ledges midway up the wall. During nesting season, the National Park Service bans climbing from routes that pass by known nest sites. It also hires El Cap climbers to locate the sites of new nests. Climbers, as a rule, are not known for obeying other people's rules, but they respect the seasonal restrictions. I think they admire the birds for choosing the majesty of El Capitan for their homes.

Wildflowers, lichen, grass and even pine trees sprout inexplicably from the granite face—a testament to their tenaciousness and a puzzler for every backyard gardener who can't keep his gardenias alive in expensive, nutrient-enriched soil.

It's not unusual for climbers to find tiny frogs living in piton cracks, thousands of feet above the ground. One evening on our climb, Corbett came across a massive column of ants. Higher up, we were swarmed by bumblebees.

Our first night on El Cap's Mammoth Terrace, Dan McDivitt, a Camp Four climber helping NBC, was dismayed to see a large rat trying to chew a hole through one of our haul bags. It's anyone's guess how the rodent got a thousand feet up El Cap, but it had obviously grown fat off its thievery from passing climbers.

When Corbett and Gwen had been setting ropes up to Mammoth Terrace before the start of the climb, Mike had a startling and ultimately sad encounter. Six hundred feet off the deck, he leaned into a wide crack and found himself eyeball to eyeball with a California ground squirrel.

It was hard to tell who was the more startled. Mike instinctively jerked backward, managing to keep his balance. The squirrel was not so lucky. Visibly shaken, it lost its grip on the rock and tumbled out of the crack. Mike lost sight of it as it plunged to earth.

Mike Corbett:

We were just settling down for the night when Gwen's voice came over the radio with some news that almost knocked me off the ledge.

"I don't know if I should tell you this, Mike, but your brother Tony called."

I was dumbfounded. It had been ten years since I'd last seen Tony, and it had been even longer since I'd had any contact with anyone else in my family. I hadn't seen my dad in fifteen years, and I hadn't seen my mom in nearly twenty.

"Uh, well... that's neat," I said into the radio. "I'll talk to him when I get down."

"Mike, that's not all," Gwen said. "Your mom, your dad, your sister—they all want to come meet you. They all recognized you on TV, and they want to get back together. And listen to this: your nephews and nieces say they'll only eat cold bagels and cream cheese, because that's what they saw Uncle Mike eating."

The implications were almost more than I could comprehend. This was a part of my past I had never mentioned to Mark or anyone else. I had never really come to terms with it myself.

My father was a career Army officer, and we had moved all around the country when I was growing up. I attended nine different schools before finally graduating from George Washington High School in San Francisco.

There had always been a lot of bickering and fighting in my family, and when my parents divorced in 1970—when I was fifteen—it was particularly ugly. My mom stayed in Houston and I moved with my dad to San Francisco. After

*finishing high school, I worked for about six months as a file
clerk for a freight company, then left home and moved to
Yosemite. I've lived there ever since.*

*My dad and I had always argued. I was the black sheep,
and I just didn't want to be part of the family any more. I
was tired of all the bickering. I had always thought my dad
was selfish, and I think some of it rubbed off on me, because
I can be that way, too. So one day I just said, "See you later.
I'm leaving."*

*But I never did see them later. The letters they sent never
reached me, and I never wrote or called. Once I phoned
directory assistance in Houston to get my sister's address,
but I never wrote her. I was living my life the way I wanted,
and it just seemed simpler not to communicate with them.
They knew I was involved in some serious rock climbing,
and, I later found out, they had just assumed I had died.*

*Now, without warning, they were coming back into my
life. I lay awake all night, staring up at the stars and
turning the situation over in my mind. Whatever bitterness
I had once felt was gone. The more I thought about it, the
more excited I was at the prospect of seeing them again. I
yearned to be part of a family again. To be given your family
back when you're thirty-five years old is an overwhelming
gift.*

*I suddenly understood that, in an unexpected way, Mark
would not be the only one bursting through personal barriers
on this climb. His were physical and mine were emotional,
but they were barriers just the same. The idea of embracing
my dad, unthinkable just a short time ago, filled me with
warmth and longing. I realized, too, that to make that
telephone call, my family must have come to terms with my
life as a climber. Because of all the publicity this climb was
getting, I hoped they could see my life in a new light and
accept it as worthwhile.*

*All this was hard for Mark to understand. He came from
a close family, and I think it was outside his realm of
understanding to go that long without talking to your
parents. My family wanted to hike up the back side of El*

Capitan and greet me on the summit, but it was too difficult a journey for them. Instead, I made arrangements over the radio to hold our reunion back in Yosemite Valley when I returned.

As the crescent moon illuminated the granite formations of Yosemite in milky light, I tried to close my eyes and get some sleep. Mark and I still had close to nine hundred feet of vertical granite between us and the summit, and I knew I had to get my family out of my head and focus on the climbing.

The relentless sun beat down on us as Mike leaned his head against the rock and let out a weary sigh. His face was stubbly and weather-beaten, and his sweat-crusted shirt was baggy on his skinny frame. If it hadn't been for his climbing harness, he would have had a hard time holding up his pants. I wondered if I looked the same. El Capitan was certainly extracting its toll from us. All day long the sun parched our throats and turned the granite blistering hot. More than half a mile straight down, we could see the cool, refreshing water of the Merced River. Tourists were splashing in it, floating on air mattresses, perhaps soaking their feet after a long hike. But up on El Capitan, the temperature was approaching 105 degrees. We had to ration every sip we took from our water bottles, and the warm water didn't even begin to quench our thirst.

Corbett and I had originally planned to reach the summit on this day, but it had been obvious for some time that we weren't going to make it. Neither one of us was concerned. The rock dictates the rules of the game, and it's just about impossible to move according to your own schedule. We had saved enough water to get us through an extra day, and there was plenty of food left in our haul bag. In this heat, our appetites were feeble. We dutifully forced down some calories each day, but eating was no pleasure.

The delay didn't bother me. The rhythms of the climb had taken over, and I was starting to feel at home on the rock. As we moved higher, the vistas opened up more and more, until we felt as if we were the kings of Yosemite, with our realm spread out beneath our feet.

Toward the end of the day, we looked up to see a body dangling on a rope above us. It was one of the NBC cameramen who had rappelled down from the summit to film us. He was the first human we'd seen since leaving Mammoth Terrace, six days earlier.

That night we camped on Chickenhead Ledge, the last ledge of any size before the top. Above us the climbing was relatively easy; we knew we had it in the bag. Several NBC cameramen met us on the ledge, and we had an impromptu little party. They brought us down a couple of cans of Pepsi.

It wasn't until we started talking to the NBC guys that we realized what a big impact our climb was having. It had been one of the top stories on the national news every night. We were amazed to hear that a huge crowd of reporters—fifty or sixty of them— was gathering on the summit in anticipation of our arrival. The networks were all there, CNN was there, everyone. They had rented every available mule in Yosemite to ferry their equipment in along the eight-mile trail up the back side of El Cap. When the mules ran out, they started hiring penniless climbers from Camp Four to carry their gear.

"There's already talk of a TV movie of the week about you guys," said Craig White, one of the cameramen.

Mike and I looked at each other and laughed. We were just two climbing bums having an adventure, and it seemed impossible that we could be capturing the imagination of the nation.

"Hey," said Mike, "we haven't done anything yet. We still have to finish the climb."

We stayed up late that night, joking and telling stories. Mike was thinking an awful lot about the reunion with his family. Around 3:00 a.m., I plopped down on my Portaledge. I looked over to see Corbett dozing off on the narrow granite shelf, oblivious to the way it sloped off toward the valley floor, now twenty-five hundred feet straight down.

Morning saw us up and moving quickly. There was an electric feeling of anticipation in the air.

"Go ahead and leave all your gear here," one of the NBC guys told us. "We'll see that it gets up."

This allowed us to move fast and light, and we were thankful. There were still four rope lengths left to go, but the climbing was easy and Mike attacked them like a man possessed. He was in a mad rush to get to the summit—not the least because he had run out of cigarettes!

Summit fever filled my arms with energy, and I cranked off the last few hundred of my seven thousand chin-ups without even pausing to rest. We were so close we could almost smell the top. The severe angle of the wall eased off and Corbett found he could scramble up it without pounding in pitons every few feet. Standing on a small ledge, he turned his back to me and bent down.

"Hop aboard," he said.

So we'd finish El Capitan the way we'd started it, with me riding piggyback on Mike. We were still on dangerous terrain, but after the absolute sheer verticality of the last twenty-nine hundred feet, it seemed like a cakewalk.

I wrapped my arms around Corbett's neck and used a carabiner to attach my harness to his. After eight days on El Cap, his body felt bony. His movements were tentative and his legs seemed wobbly, like an astronaut returning to earth after a week in zero gravity. But after all we had been through together,

I had complete and total confidence in him.

Mike moved slowly and with exaggerated care up the last steep section of the route, pausing every few feet to catch his breath. Suddenly, over our shoulders, there was an ear-splitting roar. I looked up to see a helicopter from one of the San Francisco television stations only five hundred feet above us, a cameraman leaning out the window. The pilot was flagrantly violating national park regulations, which require aircraft to stay two thousand feet above the valley rim.

The angle eased further, and Corbett tried to pick up the pace. Now dispensing with the rope altogether, he fought a battle between impatience and exhaustion. The summit couldn't arrive soon enough for either of us.

We were moving up a sloping slab of granite covered with loose gravel when it happened.

Mike's foot slipped, his legs buckled slightly, and for one horrifying moment we teetered there, on the brink. An electric current of fear jolted me out of my weariness. The circumstances were frighteningly similar to those of seven years before, when a single instant of carelessness had changed my life forever. Then, as now, it had been a few pebbles out of an entire mountain that got me.

Corbett staggered, trying to regain his balance. I held my breath. If we lost it here, there would be nothing to stop us. We'd have plenty of free-fall time to contemplate our foolishness before we smacked into Yosemite Valley at terminal velocity.

The moment passed almost before it had a chance to register in my consciousness. Corbett found his balance, and I let out my breath. The danger had passed, but that single moment, so close to success, was the scariest of the entire climb for me.

A minute later, our adventure was over. We scrambled up another slab of rock, and in front of us stood an army of photographers, television cameramen, reporters, Park Service officials and cheering friends. Someone had strung up a rope to keep them from getting too close to the cliff.

"Give 'em a salute or something," Corbett whispered to me. "Let them know we're charged up."

I thrust my fist in the air, in a sort of victory gesture, and heard the machine-gun chatter of thirty camera shutters. That's the picture that ran on the front page of half the newspapers in the country the next day.

Suddenly everyone was upon us. Surrounded by friends and well-wishers, we were laughing, smiling, thumping each other on the back, receiving warm embraces, letting the pure joy of the moment wash over us. Someone handed Corbett a magnum of champagne. He popped the cork, sprayed my hair with bubbly and took a long, thankful gulp. I took the bottle from him, gave it a shake and playfully sprayed it at the media.

By their very nature, climbing triumphs like this are usually won atop lonely mountaintops, with no one else around to share the moment. But here we were, with not only our friends but the whole nation sharing in our summit celebration. I felt like an Olympic athlete standing on the platform to receive my gold medal.

Mike carried me over to a tree, where someone had laid out a blanket in the shade. Reporters clustered around, and soon the questions were flying at us.

"How do you feel now?"

"What was the hardest part?"

"Did you ever think you weren't going to make it?"

"Why did you do this?"

"What statement does this make for disabled people?"

"What's next?"

This time it didn't bother me to answer the questions. We were no longer shooting off our mouths— we had done what we had set out to do. Our little press conference went on until the questions were starting to come around for the third and fourth time.

Then the NBC crew led us over to a spot on the edge of the cliff where we did a live interview with Tom Brokaw for the *NBC Nightly News*. It was quite a surprise for Mike, because it turned out to be a three-way interview that included his mother and sister from Houston.

When it was over, Colin Campbell, a Park Service ranger and a friend of mine, brought over a horse and I saddled up for the ride out to the trailhead. All the way out along the dusty trail it was like a victory procession. Word traveled fast among the hikers, and everybody we passed had a smile and some congratulations to add. Weary beyond words, I waved and smiled back.

I knew I'd soon be settling back into my wheelchair. I also knew that the person sitting in it would never be the same as the one who had left it eight days earlier.

Mike Corbett:

Late that afternoon I was standing around at the trailhead, waiting for them to put Mark's horse away, when Gwen pulled me aside.

"There's a woman here who wants to tell you something," she said.

Gwen introduced me to the woman, and she motioned for me to come with her. She wanted to stand away from everyone else. What she had to tell me was private.

"Six years ago today, on July 26, 1983, my son committed suicide in Yosemite," she said. "Every year on this date, I come back to Yosemite to think about my son. And every year I cry. But this year, because of what you two have done, I didn't cry. From now on, when I come back each year, I am going to celebrate the life of my son, instead of his death. You two inspired me to do that, and I just wanted you to know."

I didn't know what to say to the woman. I was moved beyond words, and for the first time I began to realize that our little adventure had come to mean so much to so many different people. El Capitan was no longer a private affair between Mark and me; it seemed to belong to everyone.

Mark Wellman, at one with nature, wades
in Lake Tahoe, CA, at the age of 4.
Credit: Wellman Collection

Already addicted to scaling the heights, 17-year-old Mark climbs Mt. Abbot, CA, in 1977.
Credit: Wellman Collection

Peter Enzminger – later Mark's climbing partner on Seven Gables – in 1980. *Credit: Wellman Collection*

For the last time, Mark walks back from the Visitor Center in Bishop, CA, after obtaining a permit to climb Seven Gables. *Credit: Wellman Collection*

Seven Gables, the mountain on which a moment's inattention cost Mark the ability to walk – and changed his life forever. *Credit: Wellman Collection*

Mark's parents, Ben and Millicent Wellman. In 1992, while Mark was representing the United States as part of the U.S. Disabled Cross-country Ski Team at the Paralympics in Albertville, France, Ben passed away. *Credit: Wellman Collection*

Mark sits with Nancy Jenks, who played a pivotal role in his life before and after the accident. *Credit: Wellman Collection*

Mark Sutherland, who inspired Mark Wellman during his recovery at Kaiser Vallejo Rehabilitation Center. *Credit: Sutherland Collection*

A year after his accident, Mark was back at his old pursuits, although doing them a little differently. Here he is seen hiking at Fallen Leaf Lakes, CA, in 1983. *Credit: Wellman Collection*

In 1984, Mark was chosen to carry the Olympic torch through Napa, CA, as a representative of the Kaiser Vallejo Rehabilitation Center. *Credit: Wellman Collection*

Mark and friends by the pool at De Anza College in 1984. *Credit: Wellman Collection*

Mark found out that, like everything else in his life after the accident, playing tennis in a wheelchair required a different approach. Here he is competing in a Chico State wheelchair tennis tournament. *Credit: Wellman Collection*

The road to recovery leads Mark to become a park ranger. Here he is seen with fellow interpretive rangers in Yosemite National Park, CA, in 1987. *Credit: Wellman Collection*

Mark and dolphin friends swimming in Florida in 1989. Dolphins seem to have an uncanny sense of a human's disability. As a result, they play an important part in many people's rehabilitation. *Credit: Wellman Collection*

El Capitan, Yosemite National Park, CA, the highest sheer granite face in the United States.
Credit: Chris Falkenstein

Mark and Mike on the way to the top of "the biggest wall of them all."
Credit: Jay Mather, The Sacramento Bee

Mark doing one of the 7,000 pull-ups that climbing El Cap required.
Credit: Jay Mather, <u>The Sacramento Bee</u>

Mark and Mike on El Cap, photographed from above.
Credit: Jay Mather, The Sacramento Bee

The view from El Cap into the valley below when Mark gave into his desire to look down.
Credit: Jay Mather, The Sacramento Bee

The much-evolved rock chaps and other climbing equipment used by Mark.
Credit: Chris Falkenstein

Mark presents President George Bush with the American flag he and Mike carried to the summit of El Cap. *Credit: Wellman Collection*

Ted Farmer carries Mark Wellman through a
rocky traverse from the shoulder of Half Dome.
Credit: Chris Falkenstein

Mark, Mike Corbett, and the support team at the base of Half Dome, getting ready to start
the climb. *Credit: Chris Falkenstein*

After the first day of the Half Dome climb, Mark and Mike camp on Dormitory Ledge.
Credit: Chris Falkenstein

Mark jumaring in the Zebra pitches on Day 2.
Credit: Chris Falkenstein

Mark and Mike on Day 11 of the Half Dome climb, when their food supply was greatly depleted. *Credit: Chris Falkenstein*

Mike on top of Half Dome's steep face, 100 feet from the summit. *Credit: Chris Falkenstein*

On Day 13, Mark Wellman climbs the last pitch, 90 feet of low-angled granite.
Credit: Chris Falkenstein

Mark and Mike on the summit of Half Dome. *Credit: Chris Falkenstein*

Mark gets ready to ski with his high-tech mono-ski. *Credit: Chris Falkenstein*

Mark, Alpine skiing at Alpine Meadows, CA, in 1992. *Credit: Chris Falkenstein*

Mark, Nordic skiing, Tahoe Donner Cross-country Center, CA. *Credit: Chris Falkenstein*

Mark and his girlfriend, Paulette Irving.
Credit: Rick Soloway

Mark Wellman finds his greatest freedom and mobility while kayaking. Here he's on the
Lower Merced River, Yosemite National Park, CA. *Credit: Chris Falkenstein*

6

A Whirlwind of Publicity

A warm glow of orange and pink spread over El Capitan as the last rays of the setting sun danced across the soaring monolith. Sitting in my wheelchair at the foot of the wall, I watched the interplay of light and shadow on the granite I now knew so well. Mike Corbett stood next to me; neither of us said a word.

We gazed up at the vertical expanse we had just finished climbing and tried to make sense of the tidal wave of thoughts, feelings and emotions flooding our heads. Both Mike and I were gaunt, haggard, and badly in need of a shower and a hot meal. I felt as happy as I ever had in my life.

A deep feeling of contentment was spreading through my body, and every nerve seemed to be buzzing. I took a deep breath of the sweet, pine-scented air. The soft grass of the meadow and the cool breeze blowing off the Merced River felt more wonderful than I ever remembered. I'd climbed enough mountains to know that the real satisfaction never comes from those few moments you stand on the summit. It emerges slowly, in the days that follow, as your heightened senses rediscover the joys of the world you left behind.

The last light of the day flickered out on El Capitan. Evening shadows were falling on Yosemite Valley, and a victory celebration awaited us back at the medical clinic. Corbett and I climbed back into the '54 Plymouth being driven by Eldon, my old swimming coach. Eldon had met us at the end of the trail, and he was giving Mike, Gwen and me a ride back home.

That night we gathered with friends at the medical clinic to eat a huge pasta dinner and watch the evening news. We flipped around the channels, and the footage of Corbett carrying me the last few feet to the summit was the lead story on every newscast. Our friends gathered around to congratulate us and hear all the stories. In our soaring emotional state, the food tasted better, the jokes seemed funnier and the bonds of friendship felt deeper.

By midnight, the adrenaline that had carried me up El Capitan for eight days was starting to run out. My eyelids began to feel heavy, so I wheeled myself wearily off to my cabin. Suddenly the idea of a soft mattress sounded irresistible. Mike, though, was still full of energy. Too hyped up to sleep, he walked the hallways of the medical clinic all night long.

At 4:30 the next morning, we were sitting in front of television cameras at the Ahwahnee Hotel as NBC technicians adjusted klieg lights, fitted earphones into our ears and clipped microphones to our collars. Suddenly, a red light on the camera went on and Jane Pauley's voice was in my ear. We were doing a live interview for the *Today* show, and to this very day I shudder at how bad we were.

Glassy-eyed and groggy from our lack of sleep, we came across like zombies from *Night of the Living Dead*. Both of us looked as if we could have nodded off at any point during the interview. At least we had showered and shaved.

"Good morning and congratulations," said Pauley's disembodied voice in our earphones. "What did you say to each other when you got to the top, Mark?"

"Well, we were real happy, that's for sure," I

stammered. "Uh, I felt, uh, a lot of relief. We were up there, it just felt, uh, great to be up there."

"Why'd you do it?" Jane Pauley's tone of voice sounded as if she were interrogating a Watergate co-conspirator instead of a rock climber.

"Uh, well, it was just a challenge, I think. Uh, you know, the rock is so beautiful and a lot of, uh, people don't really get to get up there and see it."

We were so confused that Mike answered one of the questions intended for me, and I answered one of his. If the millions of *Today* show viewers were wondering whether a lack of cerebral function was a prime requirement for climbing El Capitan, this interview probably convinced them.

Mike Corbett:

My eye was still bothering me, so later that day I dropped by to see my friend Dr. Schankerman at the Yosemite Medical Clinic.

"You've definitely got something in there," he said, shining a light in my eye. "I'm going to have to try to pull it out."

As I lay back on the table, a tiny pair of tweezers came straight at my left eyeball. My natural reaction was to shut my eye, and it took several tries before I could keep it open long enough for Dr. Schankerman to reach in and pull out the object.

He dropped it onto a metal tray. It was a tiny sliver of steel, a chip off a piton maybe half the size of a grain of rice. If it had struck my eye a millimeter to the right or left, it could have caused serious damage to my sight. Only luck had caused it to lodge where it did.

I stood up, thanked Dr. Schankerman and started to leave.

"Wait a minute, Mike," he said. "You're not done yet. I got the sliver out, but there's still some stuff in there. Your tears caused the metal to rust in your cornea, and I'm going to have to send you to an ophthamologist to have it drilled out."

My knees buckled slightly and I felt queasy. The operation sounded terrifying, like something the Secret Police would dream up to try to extract a confession. It also sounded expensive. All the attention I'd gotten over the last week hadn't changed the fact that I was a poor climbing bum.

However, I had no choice in the matter. The next day I drove down to Fresno to see the ophthamologist, and the procedure was every bit as horrifying as I'd imagined. The little drill came directly into my left eye, and there was nothing I could do—I couldn't shut my eye, I couldn't even blink. Oddly, there was no real physical pain; the human eye is not very sensitive to touch. But the high-pitched whirring and the vibrations I felt were awful enough.

After a few minutes, it was all over. The nurse handed me some antibiotic ointment to dab in my eye every hour, and I prepared to settle the bill. Dr. Schankerman had warned me it was going to cost about four hundred dollars. That would just about clean out my meager bank account.

"Aren't you the guy who just climbed El Capitan?" asked the ophthamologist.

"Yeah," I answered. "That's me."

"Well, I'll tell you what," he said. "Just sign an autograph for my son and we'll call it even."

A few days later, I was back working at the medical clinic when someone burst in the front door saying, "Your family is here!" I walked out onto the porch, and there stood the Corbett clan, looking much older than I remembered them.

Five nieces and nephews I'd never met—the children of my brother, Tony—came rushing up, wrapped their arms around my legs and screamed, "Uncle Mike! Uncle Mike!" My dad shuffled slowly across the parking lot. His face was oddly expressionless; his hands hung limply by his side.

"He's had six strokes since you last saw him," whispered Tony.

We all embraced. There was so much to say, so much to catch up on. All of them had grown and changed so much since I had last seen them. In addition to Tony, his wife, and *his five children, there were my older sister Terry, my dad, and Randy Hill, a cousin from North Carolina.*

Someone at Continental Airlines had heard about my family situation on the network news, and the airline had generously offered to fly everyone to California free. The only one missing was my mom. It was awkward for her to be there with my dad, but she sent word that she'd drive out later in the summer for a visit.

It was strange and overwhelming to be suddenly encircled by the family I had not seen in more than a decade. But so many weird and wonderful things were happening to me at the time that I just shrugged and enjoyed it. In all our catching up we never talked about the reasons I had left; they no longer mattered.

My dad didn't say much, and when he opened his mouth the words came out slowly. But I noticed that wherever I went, he made sure to stand right by my side. If I moved across the room to talk to someone, he followed. At lunch, he took the seat right next to mine, and he leaned close to hear every word I said.

We swapped old family stories, like the time when my dad had taken me to see the motorcade of President John F. Kennedy in Houston. The date was November 21, 1963, the day before his visit to Dallas.

At one point during lunch I complimented my dad on his watch, and he slid it off his wrist and gave it to me. My nieces and nephews treated me like a celebrity; I guess that's what being on television does for you. I was flattered to learn that Tony, like Terry before him, had named his firstborn son Mike.

Just as quickly as they arrived, they were gone. They had only been able to come to Yosemite for two days. But now we all write each other and drop by for visits when we can, just like a real family. My dad telephones me regularly. He never says much, but it's the fact that he makes the call that counts.

Not long after my family left Yosemite, word arrived from Washington that President Bush wanted us to come to the White House on May 4. It all seemed like a crazy dream. Until recently I had been living out of a tent in Camp Four and scrounging aluminum cans out of the trash for food money. Now I was going to the Oval Office to meet the President of the United States. What was I going to wear? I couldn't exactly walk into the White House in my ratty climbing clothes. I hadn't owned a suit in my entire life. I didn't even have a necktie to call my own.

Gwen lent me five hundred dollars, and I drove to Fresno to shop for a suit, tie, shirt, belt, shoes—the whole works. I went from shop to shop, but nobody could do the alterations immediately. Finally, in a store called the Men's Warehouse, I blurted out to a salesperson: "I'm going to the White House in a couple of days to meet the president!"

That did the trick. All the salespeople clustered around. Soon tape measures were encircling my body and chalk marks were appearing on my cuffs. The shop staff dropped everything and did the alterations while I waited.

"So this is what it's like when you've hit the big time," I thought. But things were only getting started.

As the flight attendant finished describing the plane's safety features, she made a special announcement: "Ladies and gentlemen, we'd like to give a special welcome to two people aboard our flight today— disabled park ranger Mark Wellman and his partner Mike Corbett—who just climbed El Capitan."

Corbett and I looked at each other, smiled and shook our heads as the United Airlines flight to Washington, D.C., erupted in applause. A minute later another flight attendant came by with a complimentary bottle of champagne. After we touched down at Dulles Airport, it seemed as if just about everybody getting off the plane wanted to shake our hands and pat us on the back. Over and over again, Mike and I kept telling ourselves we were just a climbing bum and a gimp from Yosemite. We didn't deserve all this.

At the Washington Hilton, the manager led us to the

Presidential Suite and swung open the door with a flourish.

"This is where you two will be staying," he said. "I hope you'll be comfortable."

As I wheeled inside, my eyes grew wide and I gasped. It was as big as a house and more lavish than any hotel room I'd ever seen. Mark and I entered the spacious living room, which was tastefully decorated with statues and original paintings. Picture windows and a balcony overlooked red clay tennis courts and a huge swimming pool.

In the center of the room was a large glass coffee table, ten feet square and covered with fruit baskets, salami, nuts and a cutting board loaded with imported cheeses and crackers. Nearby stood a fully stocked bar with a selection of excellent French and California wines, Heineken beer and just about every fancy brand of liquor you could name.

"Mark, come check this out," said Corbett.

I wheeled across the expansive living-room carpet to the doorway where he stood. It opened into the master bedroom, which contained a bed almost as big as my whole cabin back in Yosemite. There were antique dressers, a sofa and a phone.

In fact, there was a phone in each of the suite's five main rooms—in the kitchen, in the mirrored dining room, in the other bedroom, in the spacious conference room, and in each of the bathrooms. So huge was the suite that we wondered if it was a long-distance phone call from the master bedroom to the conference room.

We were still exploring when the manager came back to make sure we were comfortable. He informed us that we would have a chauffeured limousine at our disposal twenty-four hours a day. If we were hungry, he said, all we had to do was pick up the phone and call room service. As he talked, I could sense Corbett was a little nervous. No one had spelled out to us exactly who was paying for all this.

"Don't worry," said the manager. "It's taken care of."

"Just out of curiosity," asked Corbett, "if we *were* paying for this room, how much would it cost us?"

"This room costs more than one thousand dollars a night, sir."

Our jaws just about hit the marble floor. A few days earlier we had been sleeping on granite ledges and eating Beanie Weenies out of the can; now we were luxuriating in the Presidential Suite and mulling over our choice of vintage Bordeaux wines. A real Yosemite climbing bum would probably claim he was more comfortable halfway up El Capitan, but we had to admit that decadence felt good, too.

"I could get used to this," said Corbett as he folded his hands behind his head and sprawled out on the overstuffed couch.

We were so nervous about meeting the president the next day that we didn't even touch the bar. Nor did we take advantage of the limousine to go visit the Smithsonian or the various memorials. Corbett and I were starting to come down from the adrenaline high that had propelled us through the climb and the crazy week that followed. With the sights of the nation's capital beckoning just outside our door, all Mike and I wanted to do was lie down in a comfortable bed and close our eyes.

The guard at the White House gate leaned in the window of our van and said, "I'm going to have to see some identification from everybody, please."

He was a no-nonsense Marine with a big pistol, and he probably had to ask that of everybody up to and including Vice President Dan Quayle. Inside our official U.S. Department of Interior van, everybody fumbled for their wallets. Corbett and I were riding with Jim Ridenour, the department's director, and Jack Moorehead, the associate director who had formerly been superintendent of Yosemite National Park.

I patted my back pocket and gulped. My wallet wasn't there. I had switched into my Yosemite park ranger's uniform for the White House visit, and I must have left my wallet back at the hotel room. Everybody was on a tight schedule, and there wasn't time to go back and get it. I leaned forward and pointed to my official National Park Service badge.

"How's this?" I asked hopefully. "It has my name on it."

The guard shook his head, gave me an irritated look and said, "I need something with your picture on it, like a driver's license. Without it I can't let you in."

I shrugged my shoulders. The guard went away for a few minutes and made a phone call from the guard station. Inside the van, we sat in silence. Then he came back, leaned in the window and said, "OK, you can go in." As the gate was raised, he poked his head in one more time and said, "Oh, wait a minute. Do you guys have any weapons?"

"Of course not," answered Ridenour, who seemed a little surprised by the question.

We parked along the side of the building and I wheeled myself up a path through the White House lawn. Milling about were several television reporters, those familiar White House correspondents you see every night on the network news. Corbett recognized one of them and waved.

"Hey, Leslie!" he yelled. "Leslie Stahl!"

The CBS news correspondent waved back with a hint of embarrassment. She had no idea who we were.

At the front door of the White House we were greeted by Marine guards in full ceremonial dress uniforms. As they stood ramrod-straight at attention, their every muscle bulged, their every button shone. They were the perfect soldiers the Marine Corps likes to use on its recruiting posters.

I wheeled up a temporary ramp into the West Wing entrance. From a quick glance around, it looked as if the White House was only partially wheelchair-accessible, although the necessary modifications were in the process of being made.

Dominating the front room was the famous picture of George Washington standing in the bow of a boat as he crossed the Delaware River. The picture is familiar to every American schoolchild, but there was something different about this one. The paint was chipping around the edges and it was in a huge gilded frame. Then it hit me—this was the original!

We were led into a waiting room, where Corbett sat down and immediately lit up a Camel. Not for the first time, I wished he would kick that bad habit. Everybody was calling us role models for the youth of America, and it didn't look good for him to be puffing on a cigarette all the time.

Half an hour passed. Mike got up and examined a beautifully ornate old clock with interior workings made entirely of wood—could it have been a gift to Thomas Jefferson from one of the crowned heads of Europe? Keeping a watchful eye on Corbett were several big, beefy guys in blue blazers. They had ominous-looking bulges in their sports coats and cords running up from their collars into their ears. Every once in a while they'd talk into their sleeves.

Sitting at one end of the couch was a very dignified man with a goatee and a traditional Arab headdress. He looked as if might have been a Saudi prince. We continued to cool our heels. One of the Park Service officials looked at his watch and joked, "When the president has to go to the bathroom, it throws everybody off for the whole day."

Finally an official White House hostess came into the room, smiled at everyone and said, "Come with me, please." She led us down a long hallway lined with priceless art treasures. I was glad my wheelchair steering had come a long way from those awkward days when I used to bump into everything.

The hostess ushered us into a huge round room that looked out onto a rose garden. It took a second to register—we were in the Oval Office. And striding into the room from another entrance was George Bush.

The President of the United States walked up, bent over and shook my hand. I was surprised at how big he was. His hand was huge, and he seemed to tower over me. Everybody looks tall when you're staring up at them from a wheelchair, but Bush seemed like a giant.

"Let me tell you, you guys really captured the imagination of the whole country," he said, gesturing for Corbett and the Park Service officials to have a seat on the couch. The president sat down in an easy chair, and I wheeled up next to him.

"I followed your climb," Bush said, "and I just want you to know that I think what you guys did is amazing. I have a lot of respect for climbers. I don't know how you do it."

Corbett and I had brought along an American flag that we had taken to the top of El Capitan. Before we could present it to the president, someone opened a side door and a mob of news photographers and television cameramen came rushing into the room. Everyone got their pictures of Mike and me handing the flag over to Bush, and then, just as quickly, they were ushered back out of the room.

We chatted with the president about the outdoors for a few more minutes. Bush is a real sportsman, and he told us how much he loved hunting and fishing. Ridenour and Moorehead clearly were excited to have some private time with the president, and they made the most of it by talking to him about land preservation and the national parks.

After about ten minutes, it was time for us to leave. I had planned to say something to Bush about setting aside more money for handicap access in the national parks, but there was no time. Mike and I were presented with presidential tie clasps, Bush shook our hands again, and our White House hostess ushered us out of the Oval Office.

Then I discovered the White House still has a way to go before it's completely accessible to the handicapped. Our next stop was a press conference in the White House gardens. As I wheeled up to the doorway, I found my way blocked by three steep steps leading out into the garden.

A hush fell over the crowd as everyone looked at each other and tried to decide what to do. Fortunately, all those long hours of practice at Vallejo paid off. As the White House press corps watched, I popped a wheelie and bounced confidently down the stairs in my wheelchair. Everyone seemed to get a kick out of that.

That afternoon we were back in our suite hanging out when there was a knock on the door. Corbett opened it to find two women, one of them in a wheelchair.

"Hi," said the disabled woman. "I'm Erin Broadbent—the girl in the picture."

Mike and I exchanged puzzled looks for half a second, and then it hit us. Erin was the person in the wheelchair shown being lowered over the cliff on the cover of *Sports and Spokes*—the handicapped adventurer who had inspired my whole climbing career. A quadriplegic, Erin was now working for the Department of Interior as a park ranger at various monument sites in Washington, D.C.

The woman with her was Kay Ellis, who works on handicapped access and other aspects of special populations for the National Park Service. Kay had heard an interview in which Corbett and I were talking about the *Sports and Spokes* cover, and when we came to town she arranged the meeting with Erin.

you did was fantastic," Harding said over the crackly phone line from his home in Utah. "What do you think about you and me doing El Cap together?"

This was too good to be true—imagine if Willie Mays called you to say he wanted to play center field for your softball team I did some quick calculations in my head, and figured out that Harding must be sixty-five years old. He would be the oldest person ever to climb El Capitan—by a considerable margin.

"Great, Warren," I said without reservation. "Come on out here and we'll do it."

"Well, it's not that easy," Harding said. "I'm a little overweight and I'll have to get in shape. I can tell you that if I do come out I will be in the best shape possible."

I knew Harding was a long way from being in fighting shape. But after climbing El Capitan with Mark, I was so confident I knew we could pull it off. I felt honored that Warren had such confidence in me.

We did the climb in November, to coincide with the thirty-first anniversary of Warren's first ascent. My old high-school buddy, Steve Bosque, an excellent big-wall climber in his own right, came along. Warren showed up with a little potbelly, but his mind was in mid-season form. He was as tough and ornery as ever. That's what mattered.

We spent seven days retracing Warren's 1958 route. Every night he'd pour himself a cup of brandy and fill our ears with stories of the old days in Yosemite. He said all of the headwalls and ledges on El Capitan looked so much smaller than he'd remembered. I guess it's like going back to visit the house you lived in when you were a little kid. It always seems tinier than you'd remembered.

The climb went off without a hitch, and it remains one of my fondest memories. It was certainly thrilling to meet the president, but for me the greatest honor was sharing seven days on El Capitan with the man who started it all.

Not long after that, Gwen broke the news that she was leaving Yosemite to study nursing in Ohio. It was the end *for our relationship. Living in Yosemite and hanging out with a climbing bum just wasn't what she envisioned for herself. Gwen's leaving devastated me for a while. To find consolation, I did the only thing I knew. I grabbed a rope and headed for the warm granite walls of Yosemite.*

On September 6, as the Oakland Coliseum announcer called out our names, 25,037 people stood on their feet and roared at the top of their lungs. I wheeled my chair out of the Oakland A's dugout, across the infield toward the pitcher's mound. Mike was right beside me.

I was to throw out the first pitch of the game, and I was so jittery I felt as if I had a swarm of bumblebees in my stomach. When I got the invitation I hadn't tossed a baseball since Little League, and I was afraid I'd blow it in front of the huge crowd. Before we left Yosemite, Mike and I had paced off the proper distance and practiced the throw time and time again.

The roar reverberated around inside the ballpark and seemed to grow louder as we reached the pitcher's mound. Ron Hassey, the A's catcher, came out a few steps in front of home plate and got down in his crouch. I was shaking from nervousness. We were supposed to get a verbal cue, but I couldn't hear a thing. Was I supposed to throw it? I looked up at Mike for help.

"I don't know... what do you think I should do?" I said.

"Hey, just throw it," he answered.

I reared back in my chair and uncorked one of the wildest pitches the A's catcher had ever seen. It hit the infield grass halfway to home plate and took a crazy bounce. Amazingly, Hassey was able to stretch out and smother the ball with his mitt. I would have been mortified if it had gotten past him and rolled all the way to the backstop.

Three days later, Mike and I were in Los Angeles to tape an appearance on a game show called the *Third*

Degree. Hosted by Bert Convy, it was sort of a modern version of *What's My Line.* The celebrity panel identified us right away, although they were stumped by the guests who followed. At least Mike and I left with the knowledge that we were better known than the owners of the Mustang Ranch, a legal brothel in Nevada.

Every movie producer in Hollywood seemed to have our phone numbers. Corbett and I were bombarded by offers from people who wanted to turn our adventure into a TV movie of the week. Hardly a day went by without phone calls or packages arriving full of brochures, contracts and glossy pictures. Eventually, seven different studios offered to buy the rights to our story.

We decided to go with Tom Sullivan, a blind producer and actor. He is the author of the best-selling book, *If You Could See What I Hear*, and the subject of a movie by the same name. His friend, Michael Landon, had followed our climb and suggested that Sullivan produce a movie about us.

His production company paid us each ten thousand dollars for the rights to our story—enough money to live pretty well for some time in Yosemite.

Sullivan turned out to be a wild guy. Without benefit of sight, he has worked as a nightclub singer and parachuted out of airplanes. In preparation for writing the screenplay, he had Mike take him climbing in Yosemite. I liked the idea of a disabled person producing the movie because I thought he might handle it more sensitively.

He talked of signing Patrick Swayze to play me, and Corbett joked that he wanted to be portrayed by Danny DeVito. Right off the bat, though, it became obvious that neither Sullivan nor co-writer Jodie Lewis knew the first thing about rock climbing. We spent many long hours on the phone explaining the difference between a piton and a camming device and a Jumar.

One day a few months later the script arrived in the

mail. I tore it open and started reading, but the plot seemed to have only a vague resemblance to what had really happened. Apparently our story wasn't dramatic enough for television—at least not without considerable embellishment. The script I was reading portrayed Mike as someone who stole food from the cafeteria and had me almost taking a long fall during a practice session and then blaming Corbett. It had us dodging falling rocks on El Capitan and entangled in all sorts of romantic situations. Some of these things were changed in later drafts, but we both still cringed at the thought of this version of our lives appearing on television.

Eventually the producers decided that the cost of filming the climbing scenes on the vertical expanse of El Capitan was just too expensive. They killed the project, and Corbett and I breathed a sigh of relief.

It seemed as if everybody wanted to give us an award. One of the most prestigious we received was the Tanqueray Amateur Athlete Achievement of the Year award. They flew Corbett and me to New York, and we rented tuxedoes for the ceremony at the famous Explorer's Club. The award put us in some lofty company. Past winners include Herschel Walker, Olga Korbut, Sugar Ray Leonard and Darryl Strawberry. Mike's father came to the banquet and beamed with pride at his son.

So much was going on in our lives that I asked for and received a three-month unpaid leave from my ranger job. I moved to Lake Tahoe to concentrate on my skiing—a sport in which I had some big plans for the future. I ended up renting a room from the director of the Tahoe Handicapped Ski School, and I frequently dropped by the school to talk to the students.

One of the instructors was familiar to me. Paulette Irving and I had met the previous winter. She skied up with a stylish, snow-spraying stop, gave me a big hug, smiled and said hello. We chatted a bit, and as she skied off I couldn't help but notice how athletic and graceful she was. I watched her instruct the young students—paraplegics, quadriplegics, amputees, blind people—and I was taken by how well she connected with them. Not all able-bodied people can do that.

Paulette was unfailingly outgoing and upbeat with the disabled skiers, even in situations that would try the patience of a saint. Nor did she baby anyone. Paulette demanded a lot out of her students, and she usually got it.

We kept bumping into each other on the ski slopes, and soon we were spending afternoons skiing together. At the end of the day we'd go get a beer at the local bar during happy hour and munch on their free hors d'oeuvres. Paulette was really easy to be with, and her experience with her students gave her a real understanding of my situation.

The two of us began spending more and more time together, and as the first warm rays of spring spread over the High Sierra, we realized we were in love.

Mike Corbett:

In April 1991 I was driving down to Mariposa, the nearest town of any size to Yosemite, to take care of a traffic ticket at the county courthouse. Beside me was Nikyra Caltagno, a 26 year-old ranger. Nikyra and I had been together almost constantly for the last six months.

We had met through Mark, and the irony wasn't lost on anyone. Gwen had introduced me to Mark, and then Mark had introduced me to Nikyra. At that first meeting I was immediately struck by how cute and friendly she was. I overheard her saying something about rock climbing, and that was all I needed to hear.

"Would you like to go climbing some time?" I asked.

"Sure," Nikyra smiled back.

A few days later, on my birthday, I threw together some hardware and grabbed a rope. We spent the day doing some beginner's routes in Yosemite. Nikyra wasn't very experienced, but she was enthusiastic and a good learner, and we both had a great time. After that, we were together nearly every day.

Now, as we drove alongside the Merced River on our way to the county courthouse, an idea popped into my head. I blurted it out before I had a chance to lose my nerve.

"While we're getting the ticket taken care of, why don't we just go next door and get a marriage license?"

"Really? Do you mean it?"

"Why not? We can kill two birds with one stone."

So we did. The following month, on a warm afternoon in May, we gathered on a beach along the Merced River with a small group of friends and a preacher. Yosemite was at its prettiest. The trees were alive with blossoms, the meadows were green and lush, and the waterfalls were roaring with the winter's runoff.

Mark wheeled his chair down the embankment and parked next to me. He was my best man. As Nikyra and I exchanged our wedding vows, there was another major presence at the ceremony. Looming directly above us, as if it were the guest of honor, was my old friend, El Capitan.

Mike and I never intended to stop climbing after El Capitan. The world may have seen that ascent as some sort of statement I was making about disabilities, but I never thought of it that way. It's great if people can draw inspiration from what I did, but I climbed El Capitan for one reason only: the personal challenge. My accident may have paralyzed my legs, but I've never stopped thinking of myself as a climber.

Our next goal was painfully obvious. You can't stand in Yosemite Valley without feeling the presence of Half Dome towering over you like a watchful mother. One of the most recognizable rock faces in the world, its sheer northwest face looks as if it had been hacked clean by some giant meat cleaver.

That very first night in the bar, Corbett and I agreed that if we made it up El Capitan, we'd try to climb Half

Dome next. We didn't tell many people—just talking about El Cap sounded crazy enough. Now, after more than a year of accepting awards, giving interviews and signing autographs, my climbers' fingers were starting to itch again. I yearned to be back up on the steep granite, far above the world, with just the wind and the rope and Mike for company.

Corbett was all for it, even though it would be a bigger risk for him. I knew he had personal reservations about Half Dome—it had almost killed him once—but he, too, seemed to want a new challenge in his life. So, in the spring of 1991, we began laying plans.

Almost from the start, we realized things could never be the same as they had been on El Capitan. Then, we had been just two naive climbers operating on moxie and a shoestring budget. Our motives were simple and pure, and the whole adventure had a freshness we could never recapture.

The whirlwind of publicity from that climb had showered us with fame and enough money that we could no longer be called penniless. Now we had access to endorsement deals and sponsorships. Before, we had been unaffected amateurs; now, we were worldly-wise professionals.

Mike and I agreed early on to put any publicity to good use by staging the climb as a fund-raising benefit. Our idea was to bring in the Boy Scouts of America and the Yosemite Association to raise money for their disabled scouting program and park access projects.

The Boy Scouts took the lead in organizing the publicity aspects, and it didn't take long for us to feel as if things were getting out of hand. Suddenly there were guidance committees and meetings and major corporate sponsors. The Boy Scouts hired a Los Angeles public-relations firm to come up with some ideas to increase the climb's visibility. Among the things they suggested was bringing in Sylvester Stallone and General Colin Powell, the Gulf War commander. We

never learned what their roles were supposed to be—
nor did we want to know.

Our adventure soon had its own artist-designed
logo, and glossy brochures were circulated among the
media. There was even a toll-free telephone number
people could call for information on how they could
support the climb.

Eventually, officials of the National Park Service put
their foot down. Because I was a federal employee and
the climb was a money-raising project, Park
Superintendent Michael Finley required the Boy Scouts
to apply for a special permit for the affair. And the
superintendent refused to grant the permit unless they
scaled things down a little. Corbett and I were relieved.

We were not completely innocent ourselves. We had
brought in our own business manager, Emilio Reynoso,
to help us land donations of equipment and money to
help underwrite our costs. Soon we were incorporated
as "Half Dome Climb, Inc." and Emilio was circulating
press releases about us, with our own logo.

All this got to be too much, particularly for Corbett.
He had spent most of the previous twenty years living
under a tree in Camp Four, following his own path and
avoiding the clutches of Corporate America. I think he
climbed to distance himself from that world—but now
the upcoming Half Dome ascent was putting him right
in the thick of it. His consuming passion in life had
suddenly become a business.

I had mixed feelings, myself. Part of me hoped the
publicity and contacts from the project would be of use
to me in the future. For a while, the idea had been
bouncing around in my head that I could become a
full-time, professional, disabled athlete. I was already
looking beyond Half Dome to other outdoor
adventures, and I would need sponsorships.

All this caused friction between Corbett and me, and
as the summer passed, we went weeks without talking
to each other. Both of us were committed to doing the

climb, but all the pressures and demands of this circus were putting a massive strain on the deep bonds that had carried us up El Cap.

We set blast-off date for September 4, in part because the Park Service wanted us to wait until the summer crowds had left Yosemite Valley. As the day drew near, I could only hope that once we were up alone on the sheer granite face, the silence, beauty and challenge of Half Dome would ease the friction and turn us into a climbing team again.

Half Dome

**YOSEMITE NATIONAL PARK
CALIFORNIA**

1. Dormitory Ledge
5. Twilight Ledge
6. Sunset Ledge
10. The "Ramp" Ledge

A. Site of Mike Corbett's twenty-foot fall
B. Zebra pitches, four hundred feet long

1-12 Bivouac sites

7

FURTHER CHALLENGES

Many, many years ago, an Ahwahneechee Indian warrior left his home in Yosemite Valley and journeyed across the rugged crest of the Sierra Nevada mountain range to Mono Lake. There he met and fell in love with a beautiful maiden named Tis-sa-ack.

They married, and a short time later the warrior brought Tis-sa-ack back with him to live in Yosemite. They were just entering the great valley when the young bride was overcome with homesickness. She told her husband that she wanted him to return with her to Mono Lake. He refused, and their quarrel turned violent. She began to cry and ran back along the trail toward her home.

The warrior cut a green limb and chased his wife up the path, beating her. This did not sit well with the Great Spirit. For bringing anger into Yosemite Valley, he turned them both into stone. The warrior became the rock formation now known as North Dome, and beautiful Tis-sa-ack was transformed into what today is called Half Dome.

If you look closely at Half Dome's face, you can still see the head and shoulders of a Mono Indian woman, with her hair bobbed and cut in bangs. Dark water streaks run down the rock face, and Indians say they are the tracks of Tis-sa-ack's tears.

In 1863, Josiah Whitney, the first head of the

California Geological Survey, gazed up at Half Dome and called it "perfectly inaccessible, being probably the only one of all the prominent points about the Yosemite which never has been, and never will be, trodden by human foot."

It took all of twelve years for someone to prove Whitney wrong. A dare-devil sailor named George Anderson spent weeks drilling holes and placing six-inch metal spikes with eyebolts up the monolith's steeply sloping east side to reach the summit. Today the Park Service maintains a set of metal cables up Anderson's route. Every summer, thousands of hikers use them as handrails to make an airy but safe ascent to Half Dome's top.

Awed rock climbers stared up at the rock's breathtakingly sheer northwest face for years before anyone stepped forward with the skill and the nerve to climb it. The leader of that 1957 ascent, Royal Robbins, returned twelve years later to forge a daring and tremendously difficult new route directly up the face's dark water streaks.

It's considerably harder than the route we took on El Capitan and it's rarely climbed—even seasoned big-wall climbers tend to give it a wide berth. The rock is frighteningly loose, the piton placements are insecure and retreat is difficult if not impossible. All of which is to say that for Corbett the lure was irresistible. He needed another big challenge in his life, a chance to test himself against his fears and doubts. So did I. For the disabled athlete in me, there was the extra challenge of conquering something someone had once called "perfectly inaccessible."

Appropriately enough, the vertical path up the streaks of the Indian maiden's tears is called "Tis-sa-ack."

Mike Corbett:
There has always been something dark and disturbing about Half Dome to me. It and El Capitan have distinctly

different personalities. El Cap is bright, sunny and inviting; Half Dome is shadowy, unstable and sinister.

The very first time I approached Half Dome's southwest face I got a bad omen. It was in 1975, in my second year of climbing.

I had gone on ahead of my climbing partner to reconnoiter the start of our climbing route. Walking along the base of the granite cliff, I spotted a tennis shoe. My first thought was that some poor climber had lost it and was going to have to walk all the way back to Yosemite Valley in his painfully tight rock shoes.

Moments later I was startled to come upon a person lying face down in a manzanita bush. What a weird place to take a nap, I thought. But as I got closer I noticed his arm was twisted grotesquely behind his back and his fingers were badly mangled.

Splotches of dried blood spattered his down jacket, which had been ripped open. I crept closer. Peering down, I felt a wave of horror and nausea wash over me. Half his face was missing—ripped off his skull—and down feathers were stuck to the exposed meat of his cheeks and neck.

"Oh my God," I said out loud.

This man had taken an horrendously long fall off Half Dome very recently, probably within the last twenty-four hours. There was no smell of rotting flesh yet, no ants crawling over his lifeless body. I turned and ran back to camp.

It was the next day before we could get back to Yosemite Valley and alert the rangers. I was so shaken I couldn't even make the report; my friend had to do it. We learned later that the victim was a young park employee who had hiked up the cable route and had fallen to his death while trying to scramble down the steep west face. The image of his lifeless body haunted me for a long time, and I stopped climbing for several weeks. I didn't go back to that side of Half Dome for eight years.

In 1986 my name was almost added to Half Dome's list of victims.

In early March of that year, two climbing friends—Steve Bosque and John Middendorf—and I were halfway up an ascent of the huge south face when trouble came. It started as a typical spring rainstorm, but by the end of the day wet, gloppy snow was starting to fall on us.

Expecting the bad weather to blow over, we hunkered down in our Portaledges, zipped the rain covers shut and tried to wait it out. But temperatures continued to plunge the following day, and heavy, wintry snow fell even harder. At one point I unzipped my rain cover and peered out. I was horrified by what I saw. Dark, angry clouds swirled around us, and snow and ice plastered the face, clinging improbably to the vertical granite.

The reality hit me: we were trapped high up on Half Dome. There was simply no way we could go up or down in these desperate conditions. Rappelling was impossible; our ropes were frozen into solid blocks. Avalanches of snow and ice pounded us, and at midday my Portaledge buckled and collapsed from the weight. I moved onto Steve's, which was not in much better condition. The poles had bent and the rain cover had been shredded by the wind.

There was nothing we could do but huddle together, shivering. I was drenched to the bone and shaking uncontrollably from hypothermia. With hands as stiff as wooden blocks, I dropped carabiners and other equipment. Gradually I lost hope that we'd survive another day, and in my chilled and dazed condition I stopped caring.

The storm lifted the next day, but our troubles were far from over. Sunshine melted the ice that sheathed Half Dome's upper slopes, and huge chunks of it began pummeling us. One avalanche crashed directly onto the Portaledge, shearing off the bolt that anchored it to the wall. I plummeted twenty feet down the face before I was yanked to a stop by the rope. Shaken up but unhurt, I started pulling myself back up the rope.

"Jeez, what next?" I asked.

The answer came as soon as the words left my chattering teeth. I heard a whistling sound and looked up—right into

*a falling chunk of ice. It smacked me right in the face, giving
me a big fat lip.*

*Later that day, just as we were letting go of the last
vestige of hope, we heard the sound of salvation. It was the
unmistakable whir of an approaching helicopter. Somebody
was trying to rescue us! It was a chopper from Lemore
Naval Air Station, the same unit that had pulled Mark from
Seven Gables. On the copter's side was painted the name,
"Angel One." To us, it certainly looked like help from
above. But how would the crew get us off the near-vertical
wall of Half Dome?*

*We soon got our answer. In an incredible feat of skill and
daring, the pilot maneuvered the hovering helicopter right
up next to the face. The slightest miscalculation would
cause his rotor to hit the face and he and his crew would be
dead. One way or another, we'd probably die with them.*

*The pilot held the chopper in position, and a long cable
dropped out of its belly. One by one, it plucked us from our
icy perch. Within an hour we were back in the medical
clinic, wrapped in blankets and sipping hot broth. All three
of us owe a debt to those brave rescuers.*

*Over the years, I have had other near-misses on Half
Dome. It seems I can't go near that rock without trouble
following me. As Mark and I prepared to begin our adventure,
an uneasiness settled over me. I knew I would have to do
more than conquer twenty-two hundred feet of steep and
dangerous granite. I would have to conquer my personal
fears, too.*

*I had a premonition that something bad was going to
happen. Before we left, I told Mark and Nikyra that I had an
uneasy feeling I was going to fall on this climb.*

Most of Yosemite still slept in the pre-dawn darkness
of September 4, 1991, as Corbett and I faced the glare
of television lights. Our send-off press conference in
the parking lot of the Yosemite stables had drawn a big
crowd, but by now we were old hands at giving
interviews.

"We're charged up to get up there," I said into the cluster of microphones. "I can't wait to get on the face and touch the rock."

A young girl stepped out of the crowd and handed me a little medallion. I tied it onto my helmet for good luck. Corbett shouldered a pack and gave Nikyra a hug and a kiss. Then he gave her bulging belly a fond pat. Nikyra was seven-and-one-half months pregnant, and Mike was concerned about giving her a scare while we were up on Half Dome.

As Corbett set off on foot, I wheeled across the parking lot to a waiting mule. Our route to the base of the wall was a long and tortuous one, and it had involved nearly as much planning as the ascent itself.

Half Dome presented some special access problems we hadn't faced before. On El Capitan and our other climbs, Mike had been able to piggyback me to the start of the route. But Half Dome's sheer face rises from a pedestal that stands a couple of thousand feet above Yosemite Valley. Rock climbers regularly scramble up that pedestal, but it was too steep and difficult for Corbett to carry me.

Our plan was for me to ride a mule seven miles around the back side and up to Half Dome's east shoulder, where Corbett and others would carry me out along a traverse below the towering northwest face.

I kissed Paulette goodbye, climbed out of my wheelchair and pulled myself up into the mule's saddle for the first step in a journey that would lead me, if all went well, to the summit of Half Dome. We expected that seven tough days of climbing would get us to the top.

The complex approach had a special bonus for me. For the first time since my accident, I would get a chance to see some of the most spectacular parts of Yosemite's back country. The mule could take me places I'd never go in my wheelchair.

We clip-clopped along a bridal path on the banks of the Merced River and eventually joined up with the John Muir Trail. After a couple of miles, the trees parted and I got my first sight in years of Nevada Falls, roaring down a steep cliff in a rugged, glacier-formed canyon. Above it, we followed the river as it flowed lazily through Little Yosemite Valley, sunlight sparkling off its deep green pools.

There was a hint of fall in the air, the maples were just starting to turn yellow and the dogwoods were beautiful. Inside, I felt torn between the desire to get to the start of the climb quickly and the yearning to linger amid this beautiful mountain scenery. This was a real treat for me, and I tried to absorb as much of it as I could.

Further up the trail we overtook Corbett, who was puffing toward our rendezvous point.

"You certainly look comfortable," he said.

"Beats a wheelchair," I replied.

As we climbed higher up the path, I could look out through the pine trees to the jagged Clark Range and the miles of glacier-polished granite of Yosemite's high country, all of it gleaming in the morning light. The dusty trail switchbacked up through an intermittent forest to a flat ridgetop. This was the end of the line for the mule. A mile away to the west I could see the towering face of Half Dome in profile. It looked seriously steep.

Soon I was joined by Corbett and the team of climbers who would help me across what we expected to be one of the trickiest parts of our whole ascent. John Dossi, Ken Yager, Chris Falkenstein and Rich Albuschkat were all present or former members of the Yosemite Search and Rescue Team. Their job would be to help Corbett safeguard the dangerous passage out onto the base of the wall.

Ted Farmer squatted down next to me. A massive horse of a man, with thighs as big around as my waist,

Ted was one of the strongest guys I knew. He managed the gym where I worked out, and he had offered to help in any way he could, no matter how big or small. We wanted to save Corbett's strength for the climb itself, so on this section, Ted would be my legs.

I climbed onto his back and used a carabiner to attach my chest harness to his. Ted stood up, and I suddenly felt nervous. I was used to riding close to the ground while piggybacking on Corbett, who's a pretty short guy. Ted was a giant, and from his back the dirt looked a long way down.

The start of our climb was a mile away across sloping slabs covered with loose dirt and gravel. It wasn't technically difficult, but one wrong step could send you tumbling a hundred feet down. In some spots, an unchecked fall wouldn't stop until you landed in Yosemite Valley, two thousand feet below. Swaying high up on Ted's shoulders, I felt a surge of panic. I realized that the terrain was chillingly similar to the spot on Seven Gables where I had fallen.

We were taking no chances. Ted and I were roped up, and the other climbers moved with us as a coordinated team, belaying the rope off trees and large rocks. A couple of them were always darting ahead to set up the belay anchors for the next section. It was a technique they had practiced many times while evacuating injured climbers.

"Gimme a little slack!" called Ted.

"You got it," answered Ken. "OK, up rope. Let's keep it tight here."

Dossi turned to me and smiled. "Just like a rescue," he said. In this case, though, the rescue team was carrying me toward the mountain, not away from it.

It was a tense, sweaty operation, and we urged everyone to rest frequently. On a few stretches Ted took an extended breather and Corbett shouldered me. As we got closer, the giant face of Half Dome towered above us like a skyscraper, looming even bigger and more awesome with each step. It was dead straight vertical, even overhanging—a far more forbidding sight than El Capitan had been.

Four hours after leaving the shoulder, we reached the spot where a climbing rope hung down from the vertical wall. Finally we had arrived at the start of the climb. As on El Cap, Corbett had gone ahead the previous week and strung ropes up the first three pitches. Our two hundred pounds of food, water and supplies were waiting for us at our first night's destination—a ledge called The Dormitory, three hundred feet above our heads.

I reached out and touched the rock. It felt cool. After all of the planning and meetings and press interviews, it was good to finally come to grips with Half Dome. I shook hands with each member of our support team. Theirs had been a difficult, unglamorous job, and they had pulled it off without a hitch. There weren't many other people with the specialized skills and knowledge of the terrain needed for the task.

I attached my pull-up bar, gave all the knots and buckles a once-over, and hoisted myself up the first six inches of Half Dome. I looked forward to easing back into the familiar sounds and rhythms of big-wall climbing—the ratcheting of my pull-up assembly, the scraping of rock chaps against granite, the cool fluttering of a mountain breeze. As the ground receded beneath me, I felt a sense of relief that we had gotten to the start of the climb without trouble. From the very beginning, we had told ourselves that it was potentially the most difficult and dangerous part of the whole adventure.

Little did we know how wrong we were.

Mike Corbett:
A dull, hollow thunk reverberated out of the piton as I whacked it with my hammer. It wasn't the high-pitched, reassuring ring you get with a good, solid placement. Now

I remembered one of the reasons Half Dome and I never had gotten along. The granite was rotten and crumbly, and the constant insecurity ate away at my nerves.

It was the second day of the climb, and progress was maddeningly slow. What was the matter? I had given up smoking and trained hard all summer, but I just didn't seem to have any energy.

Part of it, I think, was that the commercialization had robbed me of some of my enthusiasm for the climb. But now all that was beneath us, down in Yosemite Valley, and it was just Mark and me and the two thousand feet of granite rising above us. I knew I had to get the lead out and get moving.

I reached up and carefully inserted a Friend—a spring-loaded camming device—behind a loose flake of granite the size of a kitchen table. I gave the Friend a gentle tug to test it, and it popped right out. Cursing under my breath, I jammed it farther up behind the flake, and this time it seemed to hold. I clipped one of my étriers to it and called down to Mark.

"Watch me here," I told him. "This flake feels pretty loose."

"You got it," came the reply from below.

Holding my breath, I eased my foot into the stirrup and gingerly stood up. The Friend felt as if it were wobbling around behind the flake, but it held my weight. I stepped into the top step of my étriers, stood on tiptoe and reached for another Friend to place higher. Big-wall climbing is like this—a constant repetition saved from monotony by the knowledge that you could peel off and be airborne at any moment.

I leaned out and looked up. Twenty feet to go until the end of this pitch, and that would be the end of the day's climbing. Amazingly, it had taken me most of the afternoon to work my way up this 150-foot section of Half Dome. It was disappointing, because I had planned to get much farther. Already I knew the seven-day schedule we had set for ourselves was wildly optimistic. There was simply no way we were going to make the top in a week at the rate we were going.

We were inching ourselves midway up the inside of a giant overhanging arch known as "the Zebra" because of its black stripes. It's a huge feature, clearly visible to the naked eye from Yosemite Valley, twenty-five hundred feet below. I had hoped to reach the top of this section by now, but I could see that it was going to take us at least one more full day.

I had just finished tapping in a rotten piton when I heard a voice shouting up at me from below. It wasn't Mark—it was Ken Yager. What was going on?

"I've got some bad news," yelled Ken. "Yabo committed suicide!"

Dangling there in my nylon slings, I cringed and felt sickened. Yabo was John Yablonsky, a longtime friend to me and just about every other climber in Yosemite. More than most people, Yabo had always been tormented by demons, and I suspected he threw himself into climbing as a way to exorcise them. He had been having emotional problems for some time, and the news that he had taken his own life didn't come as a big surprise. I wished Ken hadn't told me, but Yabo was such a part of our lives that he just couldn't keep the news to himself.

Black, angry-looking clouds were gathering around Half Dome, reflecting my mood. As I finished the pitch and rappelled back down to Mark, the hair on my forearms was standing up, and I knew the weather was in for a change.

"Better get the Portaledges up fast," I said. "It looks like rain."

We hurried to get our two sleeping platforms unfolded and assembled as a cold, moisture-laden breeze kicked up. Mike's double-width ledge, set up directly above me, formed such a big roof that I didn't bother with my rain cover. We were just settling in and breaking out the Beanie Weenies for dinner when the sky lit up in a blinding flash. A second later a rolling, ear-splitting boom reverberated off the granite wall. Mike and I looked at each other with wide eyes.

"That was kind of close," I said.

"Way too close," said Corbett.

Another lightning bolt crackled through the black sky and danced off the top of the cliff across the valley. The rumbles from the thunder penetrated down to our bones—a wild and spooky feeling. It occurred to me that a metal-framed cot festooned with forty pounds of iron, steel and aluminum climbing gear wasn't the best place to be watching these pyrotechnics from. But we didn't have any choice.

The clouds opened up with a heavy downpour. Down below in Yosemite Valley, tourists scrambled for cover. Amazingly, though, none of the rain touched us. Looking up, I could see why. The overhanging arch of the Zebra acted as a natural roof and protected us from the elements. Rain was pouring down twenty feet away from the cliff, but underneath the Zebra's awning, we stayed as dry as a salami.

As I tried to close my eyes, a gust of wind whipped underneath my Portaledge and goosed it a foot or two in the air, sending my heart into my throat. Inside my sleeping bag, I checked the knot on the rope that connected my harness to the piton and bolt anchor. It was going to be a long night.

At dawn I was greeted, bleary-eyed, by the sight of grey mists swirling around Half Dome. It was ironic— two years earlier on El Capitan, the sun and blistering heat had been our constant enemies. Now a little sunshine didn't sound so bad. The chill made me shiver. I pulled my sleeping bag tightly around me and waited for Corbett to wake up.

At 8:00 a.m., I turned on the radio for our regular morning check-in. The news wasn't good.

"Right now there's a low-pressure system parked over Yosemite, and the weather forecast is calling for thundershowers on and off for the next few days," said

Ellyn Windsor, our contact with the Boy Scouts.

Neither of us liked the sound of that. Already, Corbett and I had gotten the disturbing feeling that we had seriously underestimated the difficulty of climbing Half Dome. Now it looked as if we were going to have to battle Mother Nature, too.

As I was putting on my leg braces, a shout from across the expansive face of Half Dome drew my attention. I looked out to see rappel ropes being tossed into the whirling winds. There were parties of experienced climbers ascending two routes parallel to ours, and both of them were bailing out because of the bad weather.

Under different circumstances Corbett and I might have, too. But it had taken the work of so many people just to get me to the start of this climb. To carry me back would be even trickier. It seemed easier to keep going up. As Mike had said, the point of no return on Half Dome came the moment we took the first step off the ground. Turning back was unthinkable.

Besides, the eyes of the world were upon us. Referring to the massive fund-raising effort being undertaken by the Boy Scouts, Corbett picked up the radio and joked: "We can't quit now. All the flyers have already been printed."

As we packed up for the day, we watched the other climbers retreating down the granite wall. A little to my surprise, the sight psyched me up and filled me with boldness. I welcomed a chance to prove to myself that I could keep going in conditions that caused able-bodied climbers to turn back. Corbett seemed to feel the same way.

"Let 'em go," he said to me. "The old man and the gimp are going to stick it out."

Mike Corbett:

Later that day it looked as if Half Dome had decided to ease up on us. Just as we emerged from the shelter of the

Zebra onto the exposed headwall, the clouds unexpectedly lifted. A little warmth and sunshine do wonders for your self-confidence, and suddenly things didn't seem so bad.

The feeling didn't last long.

By nightfall I was bent double on my Portaledge, holding my stomach and retching over the side. A violent urgency overcame my bowels, and I fumbled to pull down my pants and open a large-sized Ziploc bag. When I had filled it, I zipped it shut and lobbed it over the side, hoping no one was standing below to be hit by the most unpleasant bomb imaginable.

A nasty case of stomach flu kept me up all night, groaning and filling more Ziploc bags. By morning I was pale, clammy and weak. Food didn't interest me. But I knew that, somehow, I was going to have to find the strength within me to keep climbing. Mark depended on me.

It was noon before I could bring myself to stand up and get back to work. Without much enthusiasm or strength I slowly nailed my way up a crack for thirty feet until I arrived at a small terrace called Twilight Ledge. That was all I could handle. Thoroughly whipped, I rappelled back down to Mark. Our upward progress for the day was going to be all of ten yards. At that rate, we would reach the summit of Half Dome sometime the following year. Already our seven-day climb had turned into a nine-day climb, and was threatening to take even longer. We would have to start rationing our food.

On this route up Half Dome, the Indian maiden Tis-sa-ack wasn't the only one shedding tears.

It was one of the gutsiest things I've ever seen. Corbett looked so sick he should have been home in bed, but he was fighting to get us higher up Half Dome. Watching his movements, all careful and sure, you would have never guessed that he had been up all night with the stomach flu.

Corbett was such an old pro that he was able to draw on his deep well of experience to keep going. As

I inched up the rope with my pull-up bar, I noticed that his eyes were glassy as he patiently tapped pitons out of the crack. It was like watching Nolan Ryan striking out batters on a day when he didn't have his best stuff.

As the day wore on, Mike began to feel better, and when he started cracking jokes again I knew he would be all right. When it came my turn to climb again, I slid my T-bar up, grunted and began pulling myself up the rope. The face of Half Dome was so steep here that the rope hung out from the wall by a couple of feet. Anything I dropped would plummet untouched for more than one thousand feet before hitting the shelf at the base of the wall. And the floor of Yosemite Valley was another two thousand feet below that.

Cranking off another chin-up, I paused to enjoy the view. By now I was used to the outrageous amount of fresh air beneath my toes, and the electric tingle I got from looking down was something to savor. Spread out below me was all of Yosemite Valley, carpeted in green and quiet with the departure of the Labor Day weekend crowds. To the east, I could see big cumulous clouds billowing up in the blue sky over the High Sierra.

As I gained another half-foot of height, I felt free and wonderfully alive and thankful to be in such a wild, spectacular place. Even in my able-bodied mountaineering days, I'd never dreamed I would one day find myself halfway up the sheer face of Half Dome.

Freed from the mental strain of lead climbing and the physical burden of hammering pitons and wrestling with the haul bags, I could concentrate on my five thousand chin-ups and enjoy the view. As on El Capitan, Corbett had to climb every foot of the route two or three times to clean out his pitons and set up the hauling.

I was able to give Mike some help raising the haul

bags, but most of the burden still fell on him. I wished there were a way for me to take over some of the lead climbing. We had talked about it, but we had never worked out a system.

Mike Corbett:

The crack was maddeningly out of reach. I stood high in my étriers and stretched as far to my left as I dared, but the crack was still several long inches away. The flake I had been climbing had petered out, and now I had to make the long reach into the next crack.

Royal Robbins, the brilliant climber who had pioneered this route in 1969, is at least six inches taller than me. Now I was paying the price for my lack of height. I unclipped a Friend from my rack and held it at the ends of my fingertips. Standing on my toes and leaning for all I was worth, I just managed to wiggle it into the crack. It didn't look at all secure, but I gave it a little tug and it didn't budge.

"It held, damn it," I yelled down to Mark.

I didn't like the look of it and wanted it back so I could try another piece—something I had more confidence in. But now the Friend occupied the crack, so I had no choice but to use it.

"I guess I'm going to have to trust this thing," I said. "Watch me closely here."

I had said something like that on just about every pitch I had climbed with Mark, and in the past the pieces had always held. I wondered if he thought I was crying wolf. I leaned over and attached a carabiner to the Friend, then threaded the rope through it. Next I clipped in an étrier and used exquisite care as I eased my weight into the stirrup.

Whew. I let out my breath. The Friend held. It must have been more solid than it looked. I stepped up slowly into the other étrier and began to plan my next move. Just then, there was a pop, then the sound of metal scraping against rock, then I was airborne—three thousand feet above Yosemite Valley.

"Whoa!" I yelled.

A million thoughts rushed through my head, but everything was happening so fast there was no time to grasp them. Sitting on his Portaledge, Mark cinched his end of the rope tight against the belay device on his harness and braced for the coming jolt.

"I got you!" he yelled.

After one heart-stopping second, I felt a jerk on my waist. The rope went tight, stretched and eased me to a stop after twenty feet. I slapped against the cold granite, unhurt and grateful.

"Are you all right?" asked Mark, who was now almost level with me.

"Yeah, no problem," I answered, trying not to let him hear me shaking.

On El Capitan and all of the practice climbs we had done together, Mark had never had to hold a fall. I trusted him as surely as any able-bodied climbing partner, and as I plummeted down, there's no denying my fate was completely in his hands. Mark did his job flawlessly. I think it cemented our relationship as a climbing team.

As I trembled from the surging adrenaline, I felt more anger than fear. We were having to fight for every inch of progress on Half Dome, and losing twenty feet was frustrating. Also, I knew I was going to have to make that same move again—and despite the sudden jerk at the end of the rope, I hadn't gotten any taller.

I quickly worked my way back up to my previous high point. This time I tried a piton. I stretched out to my left as far as my nerves would let me and nudged the steel pin into the crack with my thumb. Then I took my hammer and gave it a couple of easy taps. It let out a dull thunk. In my spread-eagle position, I couldn't swing my hammer hard enough to give a solid blow.

I took several deep breaths, clipped on the étrier, and gave silent thanks as the piton held. Without hesitating I stood up and slotted another piton into the crack. Now I was in position to take a better swing with my hammer, and I pounded the pin into the slot for all eternity.

Blasting up to the top of the crack, I anchored the rope and rappelled back down to Twilight Ledge, where Mark was waiting for me. Neither of us had said a word since the fall. As I reached his position, we looked at each other and said, "Whew!"

"Well," Mark said, "you told me you thought you were going to fall on this climb."

"I hope that's the only one," I said.

I glanced at my watch. It was still early, and there was plenty of climbing left to do. But I needed some time to regain my composure. Mentally, I was a wreck. It's never a good idea to let your climbing partner see the fear in you— especially in a situation like this, where I was the experienced guy Mark was depending on.

"Hey, man, let's just call it a day," I said.

"Fine," he replied. "You're the boss."

Mark and I sat on his Portaledge for an hour and talked about whether we should try to keep the fall a secret. These things happen all the time in big-wall climbing, but we were under such intense scrutiny that we worried the press would make more of it than it was. And I had a pregnant wife to think about.

Still, there were hundreds of people down in Yosemite Valley watching us through telescopes, and they must have seen what had happened. In the end, we decided it was best to mention it in our afternoon radio check-in. We tried to slip it casually into the conversation, but, as we expected, the media had a field day with it. It was all the television stations and newspapers talked about the next day.

Later I was able to talk to Nikyra about it on the radio. Luckily, she knew enough about climbing and enough about me that she wasn't too upset.

Our sixth day on the wall began with the worst news yet. At our 8:00 a.m. check-in, the radio crackled to life with the somber voice of Bruce Brossman, head of the Yosemite Mountaineering School. Still snuggled in my sleeping bag, I pulled out the antenna and turned up the volume.

"Half Dome, this is Yosemite, do you read?"

"Morning, Bruce," I said. "This is Half Dome. Go ahead."

"I hate to tell you this, guys, but there's more bad weather on the way," said Brossman. "There's a winter storm heading toward Yosemite with possible snow forecast down to eight thousand feet. It might get a little colder up there."

"Uh, roger, Yosemite, we read that," I said. "It's already chilly here. There's a constant thirty- to forty-mile-an-hour wind blowing. It's cold like you wouldn't believe."

Down in the San Francisco Bay Area, the TV weatherman was pointing to a satellite picture showing an unseasonable cold front bearing down on us from Canada. Sure enough, from our airy vantage point on Half Dome's face, we could see dark, evil-looking storm clouds on the horizon.

Our elevation was almost exactly eight thousand feet. If snow was going to fall, we were going to catch it. As we packed up to begin the day's climbing, there wasn't much to say. Each of us had reason to fear the cold. For Corbett, it was the memory of shivering helplessly and waiting for rescuers on this very same rock five years earlier. For me, it was the long icy night on Seven Gables as I fought to stay alive in sub-freezing temperatures.

The granite face of Half Dome felt cold to our stiff fingers as Corbett and I tied into the climbing rope. Even in the best of weather, Half Dome's face remains in shadow until the middle of the afternoon. As he started up the rock, Mike wore a thick down jacket more appropriate for Mt. Everest than Yosemite. It's hard to keep your nerve up when you're chilled, and I wondered if Mike was trying to retain his boldness along with his body heat.

We were lagging seriously behind the schedule we

had announced for ourselves. We had told everyone we planned to make the summit in a week, but now, on the sixth day, we were barely halfway up the face. Both of us knew we were climbing as fast as we could, and we couldn't let the expectations of others pressure us to move faster than was safe. I tried to give Corbett a little pep talk.

"I don't care how long this takes, and I don't care what we told anybody," I said. "This is turning out to be tougher than we thought, and if it takes us a few more days, it takes us a few more days, that's all."

Late in the afternoon, I yanked myself up the rope and pulled onto the flat shelf known as Sunset Ledge. Icy winds had been lashing us all day and the storm clouds had drawn closer, and we wondered how long it would be before the snow started falling.

With a long way left to go, we had begun to seriously ration our food. Dinner on Sunset Ledge, after a long hard day of climbing, consisted of a PowerBar and a can of Beanie Weenies. I was just scraping the last spoonful out of the can when Corbett held up his hand.

"Shhhh," he said. "Listen."

"What is it?" I whispered.

"Just listen."

Wafting up toward us from Yosemite Valley, four thousand feet below us, was the unmistakable sound of bagpipe music. I could clearly make out the slow, haunting notes of *Amazing Grace*. Immediately we knew who was behind it. It was Dr. William Bowie from the medical clinic, a friend of Corbett's who sometimes serenades Mike on his climbs. We couldn't see him, but we learned later that he was wearing a kilt and tam-o'-shanter. Down at Mirror Lake, at the base of Half Dome, Dr. Bowie had gathered with a large group of our friends and loved ones, and he was doing his best with his bagpipes to inspire us.

It was working. A chill ran up my spine and I could

feel my spirits soaring. Just knowing that Mike and I weren't alone—that friends and loved ones in the world below were thinking about us and pulling for us—helped restore our fighting spirit. Somehow, the plaintive tone of Dr. Bowie's bagpipes communicated more to us than our two-way radio ever could.

Corbett took off his headlamp and aimed it in the direction of the music. Usually we refrained from shining our lights at the valley—it's too easy to misinterpret it as a request for a rescue. But this was a special occasion. Mike flashed his bright light on and off several times to let our friends below know that Dr. Bowie's message had come through loud and clear.

Mike Corbett:
I needed every bit of that extra resolve the next day. As I started climbing above Sunset Ledge, I knew I was in for some of the loosest and most rotten rock on the entire route.

To climb up the face of Half Dome is to get an instant lesson in geology. The same forces of nature that sheered off the vertical face are still at work, peeling layer by layer, stone by stone. If you look at pictures of Half Dome taken thirty years ago, there are huge sections of rock, half the size of a football field, that are no longer there.

I reached up and grabbed the corner of a granite block the size of a refrigerator. To my horror, it rumbled and shifted. I backed away quickly, fearing it might take my head off. But it stayed put. Climbing this section of Half Dome required all the concentration and overwrought care that go into defusing a bomb. Sometimes it seemed as if a harsh word would be enough to topple a loose chunk of granite down onto Mark.

Gingerly, I passed by a particularly rotten section Royal Robbins had accurately described as a "stone fence without mortar." Higher, I put my hand against a granite pinnacle wedged into a crack. It wobbled back and forth, making a chillingly hollow sound as it scraped against the sides of the crack. A hundred feet below, Mark could hear it clearly.

Later in the day, I drove a piton into a crack and was just stepping into the étrier connected to it when the piton below it popped. I gulped. But the new piton held, and I escaped with nothing more than a scare.

In some places, the pitons were so insecure that I could pull them out with my fingers. In others, I was forced to support myself with steel hooks on tiny nubbins. It's a standard trick in big-wall climbing, but as a wintry wind lashed at me, it required all the nerve I could muster.

Still, when evening arrived, I couldn't help but be happy with the day's progress. We had climbed three pitches consisting of 450 feet of the scariest rock on Half Dome. It was by far our most productive day, and it gave me hope that the worst was behind us.

I was just finishing up the last pitch when the snow started drifting down. Thick flakes dusted my shoulders and hair. Then hailstones pelted me as the skies opened up in a furious downpouring. Anchored to the rock, I could find no place to take shelter. There was nothing I could do but stand there. It was the moment we had been dreading, but, surprisingly, it didn't seem so bad now. This storm had the feeling of a minor local disturbance; it just didn't seem to carry the wallop of the snowstorm that had hammered me five years earlier. I had the feeling that this would soon pass.

Sure enough, the snow soon let up, and by nightfall the skies were clearing. That night's radio check-in brought the welcome news that good weather was finally on the way.

Corbett rummaged around in the food sack, made some quick mental calculations, and handed me down my dinner rations: half a can of fruit cocktail and a fistful of trail mix. This was the major meal of the day, and I ate slowly to make it last.

It was our ninth day on the wall, and the summit was still six hundred feet above us. Hunger and the unrelenting steepness of the face were taking their toll. Already, Corbett was looking more gaunt than he ever had on El Capitan. His face was sunburnt, his eyes had a sunken, hollow look about them and his bony shoulders drooped. His T-shirt looked two sizes too big.

I imagined I was seeing a reflection of my own condition. My stomach growled constantly from the lack of food, and my rock chaps were feeling awfully loose. I was still able to summon the strength to crank off my three hundred chin-ups on every pitch, but I noticed it was taking longer and longer to get up the rope.

The days began to drift together, each one pretty much like the last. The weather turned warm and sunny, but Corbett and I simply didn't have the energy to make one last dash to the summit. Slowed by exhaustion, we realized we were going to have to lay siege to Half Dome, one inch at a time.

On Day Ten, Mike managed to struggle up only about thirty feet as he coped with loose rock and wiggly, twenty-one-year-old bolts. Completely spent, he anchored the rope and rappelled back down. In his fatigue, Corbett was being extra careful to test every piton and check every knot. Bonehead mistakes have been the undoing of many dog-tired climbers, and neither of us wanted our names added to the list. Dejected at our lack of progress, we spent the night at a ledge called The Ramp.

By the eleventh day, our radio check-ins were all starting to revolve around the same question: when were we going to make it to the top? The press was getting impatient, the Boy Scouts were getting impatient, and I imagine Paulette and Nikyra were feeling the same way. But there was nothing we could do about it. Half Dome and our weary bodies were dictating the pace.

"Climbing is not a spectator sport," I told Ellyn Windsor one night on the radio.

The next day our mood was brightened by a radio

call from the students at Yosemite Elementary School. Seventh grader Alexis Mayer told us she and her schoolmates were going to raise money for our charities by duplicating my effort: they were going to do five thousand pull-ups in twelve days.

"That's just fantastic, Alexis," I said. "How many pull-ups can you do?"

"Uh, two... or maybe five," she answered.

"That sounds like about what Corbett can do," I said, laughing. It was true. Even when he was in the best of shape, Mike was never going to win any pull-up contests. And now he was so weak he had trouble lifting his arms above his head.

Somehow, Corbett was able to struggle up two pitches that day, half the remaining distance to the summit. At dinner time, we had some welcome company as our friends Ken Yager and Chris Falkenstein rappelled down to our Portaledges. They were the first other humans we'd seen in ten days.

Ken delivered fresh batteries for our radio, and Chris filmed us for KPIX-TV in San Francisco, with whom we had a contract.

"Do you want some granola bars?" asked Chris. "I could leave them on the ledge for you."

"No, we can't take them," Corbett told him.

"Do you have much food left?"

"Not much."

To accept any food would constitute a rescue and violate the rules of the game that Corbett and I had agreed upon. Climbing is an odd sport, because the only rules are the ones you impose on yourself. It's probably hard for an outsider to understand, but I think the reason we refused the food was that we needed it so badly.

On El Capitan we had accepted a couple of Pepsis from the NBC cameramen, but that was different because we had ten pounds of food left in our haul bags. On Half Dome we took the spare radio batteries only so we could fulfill our commitments to KPIX and the Boy Scouts. They didn't help us get to the summit.

As Chris and Ken climbed back up to the top, they left their ropes dangling in place. It was torture to know we could just clip our ascenders onto them and have our ordeal over with in less than an hour. But that was out of the question, as long as we had the willpower to keep struggling.

That night the questions during the radio check-in seemed particularly cruel.

"So, what do you guys want most to eat?" Ellyn asked. "Pizza? Hamburgers? Beer?"

Mike Corbett:

For several days my right arm had been tingling constantly as if I'd hit my funny bone. The pain started in my wrist, with a swelling around the bone. Then a numbness spread up my arm and it began to ache, even when I was asleep. It got to the point that the only part of my body I noticed was my painful right arm.

All that hammering was exacting its price. Usually, with an able-bodied partner, I trade off leading and cleaning the pitches. On Half Dome I was having to do it all, and all those shock waves running up my arm were having their effect.

Already, I had broken my own record for the longest time I had spent on a rock face. That record had been ten days, set while climbing a new route on El Capitan in 1982.

On our twelfth morning, Mark and I felt confident enough to tell everyone we'd be to the summit by that afternoon. There were only three hundred feet left to go, and I felt sure we could tap into a pool of adrenaline that would carry us up.

By early afternoon I had reached a ledge just seventy-five feet from the summit. One more big push and I'd be on top. I might even be home with Nikyra by supper time. Looking up, I scanned the spectacular overhang that stood between us and the summit. It jutted out forty feet into space like the underside of a giant staircase, and it would require some tough climbing.

By the time I finished wrestling our lightened haul bag up to the ledge, I knew I didn't have the strength to attack the overhang. I wrapped my arms around the haul bag like a sleepy koala bear and put my head down. It was time for our afternoon radio call, and I dreaded answering the inevitable question.

"One quick question," said the voice at the other end. "Everybody's wondering whether you're going to top out today or not."

I lifted my head up and looked weakly at Mark. I hated having to say it, but I had no choice.

"No, no," I said. "Tell 'em no."

"We've got a hard lead ahead of us and Mike is really tired," Mark said into the radio. "So I think we're just going to bivy here and top out in the morning."

I desperately wanted the climb to be over—I'm sure we both did. But I had long ago used up all my energy reserves, and I had to face the fact that the summit overhang was more than I could handle that afternoon. What if I didn't have the strength the next morning? I tried not to think about it.

At dinner time I reached all the way to the bottom of the food bag before my hand hit anything. All we had left was one can of pineapple and one breakfast bar. We'd have to split the fruit for supper and save the breakfast bar for the next day.

On the morning of our thirteenth day on Half Dome, I was just stuffing my sleeping bag into the stuff sack when I saw a sight neither of us will ever forget. It was a body, and it went plummeting right past our Portaledge.

"Someone's fallen off the top!" yelled Corbett. "Maybe it's a reporter who got too close to the edge!"

We were both gripped with horror as we watched the person dropping out of sight. Suddenly we heard a *whoooof!* and a big white parachute popped out of the person's back. Corbett and I let out a collective sigh, but the daredevil wasn't out of trouble yet.

He was too close to the rock face. His chute scraped the wall, and he spun around, away from the cliff. As his descent stabilized and he floated down toward the pine trees at Mirror Lake, I picked up the radio and called the rangers' patrol desk.

Parachuting off the big walls of Yosemite is a bootleg sport that the National Park Service has spent years trying to stop. It's incredibly dangerous, and rangers get tired of scraping up the remains of those who miscalculate. The parachutist had broken the law, and as a park ranger it was my duty to report him. He landed safely and, with the help of my radio call, was later arrested.

Corbett barely had the energy to tie his shoes, but he climbed brilliantly up the awesome summit overhang. Using every trick he had picked up in his eighty big-wall ascents, he nestled pitons into unlikely cracks and unclipped the rope in key places to ease the drag. Every movement was agonizingly slow and methodical, but absolutely safe.

Above us to the left, where the rock jutted out, I could see dozens of friends and well-wishers lining the top. They were hooting, waving, snapping pictures, shouting encouragement and cheering us up those last agonizing feet.

After about an hour of delicate climbing, I saw Corbett's head and shoulders disappear over the lip.

"All right. I'm at the bolts!" he yelled down. "Yahooo!"

Next it was my turn. I clipped my pull-up bar onto the free-hanging rope, checked all my knots one final time and swung out over the bottomless void. Nearly a mile of nothingness dropped away beneath me, but I was too tired to notice. All my attention was focused on the seventy-five feet of rope above me.

I raised the T-bar up the rope, grunted and lifted myself six more inches. Summit fever gripped me and I felt an unexpected surge of energy cut through my weariness. I began cranking chin-ups with arms that were suddenly fresh and lively. Looking up, I could see Ken Yager, who was hanging off the side on a rope to welcome me.

"Only thirty more pull-ups!" he yelled. "Only twenty-nine... only twenty-eight... Hey, you're an animal, Mark. Don't ever change!"

Soon Corbett and I were together at the lip of the overhang. With our butts still hanging out over the void, we put our arms around each other and grinned. Despite Mike's total exhaustion, there was no mistaking the look of pure joy in his weather-beaten, stubbly face.

After thirteen days we were finally off the face. But there was still a long, low-angled slab left to ascend before we reached the broad summit where everyone was waiting for us. Corbett ran out the rope and I laboriously dragged myself up the rough granite until the slope eased.

From here it was just an easy scramble to the top. I looked over at Corbett for a boost, but he appeared as weak and ragged as a concentration-camp survivor. Mike could barely stand up himself, much less carry me. Instead, I hopped onto the back of Ted Farmer, the big guy who had carried me to the base of the climb nearly two weeks earlier.

A raucous cheer erupted from the fifty people gathered on the summit as we climbed the final steps to the top. Corbett waved his hand, staggered and held onto the rope for balance. If Half Dome had been five feet higher he might not have made it.

Suddenly it was over—we had climbed Half Dome. However, it was hard to tell who was the conqueror and who was the conquered. There was no denying that Half Dome was in much better shape than we were.

The television crew pulled Corbett off to the side. Nikyra was too far along in her pregnancy to make the strenuous hike and climb up the Half Dome cables, but KPIX had arranged a two-way TV hookup so they could see and talk to each other.

Paulette ran up, gave me a big hug and handed me an orange slice. Ted gently lowered me into my wheelchair, which he'd carried all the way up from Yosemite Valley. I heard a pop and looked over to see Corbett pouring champagne over his head. Someone handed me a bottle. Giving it a big shake, I sent the cork skyward and sprayed the bubbly liquid spray over everyone within range.

"The long adventure is over," I said.

Royal Robbins, the first man to climb the face of Half Dome and the first to ascend the Tis-sa-ack route:

Mark's ascent was in keeping with the classic values of mountaineering, which are to do something nobody has ever done before, to accomplish what people say can never be done, and to push the limits of the possible.

He was involved in extending a certain type of limit— that which a disabled person can do. Up to that point, people thought nobody without the use of their legs would ever get up the face of Half Dome, much less by the hardest route. Mark went out and did just that—with, of course, the supreme effort and support of Mike Corbett.

Mark reminded all of us that when the spirit is there, the "impossible" comes within reach. He showed that people can achieve great goals regardless of their situation, or even because of it.

These days, you hear climbers saying that there are no new challenges left on the big walls of Yosemite—but they're wrong. It's simply a matter of upping the ante and raising one's personal, spiritual, psychological and physical abilities to the new test. People like Mark are doing things now that even I would have said could never be done. The only limitations are those of one's imagination.

8

DOORS OPEN

We were running late, as usual, but this time it looked as if we were in luck.

As I wheeled through the front door of the Grand Hyatt Hotel in San Francisco, I was relieved to see a taxicab waiting at the curb. Maybe we'd make it to the radio station on time for our interview, after all.

"I'll go grab the guy," said Mike Corbett, who was a few steps ahead of me.

Mike and I were in the city to receive a proclamation from Mayor Art Agnos as part of Youth Excellence Day, but we had a squeezed in a couple of other appointments. Our early morning radio interview was halfway across the city, but if the cab made good time we'd be OK.

Waving his arm, Corbett dashed up to the waiting taxi and started to tell the driver where we wanted to go. But when I rolled across the sidewalk and approached the curb, the cabbie took one look at me, threw his taxi into gear and abruptly drove away.

We watched, incredulous, as the cab darted across three lanes of traffic and pulled up in front of an able-bodied fare on the other side of the street. Both Mike and I were speechless. It was a blatant case of discrimination, committed in full view of everyone on one of the busiest streets in San Francisco.

Seconds later another taxi pulled up in front of us.

The driver had seen the whole thing, and he was irate.

"What that guy just did to you was not only rude— it was illegal," he said as I popped the wheels off my chair and tossed it in the back seat. "Guys like that give all of us a bad name. You ought to fill out a report on this, and I'll deliver it to the police department's cab detail for investigation."

The driver was right. In San Francisco, as in many other cities, it's illegal for a cab driver to refuse to convey someone in a wheelchair. But if you talk to any disabled person, you'll hear stories of incidents like this—of cabs that darted away, of restaurant reservations that disappeared, of jobs that vanished.

Over the years, it seems as if I've been luckier than most. I can't think of too many times I've been discriminated against because of my wheelchair. The few times it has happened, I've just shrugged my shoulders and gone on with my business. Many people, in all walks of life, face discrimination every day, and the few instances I've run up against have been minor.

Corbett and the second driver were more steamed about this incident than I was. I was willing to give the first cabbie the benefit of the doubt. Maybe he was just abandoning us for what looked like a more lucrative fare. Mike and I certainly didn't look like big tippers.

"Let's just drop it," I said as we pulled out from the curb. "It's no big deal, and besides, we've got to hustle if we're going to make it to the radio station on time."

It was three weeks after Mike and I had reached the summit of Half Dome, and it was obvious the hoopla wasn't going to be anywhere near as great as that following El Capitan. That sort of thing happens just once in a lifetime. Chauffeured limousines and presidential suites were a thing of the past.

We discovered this quickly. Not long after the climb, California Governor Pete Wilson invited us to the state capital for a little award ceremony. A crowd of reporters gathered around, but from the very beginning it was obvious they weren't interested in our ascent.

One reporter dashed up, reached right past my nose with his microphone, and blurted out, "So, Governor Wilson, what do you think about the legislature's latest reapportionment plan?"

The second and third questions dealt with state politics, too, so an embarrassed Wilson rushed us out of the room and into his office. Waiting for us there was Wilson's stepson, who was a rock climber himself. So we discussed the climb with Wilson and talked shop with his stepson for twenty minutes. It turned out his son had even built an artificial climbing wall behind the governor's mansion.

Later, Wilson presented Corbett and me with medals that had the governor's seal on them.

Even though the hoopla was muted the second time around, there were still plenty of doors opening for me. Corporations wanted me to give talks to their employees and endorse their products, schools invited me to address their students and outdoor firms offered to help sponsor my next adventure, whatever it might be.

I started adding up numbers and making calculations, and I concluded I could probably support myself on the income from these projects. I wrestled with the decision for a while, but in the end I made up my mind: I would quit my job as a Yosemite ranger and try to make a new life for myself as a full-time adventurer.

Ever since my first nervous forays off the ground with Corbett, I had been rediscovering the deeply satisfying pleasures of the wilderness, and now I knew there was nothing stopping me from living out my dreams. I had developed an insatiable appetite for more mountain adventure—an appetite, I knew, that couldn't be satisfied by working at the

Yosemite information center forty hours a week.

My imagination was filled with new challenges. I wanted to become the first paraplegic to ski across the Sierra Nevada. I wanted to navigate wild rivers in my kayak. I wanted to find new ways of pushing into the back country in my wheelchair. And I wanted to represent my country as a member of the U.S. Disabled Ski Team. To do these things would require my training nearly full-time as a serious athlete.

The idea of quitting my ranger's job, though, was a little scary. Only a few able-bodied athletes have been able to eke out a living as full-time adventurers, and, as far as I knew, no disabled person had ever tried it. Sponsorship money was tight, and the competition for it was intense.

But if climbing El Capitan and Half Dome had taught me anything, it was that my dreams would always remain just that—unless I took the risk and put in the hard work to make them come true. I knew that the first thing I had to do was to take that first frightening step off the ground.

So I called up my boss in Yosemite and told her I was going to leave the Park Service. I had worked hard to get the job, and had proudly worn the uniform for six years, but now I felt I had taken the position as far as I could. The opportunities I had in front of me didn't come very often, and I knew I had to make the best of them.

I left Yosemite at the end of October 1991. As my last day approached, I realized how much I was going to miss the tight-knit community of park employees, climbing bums and colorful characters that is unique to the national park. I knew I would also miss being able to stand outside my front door and gaze up at Yosemite Falls and Half Dome.

My colleagues threw a little going-away party for me, and all my friends showed up. One who meant the most to me was a ranger named James Gervasoni. A

year earlier, he had been riding his bicycle down a
steep hill in the valley when he hit a rock and tumbled
over his handlebars. His head slammed into the
pavement. James was in a coma for three days, and his
body curled up into the fetal position.

A few months after regaining consciousness he had
had a brain seizure, and I had been by his side as they
loaded him into a helicopter to evacuate him out of
Yosemite Valley. Since then he had been working hard
every day to recover. I had watched with admiration
as he underwent the painful struggle of learning to
walk again. Now, a year after his accident, he still
showed a few signs of his head injury, but he had
regained most of his physical abilities.

James stood up slowly to say a few words about me,
and I choked up. In his own quiet way he had conquered
something as difficult as the vertical face of Half Dome.
I realized how much strength I had drawn over the
years from all the bold Yosemite people like him.

As Paulette and I climbed into my van and drove out
of Yosemite Valley, Half Dome dominated the view in
my rearview mirror. At El Capitan Meadow, at the
western end of Yosemite Valley, I pulled over and
parked. I rolled my wheelchair across the grass to a
spot with a clear view of the summit, and Paulette and
I ate our picnic lunch beneath the soaring wall.

These massive towers of granite had dominated my
life over the last two years, drawing me to them and
allowing me to discover the secrets of nature and of
myself. They had reawakened the mountaineer in me
and taught me I was capable of some remarkable things.
As they receded behind me, I knew I'd always be
thankful to them.

One of the sponsors that allowed me to pursue my
dream of being an outdoor adventurer was Health
South Rehabilitation Corporation, a chain of private
medical facilities in Texas and throughout the southern

United States. Over the years they have flown me out to several of their hospitals to cut grand-opening ribbons and demonstrate my climbing techniques for the patients.

Health South stresses sports in its rehabilitation programs, and the gym is always the focus of the hospital. Some patients are athletes who have suffered severe sports-related injuries; others are paraplegics and amputees who are using sports to develop the strength and skills to navigate their way through the world.

It was while attending the opening ceremonies at a hospital in Miami that I had one of the most unusual and exciting experiences of my life. Several of us piled into a van and drove down to Key Largo, the home of the Dolphin Research Center. All sorts of people—autistic children, in particular—gain surprising benefits from contact with dolphins.

Some of the dolphins had been wounded after being caught in drift nets; others are performers retired from aquatic parks. They swim in a big lagoon that is open to the ocean. There are various pens separated by nets, but the dolphins can easily jump over these and are free to leave at any time. Many of them, though, choose to hang around the research center. They know they'll be fed there, and they seem to enjoy their contact with humans.

I wheeled my chair out onto a catwalk that stretched out into the lagoon—it looked a lot like the dock in the TV show, *Flipper*.

"Somehow, the dolphins will be able to tell that your legs don't work," said one of the researchers. "We don't know how they figure this out, but they seem to know it. Maybe their sonar is able to pick up the metal rods in your back."

I parked my chair, pulled myself over to the edge of the catwalk and slid into the warm lagoon.

"Now what do I do?" I asked.

"Slap the water with the palm of your hand," said the researcher.

I gave the water a smack, and moments later two dolphins swam up next to me. Even with a snorkeling mask it was hard to see them because the water was so murky, but I could feel them. Their skin was slick and slimy. Having these four-hundred-pound creatures so close was a little unnerving. I kept thinking of sharks.

"Hold your hand out in front of you," said the researcher.

I did that, and one of the dolphins put his snout up right next to my hand. I slowly drew my hand closer to my face, and the dolphin followed until we were literally eyeball to eyeball. I was amazed at how gentle and intelligent the sea mammal was. It seemed to be giving me the once-over as I checked it out. It seemed as friendly and playful as a big dog.

"Grab onto the dorsal fins," the researcher said.

With one hand on each dolphin's fin, I held on tightly as they dove down six feet under the surface. With their tail fins flipping back and forth they swam back up and towed me along the surface. I swam with them for nearly twenty minutes, grinning at the outrageous thrill of it. The dolphins seemed to be having fun, but not nearly as much as I was. Finally, they towed me gently back to the catwalk and dropped me off right next to my wheelchair.

I've also continued to work with the people at Fortress to design new wheelchairs—which is a little ironic, because I'm best known for the things I've done when I haven't been in my chair.

Of course when I'm not climbing, which is most of the time, I think of my wheelchair as my legs, my mobility and my ticket to freedom. Like most paraplegics, I spend most of my waking hours sitting on my wheels. Whether I move through life as deftly as a dancer or as clumsily as a bull in a china shop depends, in large part, on subtle design features of my wheelchair.

From my earliest days of crashing into gurneys and trash cans with my ungainly hospital-issue wheelchair, I've appreciated what a light and nimble chair can do. It's like the difference between playing basketball in steel-toed work boots and playing in Air Jordans.

From the time I left Vallejo through the El Capitan climb, I had been rolling through life in an X-L sports wheelchair. At the time I bought it, it was one of the more maneuverable chairs on the market. After six years of constant and hard use, though, it was badly battered and technological advances had dated it. But wheelchairs are expensive—a good sports model can cost from twelve hundred to three thousand dollars—and I simply couldn't afford one on my park ranger's salary.

Within days of reaching the summit of El Capitan, I got a phone call from the people at Fortress and an invitation to stop by their wheelchair factory in Clovis, near Fresno. Corbett and I dropped in on our way to the White House.

Waiting for me there was a shiny new wheelchair.

"This is for you, Mark," said Jim Papac, the head of marketing. "We'd like to have you ride in one of our chairs."

I pulled my old wheelchair up next to it, transferred into the new chair and gave it a quick spin around the room. An all-purpose "Edge" sports chair designed for basketball and tennis, it was the wheelchair equivalent of cross-training athletic shoes. It was much lighter and more responsive than anything I had sat in before. Even though I wouldn't be using it much for competitive sports, it was a huge step forward for me in everyday mobility.

One reason good sports chairs are so expensive is that every one of them is custom-built. Wheelchair athletes have exacting requirements for back height, wheel angles, widths, footrest positions, wheelie bars, brakes and upholstery. There are probably thirty different variables, and a top-performing athlete has to have every one of them just so. For instance, some top tennis players need to have the push rims farther away from the hub rims to accommodate hands that are also carrying a racket.

Since my first visit to the factory, I've been working with the Fortress designers on new products to help disabled people push out into previously off-limit areas of the wilderness. I want to help wheelchair people get to their favorite fishing spot or negotiate an easy hiking trail.

We're currently considering development of an off-road chair that would incorporate some aspects of mountain-bike technology. But it will be designed for general-purpose use indoors and on cement, too. Most disabled people have only one chair, and a special-purpose model with limited use would be more of a luxury than most could afford.

The engineers at Fortress have also been working with me to develop a cross-country ski frame. It's a lightweight tubular aluminum frame and plastic seat that screw right onto standard Nordic skis. By pushing with special ski poles in each hand, I can move across the snow at a surprisingly good clip.

Unless I miss my guess, cross-country skiing will one day prove to be the most popular way for disabled people to travel in the wilderness. I remember my first excursion with the West Valley College mountaineering class. Even using a cumbersome sit-ski not designed for the purpose, I could cover much more terrain in the winter than I ever could have in my wheelchair in the summer.

From the mail and phone calls I've received, I know there are many paraplegics and quadriplegics out there who are itching to break away from the world of concrete and return to the wilderness. By working on designs for off-road wheelchairs and cross-country skis, I hope I'll be able to give them the tools to do just that.

The gear donated to Corbett and me by The North Face allowed us to survive the nasty weather on Half Dome in relative "comfort." They also created the fourth-generation set of rock chaps I wore on the climb. Made of tough ballistics nylon and incorporating a Yates harness on the outside and wider leg loops, they were a huge improvement over their predecessors. They were so easy to put on that I could do it by myself on my Portaledge, with no help from Corbett.

The North Face has continued to support me. Their designers are working on a one-piece ski suit for me, quite an undertaking, since my dimensions and needs are different from those of most skiers. Mine will have narrow pants to accommodate my atrophied legs, and plenty of insulation there to prevent frostbite. I'll need more room in the arms, chest and shoulders because all my muscle mass is concentrated there. I'll also need special patches on the cuffs to keep them from getting cut by the outrigger poles I use in downhill skiing.

The makers of PowerBar, a high-performance food for athletes, have also supported me. Their product helped fuel Corbett and me up Half Dome, and their financial backing has allowed me to pursue new outdoor adventures. PowerBar uses me in some of its advertising, and it's an example of what I hope is a growing trend. Wheelchair athletes these days are popping up in commercials for everything from banks to beers.

With the knowledge that I could stay solvent for a while on the income from these and other sponsors, I drove my van out of Yosemite, turned north and headed for Lake Tahoe. Rolling down my window, I could feel a distinct chill in the late afternoon air. Winter would be here soon, and with it would come a new chapter in my life as an outdoor adventurer.

I immediately felt at home at Lake Tahoe. Its clean air and mountain scenery attract some of the country's best skiers and other outdoor athletes. And, as I soon learned, it was the training site for a lot of disabled athletes, too. It was common to see roadracers rolling down the side of the road in their competition wheelchairs and sit-skiers carving up the ski slopes. I wouldn't be the only gimp jock in town.

I quickly became friends with many of them, including Candace Cable, a top wheelchair marathoner who was hoping to compete in the summer Paralympics in Barcelona; and Michael Bixby, her able bodied boyfriend, who was the ski coach of Team Tahoe. Bill Bowness, a champion disabled water-skier and instructor at the Tahoe Handicap Ski School, was an old friend of mine from my days in Vallejo.

With Bill's girlfriend, Karen Witt, I tried disabled water-skiing for the first time at chilly Donner Lake. The ski consisted of a metal frame with a nylon sling for a seat mounted on a single slalom board that is a little bit wider than a standard water ski.

Floating in a wet suit and a life preserver, I maneuvered my way into the nylon sling seat. It was fairly easy for me, but I could see how it would be tough for someone with less feeling in their legs and less balance. Karen moved the boat forward until the slack was out of the line, and I yelled "Hit it!"

The boat took off. I surged forward in the water— and then cartwheeled sideways, sending up a big spray and swallowing a few gulps of lake water. On the second try, though, I got up on the ski. Before long I was carving turns back and forth across the boat's wake and feeling the spray in my face.

Later, Karen told me she'd never seen a paraplegic pick it up so fast. For me, it reinforced the notion that

I could handle any sport if I set my mind to it and found a way to go about it.

For a month, Paulette and I lived together in a tiny cabin on the north shore of Lake Tahoe. It was the same size as my ranger's cabin, which is to say much too small for two people—especially when one of them is in a wheelchair.

Immediately we started looking for something bigger. Touring the area with real estate agents, we inspected house after house, but they all had the same flaw. Lake Tahoe is nestled in a mountain basin, and just about all the houses are built on steep hillsides. Every house we looked at had two or three floors—and steep staircases.

I can drag myself and my wheelchair up or down a set of stairs if I have to, but the thought of doing it half a dozen times a day was too much. We despaired of ever finding a suitable place to live until Paulette found a large house with most of the rooms on one floor. It was located just outside the old Wild West town of Truckee and only a mile from the Tahoe Donner Ski Resort where I did my cross-country training.

The one remaining problem was the set of five steps leading into the entrance, but we solved that by paying a friend to build a ramp out of plywood and two-by-fours.

In December I flew to Chicago to receive the Arete Award for "courage in sport," and I was in prestigious company. Among the other recipients at the awards banquet were Bo Jackson and Mario Andretti.

The presenters had promised to have a rented tuxedo ready for me, and it arrived two hours before the banquet began. I took one look at it and knew I was in trouble. The jacket had a traditional cut, which is a disaster when you're in a wheelchair. The long coat gets all tangled up in your spokes.

What I needed was either a short "Eisenhower" jacket or a "Spencer" cut, which stops just below the lapels. Many tuxedo shops carry these, but they can be hard to find on short notice. The hotel began making phone calls. Now there was less than an hour to go, and it was looking like a long shot.

Another thirty minutes passed, and I had visions of wheeling across the stage in front of the black-tie crowd while pulling my grease-covered tuxedo jacket out of my spokes.

Finally, at the last possible moment, a delivery van from a menswear store pulled up with a short-cut jacket. I tossed it on, checked myself in the mirror and wheeled into the elevator.

My award was presented by former Pittsburgh Steeler running back Rocky Bleier. It was appropriate, because he had been wounded in Vietnam and was told he would never run again. Not listening to the experts, he had worked hard in rehabilitation and had gone on to win a couple of Super Bowl rings. I admired his courage.

At the party afterwards, I found myself explaining to Mario Andretti how Corbett and I had slept in Portaledges and climbed up the ropes with our mechanical ascenders. He told me about the speed-thrill of driving an Indy car, and about the growing rivalry of his sons, who are also race-car drivers.

Bo Jackson may have been an ace at a number of competitive sports, but, as I talked to him, he seemed astounded at the notion that rational human beings would want to spend a week or two inching their way up a rock face.

"Bo don't know climbing," I said.

"You got that right," he replied, grinning.

It was thrilling and a little unnerving to be rubbing elbows with athletes of this caliber. I didn't consider myself in that league—not by a long shot. But I felt honored that the sponsors of the ceremony, the

Children's Memorial Medical Center of Chicago, would consider the accomplishments of disabled athletes in choosing recipients for their awards.

9

1992 Paralympics

It's almost April, but there's a winter chill in the breeze as it blows down the French Alps and into the entrance to Olympic Stadium. I'm lined up there with the other forty members of the U.S. Disabled Ski Team, and we're all shivering as we await our cue to enter the stadium.

Parked in a neat row alongside me are seven other athletes in wheelchairs—paraplegics and double amputees. We're all sitting up straight and proud and rocking nervously back and forth on our wheel rims. Lined up behind us are all the blind skiers and single amputees.

We're all wearing the same Team USA uniform that the able-bodied U.S. Olympic athletes wore at the Albertville games a month earlier. The only difference is that the ceremonies for the Paralympics are being held at Tignes, an hour's drive up the valley.

Is it the icy temperature or the unsurpassed thrill of the moment that makes us shiver? For each of us, it is the honor of a lifetime to be representing our country at the highest level of competition available to us. This is the goal we set for ourselves during those countless sweaty hours of training in the gym and those grueling practice sessions in the snow.

Reaching the summits of El Capitan and Half Dome was a personal thrill for me, but I feel an extra measure of pride to be wearing the uniform of the U.S. team. Now it's not just me I'm competing for, but also my country and my teammates.

An official gives us the signal, and it's time to enter the stadium. Leading the procession and carrying the U.S. flag is Reed Robinson, one of the most remarkable athletes on the team. A promising ski racer before losing his right arm to cancer at age twelve, he made history by winning medals in both alpine and Nordic events two years ago at the U.S. Disabled Ski Championships. That's something no able-bodied skier has done for a long time.

I squint into the high-altitude sunshine as I clear the tunnel entrance. Simultaneously, all of us in wheelchairs lean back and pop wheelies, and a huge roar goes up from the ten thousand spectators. We roll slowly past the reviewing stand, where French President François Mitterrand is on his feet applauding us. Next to him is the five-ringed symbol of the Olympics, and the sight of it sends a shiver down my spine.

Team USA is one of the last of the twenty nations to enter the stadium, and after we march slowly around the perimeter track, waving to the crowd, we take our place next to the athletes from Norway, Switzerland and all the other nations, including the Unified Team of the former USSR.

"Hey—check it out," someone says, pointing up to the sky. Shielding my eyes from the bright sunlight, I look up to see twenty paragliders descending toward the stadium. Their nylon chutes are painted with the flags of every participating country. They make pinpoint landings on the infield, and the crowd goes crazy.

Thousands of balloons float up into the blue alpine sky, and then an even louder cheer goes up as a disabled French skier on a mono-ski makes his way down the ski slope behind the stadium with the Olympic torch in his hand. At the bottom of the hill he hands it off to a blind skier, who holds it proudly aloft as he jogs one lap around the stadium with a guide.

The roar inside the stadium is thunderous as the blind skier climbs up the steps to the giant torch and ignites the Olympic flame. The 1992 Paralympic Games have officially begun. I sit up in my chair and cheer along with the crowd, savoring the thrill and trying to press the details of the moment into my memory.

Now it is time to get down to business, I remind myself, because I want more than anything to return home with a medal around my neck.

I started thinking about disabled skiing before I even knew for sure that I had broken my back. In fact, I started thinking about it, during that cold and torturous night following my accident on Seven Gables. Six months earlier I had seen my first sit-ski, and at the time I had thought it an interesting but unlikely looking device. However, it had opened my mind to the idea that a disabled person could actually ski. As I lay there shivering on the mountainside with my legs paralyzed, the notion that I would be able to ski again one day— no matter how things turned out—gave me some of the hope that helped me survive the night. Skiing had been as much a part of my life as climbing.

The first time I ever went skiing I was five years old, and it was such a disaster I'm surprised I ever went a second time. My family took me to the Badger Pass Ski Resort in Yosemite, and I remember being terrified at all the diabolical-looking machines that were supposed to take me to the top of the hill. Forget the chairlift— I wasn't big enough to subject myself to that. First I tried the rope tow, and I remember the smell of burning wool as the thick rope slid through my mittens.

"You've got to grab it tighter," said my dad.

I did as I was told, and suddenly I was lurching forward—right onto my face. At least I had the sense to let go of the rope. Blinking back tears, I wiped the snow out of my face and made my way over to the T-bar, which looked a little easier.

The result, though, was the same. I ended up nose down in the wet snow again. At that point I wanted to get in the car and go home, but my parents insisted I make at least one ski run. Finally, I took off my skis and carried them in my little arms as I walked to the top of the hill.

It was only the bunny hill, but looking down from the top I felt as if I were standing at the top of a vertical cliff. I wanted to take my skis off and walk back down, but my parents wouldn't hear of it. So I gulped deeply, held my breath and pushed off down the hill. Instantly I was going faster than I wanted to. I tried to remember what they had said about the snowplow turn, but I was out of control. I went down on my side, slid a few feet and stopped.

I was chilly and wet and I wanted no part of this stupid sport. I stood up, skied ten more shaky feet and landed on my butt again. This was the process I repeated all the way to the bottom of the hill.

It was many years before I had the urge to try it again. When I was in junior high school another family took me skiing with them, and I was amazed at the difference. I was bigger and stronger and more coordinated, and I found I was able to make my skis turn and point me in the direction I wanted to go, more or less.

I found that I liked the dynamic sensations of movement and balance, and the sound of the snow rushing by beneath my skis. A little to my surprise, I also discovered that I liked the thrill of going fast.

All through high school I went skiing every chance I got, and I improved constantly. I learned to synchronize the movements of my knees, hips and upper body with my ski edges to carve graceful parallel turns down increasingly steep ski slopes. Every winter my nose was permanently sunburned.

When my friends and I got our driver's licenses, we began making the four-hour drive to the resorts near Lake Tahoe just about every weekend of the ski season. By then I was able to negotiate all the black diamond runs, the steepest and most difficult trails at the time.

Skiing was another facet of my lifelong love affair with the mountains. It was a way to appreciate their beauty in different moods and seasons, and it opened up new avenues of experience I hadn't been able to get from backpacking and mountaineering.

I loved downhill skiing, but I began to yearn for a way to get away from all the noisy crowds, chairlifts and ski lodges. It was hard to savor the silence of the wilderness with all the skiers whooshing by me in their Day-Glo parkas.

The answer was cross-country skiing. Back then the gear and techniques were crude compared to today's, and the people pushing out into the back country were mostly out-of-season mountaineers, like me.

I bought a used pair of metal-edged telemark skis and mounted *randonee* bindings that allowed the heels of my beefy mountaineering boots to lift for normal cross-country skiing and lock down tight for downhill runs.

Using that gear, I once skied out into the teeth of a mid-winter storm with a group of friends in the Desolation Wilderness near Lake Tahoe. True to its name, it was harsh country, with lots of jagged granite peaks and few trees to cut the wind. With snow blowing all around us, we navigated our way through the drifts until we came to an old cabin along the shore of Fallen Leaf Lake. It was half buried by the snow, and it took us some time to dig out the entranceway before we could get inside to escape the storm. We barely slept that night as the wind howled and the windows rattled.

On another occasion, as I mentioned earlier, another

group of friends and I skied halfway across Yosemite National Park in the springtime to climb Mt. Lyell, the park's highest mountain. Delighting in the wild scenery, we skied down the mountain's back side, carving elegant turns through the virgin corn snow all the way back to camp.

These were some of the best times of my life, and I was starting to feel like a real all-around mountaineer—someone who could journey through the mountains in any season. It's hard to say whether I enjoyed climbing or skiing more. I loved them both, and each had its own time.

One day in 1982, while I was working at the Ski Hut shop in Palo Alto, the doors swung open and a man came rolling in in a wheelchair. His face was tan and his hair was sun-blond. It was obvious he spent a lot of time in the outdoors.

"Hi, I'm Peter Axelson," he said. "I'm here to pick up the skis you mounted for my wife."

"I've got them right here," I answered. "I'll carry them out to your car for you."

Peter was strong and athletic, and I was impressed by the way he could open the heavy front doors from his wheelchair. It obviously required substantial upper-body strength. He told me he had broken his back in a mountaineering accident while in the military six years earlier. Now he was an engineer with his own company, Beneficial Designs, in Santa Cruz, California.

I followed him out to his van and watched, fascinated, as the door opened and a mechanical lift lowered out of the doorway. As I stashed the skis inside, I noticed a strange device that looked like a sawed-off kayak.

"Hey, what's this thing for?" I asked.

"That's a prototype of a sit-ski I'm working on," Peter said. "Pull it out and I'll show you."

It had a fiberglass body, about four feet long, with

metal runners on the bottom. In the sunlight it looked almost like the front half of an Olympic bobsled.

"You can really ski in this thing?" I asked.

"Sure," he said. "I've already tested it a few times. I've still got to make a few adjustments, but basically it works."

"How do you turn?"

"You use your poles," he said. "That's one of the things I'm working on."

As Peter drove away, I smiled and shook my head at the thought of his oddball-looking device. It was hard to picture a handicapped person actually skiing with it. I walked back into the store and didn't think too much more about it—until the night, six months later, when I lay bruised and paralyzed on Seven Gables.

Fifteen months after my accident, I felt physically and mentally ready to start thinking about skiing again. That's considered rushing it in the rehabilitation process, but I couldn't wait. As fall turned to winter in northern California, ski racks were beginning to appear on car roofs and snow-condition reports were popping up on the radio.

De Anza College, which I was attending, had a Ski Club and a Disabled Student Union, and I approached them about teaming up to buy one of Axelson's sit-skis, which he was now marketing under the name of Arroya. To my delight, the two organizations agreed to put up the full fourteen-hundred-dollar purchase price. As soon as it was available, I was the first person to check it out for the weekend.

I've already related that first disappointing outing to the Dodge Ridge Ski Resort. To me, the worst parts were the hassle of being loaded on and trapped into the ski lift, and the initial need to ski tethered to an instructor. Skiing for me had always represented freedom and unencumbered movement, and this process seemed just the opposite. It's hard for an able-bodied person to understand how much people like me loathe being dependent on other people.

Also, it felt more like sledding than skiing. Even with ski poles, it was difficult to carve precise turns down the fall line. I realized that the Arroya was new on the market, and the whole concept of skiing for paraplegics was still in its infancy. This wasn't like able-bodied skiing, where the equipment has been improved and perfected over generations.

So I began to experiment. It dawned on me that there was always another way to do things, and I didn't have time to wait around for someone else to solve the problem. If I couldn't carve turns the way I wanted with the existing equipment, I'd have to find a new way myself.

In this instance, the solution turned out to be fairly simple. I discarded the long ski poles Axelson recommended and instead used two poles that had been radically shortened to the length of daggers. By planting one firmly into the snow, almost as if I were setting a pick, I found I could pivot the sit-ski around it and carve a pretty crisp turn.

Once I had made that adjustment I found I could start skiing steeper and more challenging slopes with more style and confidence. By the time I landed my job as a Yosemite ranger, I was able to negotiate the most challenging runs at the Badger Pass resort with as much control as a typical able-bodied skier.

I even spent one day a week as a skiing ranger, a sort of cross between a back-country ranger and a ski patrolman. I performed first aid on injured skiers and made sure people didn't wander out of bounds into the unpatrolled areas. Still, my rig required the operators to stop the ski lift and have two people physically lift me up into the chair. I longed to find a way that would give me more independence.

It wasn't until after I had climbed El Capitan that I

found one. In the heady days following that climb, I had a phone call from the representative of a group of businessmen and land developers in Fresno. I couldn't believe what I was hearing: They were offering to put up the three-thousand-dollar cost of buying me a mono-ski.

I'd been hearing about mono-skis for a while, and I knew they were supposed to be a radical step up from sit-skis. But their hefty price tag had put them far beyond the reach of someone on a park ranger's salary. Now, though, with these generous businessmen footing the bill, I'd be able to try one out for myself.

They flew me twice to the Los Angeles headquarters of J and K Mono-Ski for fittings for the customized plastic seat. The ski frame itself was cunningly engineered and complex-looking. There were shock absorbers and levers and binding assemblies everywhere. As the engineers demonstrated the various features, I felt like James Bond being issued his new high-tech spy gear by Q.

"What's this lever for?" I asked.

"Pull it up and see for yourself," someone said.

I did, and a scissors mechanism raised the whole seat assembly by eighteen inches. It took me a second to grasp the reason for this. Then it dawned on me.

"It's to ride the chairlift, right?" I said.

"That's right," answered one of the designers. "The idea is that you just ski up to the front of the lift line, and the lever raises your seat so the chair slides right under you. Some people can do it without even having them slow down the lift."

I loved the idea of that. Next my eyes moved down to what looked like a motorcycle shock absorber between the seat and the ski. This, the engineers told me, would do the job that an able-bodied skier's knees do. It would allow me to move up and down to weight and unweight the ski, and it would cushion the blows that come from banging through moguls. I could adjust the compression and rebound for different kinds of terrain and different styles of skiing.

The ski itself looked just like a ski any able-bodied skier would use, the only difference being that there was only one. Mounted below the shock absorber, it had a camber and a side cut, and it looked as if it could carve a perfect turn in just about any snow condition.

Finally, the poles were radically different from any I had used before. They were twenty-inch-tall outriggers; the tops had metal-braced forearm-like crutches, and the bottoms had little ski tips.

On my very first ski run back at Badger Pass, I could see that the difference between my old sit-ski and my new mono-ski was like the difference between a school bus and a Ferrari Testarossa. I was able to carve snappy turns straight down the fall line, sending up a rooster tail of snow behind me. At the bottom of the run, my cheeks hurt from grinning at the thrill of it all. For the first time in eight years, I was really skiing again.

The loading lever worked like a charm, too. I skied into place at the loading line, levered my butt up a foot and a half, and watched as the chairlift seat slid under me—just like in the old days. Best of all, I could do it all by myself.

That season I skied run after run until I could handle anything the northern California resorts could throw at me. I found myself skiing double diamond runs, the toughest level. On my mono-ski, I was as good a skier as I had ever been in my able-bodied days.

Suddenly there was a whole world reopening to me, one that I thought I had lost forever. With a little bit of money in my pocket from the aftermath of the El Capitan climb, I couldn't wait to get on the road and visit the hallowed shrines of skiing—the big powder resorts in Colorado and Utah.

With Paulette accompanying me on many of the trips, I blasted through the champagne powder of

Breckenridge, Steamboat Springs, Alta and Vail. Venturing further, I skied at Mt. Hood in Oregon and even Lake Placid in upstate New York.

At Vail, Paulette and I followed one of the local hot shots on a high-speed kamikaze run through the trees. At the bottom, he expressed surprise that a gimp skier had been able to keep up with him. He spent the rest of the day showing us some of the most radical, heart-in-your-throat terrain on the mountain.

I skied the steepest faces, jumped off five-foot cornices and careened through giant mogul fields, accompanied on the latter by a group of pro skiers from the mogul ski circuit.

That day I pounded myself as I never had before, and at night I felt it. My back was stiff and sore, and I could feel the metal Harrington rods rubbing on my backbone. When I got home I went to see a doctor, who felt up and down my spine and took some X-rays. He pronounced me fine, although I sure didn't feel that way. In fact, it was summer before the pain went away and my back felt normal again.

I realized I had been trying too hard to make up for all those years of lost skiing after my accident. Since I had gotten my mono-ski, I had been feasting on the freedom of the slopes like a man just released from prison. I had to remind myself to take it easy; I had a lifetime of skiing ahead of me.

Not long after the El Capitan climb, I had received another phone call that opened a new world to me.

"Hi, Mark," said the voice at the other end. "This is Kendall Butts, head coach of the U.S. Disabled Cross-Country Ski Team. I followed your climbing on TV, and you look like you're a hell of a disabled athlete."

"Well, thanks."

"We could really use someone like you on our team," he said. "We're looking for athletes with great stamina and a good aerobic base, and we're always looking to get more wheelchair people involved. What do you say?"

"I haven't really done all that much cross-country skiing," I told him. "Mostly I'm a downhill skier."

"If you're willing to give it a try, we're willing to work with you," Butts said. "We're going to be sending a team to the Paralympics, which are going to be held in Albertville, France, right after the able-bodied Winter Olympics. You'd be representing your country."

The sound of that made me sit up a little taller in my wheelchair. I definitely liked the idea. I knew there wasn't much chance of me making the team as an alpine skier, because the roster was full of athletes who had been top-flight racers before suffering their disabilities. But the field for the cross-country team was wide open. Otherwise, they wouldn't have been calling me.

"OK," I told Butts. "Count me in."

The thermometer read eight degrees Fahrenheit when I climbed, shivering, out of my van at West Yellowstone. It was Thanksgiving 1991, and I was there for the start of the ten-day U.S. Disabled Cross-country Ski Team training camp. My breath formed into billowing clouds and my wheels squeaked and creaked as I rolled across the snow-covered parking lot. Overhead, the big Wyoming sky was a somber grey. It felt as if more snow was on the way.

Warming themselves around the fire inside Three Bears Lodge were the other team aspirants. These athletes represented just about every category of disability you could imagine. Dorothy Yucha, a four-year veteran of the team, has been blind since suffering an accident at age seven. Bill Henry, who was hoping to compete in both the winter and summer Paralympic Games, had lost the use of his left arm after being hit by a car. Janet Penn, a cross-country ski instructor at the Royal Gorge Resort near Lake Tahoe, had lost her left foot in a dirt-bike crash.

As I looked around the room, I noticed only one other person in a wheelchair. Immediately, I knew who he was. This big guy with his massive shoulders, bulging biceps and air of quiet confidence would be my competition. Beating him in a ski race was a challenge bigger than climbing El Capitan, because Jeff Pagels was unquestionably the best paraplegic cross-country ski racer in the world.

A Nordic ski racer from frosty Green Bay, Wisconsin, Jeff had competed in seven American Birkebeiner ski marathons before a falling tree broke his back in 1984. Paralyzed from the waist down, he became the first and most successful "sit-skier" on the U.S. team. At an age when most athletes have hung up their competitive skis, the forty-three-year-old Pagels was just reaching his peak. He was coming off a year in which he had placed first in every U.S. and international race he entered. The previous April, in Beitostolen, Norway, he had beaten the best European skiers in their own backyard.

Pagels was a real "do-as-I-do" leader and a no-nonsense guy who commanded the respect of everybody at the training camp—especially me, since I was the only one who would be racing head-to-head with the guy.

Disabled athletes compete in categories based on their disability. There are three classes of blind and partially sighted skiers, and up to twelve different classes for those of us who are physically impaired. Your category is based on whether your amputation is above or below the knee, or, in the case of paraplegics and quadriplegics, how much mobility you have left in your lower body.

I was categorized as an LW-11, which meant I had a little movement in my legs. In international competition, I was told, I would be skiing mostly against polio victims. Pagels was an LW-10, with virtually no feeling below the waist. Technically, we'd be competing in different classes. But every day we'd be out on the track together in our sit-skis, and Pagels was the man I'd measure myself against.

Disabled skiing got its start in Europe after World War II, when Austria, Germany and Switzerland began organizing rehabilitation programs for amputees and other crippled veterans. It moved to the United States in the 1950s as a recreational sport, but it has since evolved into a highly competitive and organized sport in its own right. In recent years, the United States has dominated world competition. At the World Disabled Ski Championships two years ago, American alpine skiers took home an incredible eighty medals. The biggest problem for the coaches this year was deciding who would make the team. New international rules had cut down each country's number of entrants per category from three to two. This left open the possibility that the team would be leaving downhill skiers at home who could have beaten just about anybody else in the world.

I think there are two main reasons for America's dominance in disabled skiing. First, the team is treated like an integral part of the U.S. Ski Team, and not just as some gimp sideshow. We work out at the same training facilities, eat at the same training table and wear the same uniforms as our able-bodied colleagues. This is not always the case in European countries, and I think it shows at the finish line.

Second, the U.S. team doesn't baby its disabled skiers. The cross-country tracks we train on are hilly and challenging. By contrast, many of the European courses are relatively flat and gentle, as if disabled skiers couldn't handle anything tougher. I hoped this difference would give my chances a big boost at Albertville.

On a crisp, bright morning, Pagels and I set out on an easy practice ski into Yellowstone. My Arroya sit-ski is unsuited for competitive skiing, so I borrowed one of Jeff's homemade models. This consisted of a welded aluminum frame with a plastic cafeteria set and a GM seat belt, all mounted atop a pair of standard single-camber racing skis. It wasn't aesthetically pleasing, but the difference between it and my Arroya was amazing. I pushed behind me with my ski poles, and the sit-ski zipped forward in the prepared track.

As Jeff and I glided down the trail, I noticed that moving across flat ground was a snap if my skis were waxed correctly. Climbing even a small hill, though, was another matter. I had to push and strain against my poles, and a second's relaxation meant lost ground. I was also gulping huge amounts of the super-cold air. I was proud to be able to keep up with Pagels, but I noticed he wasn't even breathing hard.

Coming around a turn, Jeff pointed off to the left with his ski pole. There was a huge bison, standing twenty feet off the track and looking primordial. Icicles hung off its fur and steam jetted out of its nostrils as it gave us a wary eye. The thrill of being out in the wilderness in such close proximity to this wild beast put a little extra snap in my poling.

Further up the trail, we passed a frost-covered moose standing incredibly tall and alert next to an ice-choked stream. We saw elk and bald eagles, and our track was crisscrossed by the footprints of other winter creatures.

Back in the toasty-warm lodge, Pagels congratulated me for keeping up a good pace all day. I had been able to match him stride for stride, but I suspected he had been saving his real stuff for when the stopwatches came out.

A couple of days later I found out how right I was. Jeff and I were lined up at the start of a four-kilometer timed trial. As he rocked back and forth on his sit-ski, there was a flaming intensity in his eyes I hadn't seen before. Kendall Butts, the coach, gave us the signal, and Pagels' powerful shoulders propelled him forward like a bullet out of a gun barrel.

Soon, all I could see was his back. Not long after that I was lucky to get a glimpse of him off in the distance. I poled as hard and as fast as I could, and even then I continued to lose ground. By the time I reached the finish line, I was a miserable ten minutes behind Pagels.

Nordic skiing, I was learning, was a lot different from cranking off pull-ups on El Capitan. On a vertical rock face I gained elevation with quick bursts of arm and shoulder strength. But I could move at my own pace and take a breather whenever I wanted. Skiing across the icy Wyoming snow, my challenge was not against gravity so much as against the impatient clock. If I wanted any chance of winning a medal at Albertville, I would have to train myself to give it my all over a long period of time.

Even with my disappointing showing, I landed a spot on the U.S. Disabled Cross-country Ski Team. They needed another paraplegic who was crazy enough to try to keep up with Pagels, and I was it.

My next hurdle was earning a spot on the Paralympic team and going to Albertville. To make the team, Butts decided, disabled skiers needed to post times that were at least sixty percent of the top able-bodied skiers' times. My personal benchmark was to reach the finish line with a time no more than fifteen percent behind Pagels'. This would require a major leap forward on my part.

All summer and fall I redoubled my efforts in the gym, pounded the pavement in my row-cycle and swam lap after lap after lap in the swimming pool. The thirteen days I had spent on Half Dome with Corbett helped me shed my residual body fat and taught me how to summon the willpower to bring out the extra reserves of strength that lie on the other side of exhaustion.

In January 1992, I felt ready for the Disabled Olympic trials in Biwabik, Minnesota. Not only was I in the best aerobic shape possible, but I also had a sleek new ski frame. It had been built for me by the engineers at Fortress out of light aircraft aluminum, and it was fast and nimble.

During the time trials, everything came together. My new ski rig worked beautifully and I shook off my nervousness to ski faster and stronger than I ever had before. I still couldn't catch Pagels, but at the ten-kilometer finish line I was only five minutes behind the guy.

It was good enough to make the team. I was going to the Olympics!

Eight of us were lined up in wheelchairs in the jetway at JFK Airport in New York, waiting to board the Air France flight to Lyon. Everyone was wearing his or her Team USA jacket. One by one, we slid out of our wheelchairs and into the seat of an "aisle chair," a forklift-like device that is narrow enough to negotiate the plane's aisles. While the athletes were being delivered to their seats, their wheelchairs were being loaded into the plane's cargo hold. With eight people, it took a long time to load everybody. It's even slower when a wheelchair basketball team travels, since teams can carry up to twenty players.

After a seemingly endless flight and an hour-long layover in Nice, the U.S. Winter Paralympic Team arrived in Lyon. Getting off the plane were forty athletes as well as ten coaches, doctors and other staff people. The pride we felt to be wearing our Team USA uniforms was mixed with a glassy-eyed grogginess from crossing too many time zones with too little sleep.

Unfortunately, our hotel hadn't been chosen with wheelchairs in mind. In our rooms, there wasn't enough space between the beds and the walls to maneuver. If you somehow got as far as the bathroom door, you were stopped cold. It was too narrow to allow you to roll any further. The bathtubs had high sides, which presented a formidable barrier. Because we were athletes, most of us were able to overcome these hurdles, but I pity any nonathletes in wheelchairs who try to vacation in rooms like that.

That night, we stuffed five skiers and two wheelchairs into a taxicab and drove through the streets of Lyon into the old part of town. Sure, we were still in training, but you don't get that many chances to sample real French cuisine.

We caused a minor stir at the restaurant, but it wasn't long before the maitre d' was leading us to a good table. Picking up the menu, I asked: "OK, who speaks French here?"

"Not me," said Jeff Pagels.

"Me neither," said his wife, Jane.

"I'm no help," said Matt Cutt, a Nordic skier with deformed arms and hands.

"I at least know *escargot* means snails," said Michelle Drolet, a blind skier. "And *lapin*, I think that's rabbit."

Beyond that, nobody had a clue. We were just going to have to order blind and hope for the best. I scanned the menu one last time, and something jumped out at me.

"Hey, they have *steak tartare* here," I announced. "I've heard of that, and it's supposed to be pretty good. That's what I'm going to have."

"Sounds good," said Pagels. "I'll have that, too."

A little while later the waiter returned from the kitchen and set our dinners down in front of us. Pagels and I took one look at our plates and exchanged puzzled glances. There had to be some kind of mistake. On our plates were raw hamburger and a raw egg.

"I can't eat that," said Pagels, pushing his plate away.

"Neither can I," I said.

"Hand it over here, boys, I'll eat it," said Cutt, who proceeded to bend his head down and, without the use of his arms, dig into the food like a contestant in a pie-eating contest. We all got a good laugh out of this, as we did when Matt told us to call him by his nickname: "Flipper."

This might seem unspeakably cruel to an outsider, but it's all part of the camaraderie amongst gimps. We poke fun at ourselves and our circumstances, but it's always with warmth and compassion for each other.

Laughing in the restaurant with my Olympic teammates and not worrying about what the other diners thought, I certainly had come a long way from that first awkward outing at the steakhouse ten years earlier.

The next day we boarded a bus and drove through picturesque farmland up into the French Alps. The peaks were radiant under their winter coatings of snow and ice, with granite spires jutting up like sharks' teeth and glaciers tumbling down their flanks into the valleys.

"Hey, check it out!" yelled someone, and we all pressed our noses to the bus window. It was the five-ringed Olympic symbol welcoming us to the village of Tignes, and the sight of it sent chills up my spine.

Tignes, a few miles from Albertville, is where we would stay and where the festive opening ceremonies were to be held the next day. Everyone was impressed with the reception we got. The French treated the Paralympics as almost as big a deal as the able-bodied games that had concluded a few weeks earlier. There was an hour or two of coverage every night on television. By contrast, I'm not aware of a single minute of coverage that was aired on U.S. television.

I had four days to cool my heels before my first race. I was entered in both the five-kilometer and ten-kilometer races, and one of the first things I did was catch a ride down the valley to inspect the track. At the first sight of it, my confidence soared. Just as we had suspected, it was flatter and gentler than the courses we had been training on in the United States. With all that extra training on the hills, I told myself, I ought to be able to blast past the competition.

I watched the European skiers gliding around the track, and my cockiness grew. These guys really didn't look that fast. In my weaker moments I allowed myself to daydream about rolling up the ramp to take my place atop the medal platform.

We got in several training runs. The toughest part of the day always proved to be loading the team onto the bus. Paraplegics like Pagels had to sit backwards on the bus steps and drag themselves up into the coach and down the aisle to their seat. Luckily I had enough residual leg strength to stand and drag myself down the aisle. The other paraplegics had a miserable time dragging their butts through the inevitable snowmelt puddle in the aisle.

The night before my first race I huddled in my room with Chris Waddell, a paraplegic on the men's alpine team. We were gulping down vitamins and drinking bottled water. After my culinary disaster in Lyon, I was keeping a safe distance away from all that sauce-heavy French food—at least until my race was over.

Watching the foreign athletes eating that rich fare, smoking endless numbers of cigarettes and washing it all down with copious amounts of red wine, I felt more sure than ever about my chances for success.

We were up at dawn on race day. After a few bites of food and some sips of bottled water, I helped load my gear on the bus and we drove down the valley to the racecourse. Even at that hour, spectators were starting to line up along the track, and the sight of them sent the first tinges of nervousness into my stomach.

A big tent was waiting for us there, and inside it were our skis, which had been waxed earlier by our coaches. I slipped into a pair of neoprene booties to protect my feet from the cold, and pulled on my sleek racing uniform. As I started my warm-up exercises, I noticed a tightness in my body that had nothing to do with the cold weather. I was tense, there was no doubt about it.

As the minutes ticked down toward starting time, the butterflies in my stomach started rumbling like an angry hornet's nest. What had happened to all that cockiness I had been feeling before? Someone gave me a signal, and I pushed myself slowly out of the tent and up to the starting line. An Olympic official came along and measured my skis and frame to ensure they were within the official guidelines. Then he marked my skis to make sure I didn't switch boards halfway through the race.

Suddenly I could see various coaches coming out of the tent and saying things to skiers in languages I couldn't understand. The athletes all looked disappointed. Finally, one of the U.S. coaches delivered the news to me.

"The race has been canceled today, Mark," he said. "It was too cold last night, and they weren't able to set the course properly. They're going to try again tomorrow."

I had twenty-four hours to let the tension build in my gut. All day I wheeled myself around the little Olympic village in Tignes, looking for diversion amid the hustle and bustle of the other events. The American downhill skiers were racking up medals at a pretty good clip, and I tried to take their moments of victory and visualize them as my own.

After an awful night of tossing and turning, I heard the alarm go off at 5:30 a.m. A coach came jogging up as Pagels and I were boarding the bus.

"The weather was good last night and they were able to set the course," he said. "You'll be racing this morning."

At the starting line I kept telling myself I wasn't

nervous, but it was an empty attempt at self-deception. I looked around at the other athletes. The Norwegians and Finns who had seemed so lackadaisical and pokey in practice now looked strong and confident—and fast.

There were still a few minutes to kill before we started. I checked out their ski rigs. The Finns had an aluminum frame similar to the one built for me by Fortress. The only difference was that theirs contained an ingenious-looking binding that allowed them to steer by leaning to the side in their plastic bucket seats.

The Germans were using what looked like racing wheelchair frames mounted on skis. Like wheelchair marathoners, they raced with their knees tucked up tight against their chests. It looked awkward and uncomfortable, but, as I was to find out, it worked quite well.

"Get a load of the Swiss over there," said Pagels, nudging me with his ski pole.

The Swiss certainly had the oddest rigs of all. Mounted atop their skis were plastic carriages that looked almost like soapbox derby cars. They looked slow and cumbersome, and they proved to be just that.

I was disappointed that there were no skiers from the Unified Team, the former Soviet Union, in our race. It turns out their Nordic team concentrated on the blind categories, where they won just about every medal there was.

International competition is so limited for disabled skiers that no one really knew who the favorites in this class were. As I had been told, many of the nineteen skiers in my class were polio victims. Looking them over, I was struck for the first time by just how powerful their upper bodies were.

"Jeez, Pagels," I said. "These polio dudes look wickedly strong."

"So do you," he said. "Just focus on skiing your own race and you'll do fine."

The course was 2.5 kilometers around, and the race

called for us to complete two laps. They started us at thirty-second intervals. As my time approached, I tried to go over a mental checklist, but my head was being overrun with surging adrenaline. I pushed myself up to the starting line, waited for the timer to tick down to zero and pushed off.

Spectators lined the course, and everyone was shouting and waving as I poled myself down the tracks. I tried to take all my nervousness and transform it into extra energy. Focusing on the skier ahead of me, I tried to narrow the gap between us. This was intense aerobic work, harder than anything I had done on El Cap or Half Dome. I realized now that I had been sandbagged during the training runs. These other guys had been holding back, unwilling to show their real speed. Now I was seeing it firsthand.

Still, I was holding my own with the big boys. As I rounded the turn and finished the first lap, a coach yelled out to me.

"You're in third place right now, Mark," he said. "Keep pouring it on!"

I poled a little harder. If I could just maintain my position, I'd win a bronze medal. Did I have the strength to push hard enough for a silver or a gold? Now was the time to find out.

Early in the second lap, I knew I was in trouble. I felt myself starting to fade, and I looked up to see I was losing ground to the skier in front of me. The skier behind me was gaining on me rapidly. I fought to regain my pace, but it was no use. The strength just wasn't there.

By the time I glided across the finish line, I had dropped all the way back to eleventh place.

Finnish skiers captured the gold and silver medals in the LW-11 category, and a Norwegian took the bronze. To the delight of all his teammates and the surprise of no one, Jeff Pagels won the gold medal easily in his class.

I applauded with everyone else as the medalists rolled their wheelchairs up the ramps and onto the winners' platform. As the medals were draped around their necks, the loudspeakers played the Olympic theme song instead of their national anthems. That's the way they do it in the Paralympics, and I hope it will catch on in the able-bodied games. I began then to feel that the games are about athletes competing against each other, not about nationalism.

Three days later I had another shot at a medal. This time the race would be ten kilometers, and I figured my chances were better. With four laps around the course, there would be time to ski out my nervousness and work into a good aerobic pace.

I got a decent night's sleep this time, and as I pulled up to the starting line I had a better idea of what to expect, and a better sense of what I had to push my body to do. My cockiness had disappeared quickly in the first race; now I felt a quiet confidence.

With the signal from the French starter, I was out fast and hard. I was making good time around the course—when disaster struck. As I was rounding a turn in a downhill stretch, I pushed too hard and tumbled over on my side. I thrashed frantically with my poles to right myself, but before I could do it, a German skier blew by me.

Mad now, I managed to tip myself back up and get into the tracks. I poled hard with all my strength, got right on the German's tail and stayed there. Near the end of the first lap I put on an extra burst of speed and passed him.

I made excellent time in the second lap, and matched it in the third. With one lap to go, I knew I needed a superhuman effort to get myself back into contention for a medal. The crowd was roaring for all of us, and I tried to use their energy to psych myself up for one last push. I strained for every last bit I had, but I couldn't increase my speed. I was already giving everything, and I just didn't have the reserves to kick it up a notch. I crossed the finish line in a disappointing ninth place, cursing myself for my bad luck. Would I have won a medal if I hadn't fallen? It's possible, but there's no way to know.

The same three skiers took the medals in the ten-kilometer race, but this time the Norwegian won the gold and the two Finns captured the silver and the bronze. In the LW-10 category, Jeff Pagels took home his second gold medal of the games.

We all stayed for the closing ceremony, which was as full of lavish pageantry as the opening, but a little rowdier. All the athletes gathered in the stadium, and I rolled around in my wheelchair, taking pictures and slapping high-fives with the French *gendarmes*. Everyone was in a festive mood. Paraplegics, amputees and blind athletes from different countries traded pins and warm-up jackets with each other. I sought out the Finnish Nordic medalists, congratulated them and swapped my warm-up jacket and pants for a set of their mysterious bindings.

As the winter games closed with a fusillade of fireworks, I hoped the bursting flashes wouldn't reveal the disappointment in my face. I had wanted to take home a medal, and I hadn't done it. But I realized that if you always succeed on the first try, you're not setting your sights high enough. I now had a new challenge facing me, and I would have two years to prepare myself for it. The next winter Paralympic Games would be held in Lillehammer, Norway, in 1994, and, like most of my teammates, I planned to be there.

If climbing El Capitan and Half Dome had taught me anything, it was that my supposedly disabled body could accomplish anything I set out to do, if my will was there.

10

MAKE IT HAPPEN

I get a lot of attention for what I do because I'm supposedly disabled. Yet each of us is handicapped in one way or another. I'm handicapped, you're handicapped, even an athlete like Michael Jordan is handicapped. (OK, maybe not Michael Jordan.) The important thing is that the rest of us recognize these handicaps and understand that we have within ourselves the power to transcend them.

My disabilities are physical and quite obvious. When your legs stop working, it's fairly easy to focus on the problem and put together a plan for regaining your mobility. Actually making it happen requires hard work, but at least you know what you have to do.

Maybe your disability is harder to detect. But chances are there are things, unseen and not completely understood, that are preventing you from climbing your own mountains in life. Something is holding you back from proposing that new project at work, or enrolling in that MBA program, or pursuing a job opportunity in a new city, or asking that special someone out on a date. The handicaps that hold you back in life are harder to see than the one that keeps me in a wheelchair, but they're no less real.

It could be that you are handicapped by inferior schooling or unsupportive parents or racism or self-consciousness about your looks or voice. It doesn't really matter what the handicap is. What's important is that you realize that no one else is going to break down your barriers or climb your mountains for you. You are going to have to do that yourself.

Sometimes I think back to the time when I was lying flat on my back in the hospital in Redwood City. It's hard to exaggerate how depressing it is for a twenty-two-year-old man to realize he no longer has even the ability to sit up in bed.

I had been a mountaineer in the prime of my health, and I had climbed to the highest summits from the Sierra Nevada to the Alps. But as I lay there in my hospital bed, I was as helpless as a newborn baby. It was as if my entire being had been set back to zero and all the rules of the game had been changed.

It's hard now to remember when the realization hit me, but eventually I came to know that, for the rest of my life, nothing good was ever going to happen for me again—unless I personally made it happen.

Just regaining the ability to sit up in bed took days of strenuous and agonizing effort that left me feeling drained and dizzy. More sweat and strain were required before I could learn to slide into the seat of a wheelchair. Then it took months of practice before I could negotiate a room in my chair without crashing into chairs and tables. After that there were all the long hours of pumping weights in the gym to build my muscles, straining until I was red in the face.

By then I had grasped a powerful idea, one that can change lives: I could no longer drift through life, taking whatever the future brought me. Instead, I had to create the kind of future I wanted for myself.

I had begun to see the undeniable connection between setting a goal and working like a mad dog until I reached it. Eventually I was strong and skilled enough to rejoin the "real world," but I didn't want to stop there. I wanted to be able to do more than just roll down a hall in a wheelchair. I wanted once again to play tennis, climb mountains and carve turns down ski slopes.

Luckily, nature gave me some gifts that helped compensate for the loss of my legs. I have a certain stubbornness and singleness of purpose that allows me to put my head down, shut out the distractions and keep plowing ahead until I reach my goal—whether it's lifting weights in the gym, mastering a biology textbook or doing seven thousand chin-ups on El Capitan.

I knew I never was going to reach my dreams until I took that first step off the ground. Once I did that, once I threw myself into the task, things immediately started going my way. It's an amazing phenomenon that some people never discover, but it's something all mountaineers know instinctively. A.F. Mummery, the great nineteenth-century British alpinist, expressed it about as well as anyone has:

"Until one is committed there is hesitancy, the chance to draw back, always ineffectiveness. Concerning all acts of initiative (and creation) there is one elementary truth, the ignorance of which kills countless ideas and splendid plans: that the moment one definitely commits oneself, then Providence moves, too. All sorts of things occur to help one that would never otherwise have occurred. A whole stream of events issues from the decision, raising in one's favor all manner of unforeseen incidents and meetings and material assistance, which no man could have dreamt would have come his way."

In other words, by the very act of committing ourselves to our goal, all sorts of unexpected breaks will come our way.

What allows some people to take that first committing step, while others hang back in hesitation? For me, in the dark days after my accident, it was regaining my sense of hope. Psychologists have found ways to measure hope, and their studies show conclusively that a positive attitude gives you a measurable and surprisingly big advantage in everything from your grades in school to your ability to fight off illness.

In many cases, it's this sense of hope, rather than any other factor, that determines how well you perform in difficult situations. Of course, hope can be translated as having a positive attitude, having self-confidence, believing in yourself or being an optimist.

Psychologists, though, have come up with a more concrete definition. Dr. Charles Snyder, a psychologist at the University of Kansas, defines it as having both the willpower and the ability to accomplish your goals. He has even developed a scale to measure this. It evaluates a person's willpower by measuring the amount of energy he or she puts into reaching goals. To test a person's ability, it asks whether they are usually able to figure a way out of difficult situations or solve problems that have defeated others.

Hope turns out to be a powerful indicator of how well someone will perform in life. In a study of nearly four thousand college students, Snyder found that the level of hope among individual college freshmen turned out to be a surprisingly accurate way to predict their eventual college performance. Those with the most hope—not necessarily those with the best high-school grade-point averages or SAT scores—tended to get the best grades.

However, where there's a will, there's not necessarily a way. And vice versa. Snyder studied seven thousand people and found that less than half of them felt they had both components of his definition of hope: the willpower and the means to accomplish their goals. About twenty percent said they had the willpower but not the ability, and roughly the same number said they had the means but not the energy.

So hope is more than just keeping a sunny outlook

on life. You have to believe that the solutions to your problems lie within your grasp, and that you have what it takes to find them.

Another study, conducted by Dr. Timothy Elliott, a psychologist at Virginia Commonwealth University, revealed something I have known for a long time. It found that people with a sense of hope bear up far better after being paralyzed from a spinal-cord injury.

The study, which looked at fifty-seven paraplegics and quadriplegics, found that those with hope had less depression, more mobility, a greater number of social contacts—and even a better sex life.

I didn't participate in the study, but if I had I believe my results would have been right in line with those found by Dr. Elliott. When I think back to my first dark weeks in the hospital, I recall the initial feeling of utter hopelessness. I remember wanting to hurl myself out the sixth-floor window. Only the fact that I couldn't move myself out of my bed kept me from doing that.

Everything changed dramatically once I found a sense of hope. Initially that sense came from Mark Sutherland, the quadriplegic who showed me you could still be cool in a wheelchair. Sutherland helped me through the blackest times and showed me what I could become if I were willing to work for it.

Once he helped me turn that corner, everything started changing for me. I started to look at the life ahead of me not as a series of insurmountable obstacles, but as a succession of challenges I could conquer. Once I regained the belief that I could succeed, I attacked those problems with vigor and enthusiasm.

I've said that no one else is going to climb your mountains for you, but that doesn't mean you can't accept help from people. In my case, the most obvious example was Mike Corbett, without whom I could never have made it up El Capitan or Half Dome. It was not only Mike's climbing, but also his wild-eyed enthusiasm and drive early in the game that made those adventures become reality.

There have been others. Sutherland, as I have said, was my mentor and guide in the strange new world of the disabled. Our late-night talks in his hospital room gave me the courage and practical knowledge to take my first hesitant steps out into that world. Later, at De Anza College, Jeff Forman became my coach and friend as he helped me build the strength to live the kind of life I wanted. At West Valley College, John "Smitty" Smith and John Nicholas gave me the encouragement to become a ranger. Countless others along the way have helped me with their advice, support and hard work.

It's a shame so many people go through life being too proud or independent to accept help and guidance from friends, teachers, coaches and mentors. They're out there, they're willing to help, and often all it takes is the ability to open yourself up to them.

As I began to build a new life for myself, I soon learned I had to start looking at every problem in a new light. When you're wheelchair-bound in an able-bodied world, you quickly realize that you've got to find another way to do things. I suspect that's true for most people, in most walks of life. When there's a big hurdle in front of you, the best thing to do is to find a way to step around it.

Most of us are so used to looking at the world in a fixed, rigid sort of way that we don't realize what can be accomplished with a little adjustment. Sometimes all it takes is a little creativity, a new outlook, a different approach.

For me, it's mostly been a matter of adapting tools, machines and techniques to my own use. The most obvious example is my wheelchair, which has taken over the function of my legs. Through a great deal of hard work in the gym and with the use of crutches, I can actually walk across a room now. But it's a slow and difficult process. Most of the time it's far easier to use my buggy.

After some experimentation, I found that a sports wheelchair gives me the kind of quick-and-nimble mobility I want. Ramps help me wheel up stairs, and the ability to pop a wheelie gets me over curbs where there are no curb-cuts. I can get just about anywhere an able-bodied person can go—with a few big exceptions—and I'm working on those. Sometimes I can even cover ground more quickly than a person with working legs. Remember, the top wheelchair marathoners routinely post times faster than the best able-bodied runners.

When I started thinking about climbing again, I knew that scaling the rugged peaks of the Sierra Nevada or the Rockies or the Alps would probably be beyond my reach. It would have been easy to dismiss as impossible the idea of climbing the sheer, vertical cliffs of Yosemite. Certainly, rock climbing in the traditional style was out. But Mike Corbett and I set out to find another way. It took experimentation and many trips back to the drawing board, but eventually we adapted some standard climbing and caving techniques into a system that worked pretty well for me. I doubt it's a sport that will catch on in a big way among disabled people, but it has allowed me to return to the high and wild places I love so much.

It's been the same story with skiing and bicycling and kayaking. By finding another way, I've been able to enjoy these sports and practice them at a level every bit as advanced as I had reached as an able-bodied person. Of course some sports require more adaptation than others. My hand-crank bicycle works beautifully but looks like something Rube Goldberg would have cooked up. My kayak, however, is close to an off-the-rack, standard model.

Even if you're not physically disabled, it helps to be

able to find another way. Sometimes problems that seem insurmountable will yield easily if you take a step back and look at them differently.

If you've been trying to bull your way through a difficult situation, try chipping away at it patiently instead. Mike Corbett likes to tell an old Yosemite Indian legend that reveals a lot about this approach.

Many years ago, the legend goes, two bear cubs fell asleep on a rock along the Merced River. While they slept, the rock grew and grew until it reached the sky. Their mother frantically assembled all the animals in Yosemite to mount a rescue.

The grizzly bear tried to sink its mighty claws into the granite and wrestle it to the ground. He failed miserably. The massive elk tried to butt it over with its powerful antlers. Still, the rock didn't budge. The lightning-fast mountain lion took a running start and tried to leap to the top. It fell halfway, leaving claw marks as it plunged back to earth.

Just when the mother was giving up hope, the humblest of all forest creatures, little Too-tok-a-nah the measuring worm, came along. Inch by inch, he began working his way up the cliff that had defeated Yosemite's mightiest creatures. Day turned into night as tiny Too-tok-a-nah kept inching his way to the top. Finally, he reached the summit and led the two bear cubs down to safety. In the inchworm's honor the Ahwahnee people of Yosemite named the towering rock "Too-tok-a-nah-lah." Today, the white man calls it "El Capitan."

Finding a different way has helped me inch myself up two pretty big mountains. Along the way I've learned that it's the personal challenge of overcoming your limitations, not the short time you spend on the summit, that really matters.

As I look into the future, I see plenty of other challenges out there waiting for me.

For example, some time soon I am hoping to spend three days paddling my kayak all the way around Lake Tahoe. (Kayaking is the one sport where I'm on equal footing, so to speak, with able-bodied people.) It promises to be an interesting and varied journey around one of the real jewels of the High Sierra. As I float through isolated, pine-studded coves, I'll see some of the finest scenery nature has to offer. As I paddle past the neon-lit casinos of the California–Nevada border, I'll witness some of the gaudiest monuments man has ever erected.

Most of all, I look forward to the freedom and mobility I'll have as I slip through the crystal-blue waters, with only the gentle lapping sound of my paddle to break the silence.

Looking further ahead, I have been invited to participate in the official five-hundredth-anniversary ascent of Mont Aiguille in France. It's a huge limestone tower near Grenoble that has been called the "Plymouth Rock of mountaineering."

It was there, in the same year that Christopher Columbus set sail for India, that representatives of King Charles VIII accomplished the first technical rock climb in recorded history, a deed that predated the birth of mountaineering as a real sport by nearly three hundred years.

It happened like this: During a pilgrimage in the area, the king had been struck by the sight of what was then called Mont Inaccessible. The local peasants filled his ears with all sorts of wild stories about the giant rock citadel and told them they had personally seen the tunics of angels drifting around the walls.

Deciding to look further into the matter, the king gave the job to his trusty chamberlain, Antoine de Ville of Grenoble. De Ville in turn rounded up a crack team of specialists for the task. It included a professor of theology, a clerk, a lackey, a carpenter, an almoner and one Reynaud Jubie, the "ladder-man to the King."

They ascended the mountain in June of 1492. In his official account, de Ville says only that his team used "subtle means and engines," and noted that the route they climbed was "terrible to look at, and is still more terrible to descend than ascend."

No angels were waiting for them on the flat summit, but, incredibly, they found a verdant, flower-dotted meadow and a herd of chamois. No one could explain how the herd of goat-like antelope got there, since the tower was absolutely sheer on all sides.

De Ville camped on the summit for close to a week and sent away to Grenoble for official witnesses who would testify that he had reached the summit. At the end of his stay, he baptized the mountain and changed its name to the current "Mont Aiguille," which means "needle" or "spire." As he had proved, it was no longer "Mont Inaccessible."

As one who has been working hard to gain access to formerly inaccessible places in the wilderness, I was honored to be invited to the official celebration of de Ville's ascent. His accomplishment was brilliant and remarkable, especially when you consider that nobody got up the nerve to repeat it for another 342 years. Even today, with modern equipment and techniques, Mont Aiguille is considered fairly difficult.

The sponsors of the anniversary ascent have arranged for a horse to carry me to the base of the tower. Expert guides from the *Club Alpin Français* will lead the route and trail ropes that I'll climb with my pull-up bar ascender, just as I did on El Capitan and Half Dome.

Mont Aiguille rises about one thousand feet above its base. For me, that's about two thousand chin-ups. I'm sure if he were here today, Antoine de Ville, the man behind the "subtle means and engines," would find my style of climbing equally hard to comprehend.

In the spring of 1993, I am planning to ski across the snow-covered Sierra Nevada mountain range with Jeff

Pagels, my teammate from the U.S. Disabled Cross-country Ski Team. For this adventure, there will be no able-bodied people around to help us. It will just be two gimps alone amid the ice-covered peaks and high passes.

Leaving from the town of Lee Vining near Mono Lake in eastern California, we plan to follow the same route over 9,945-foot Tioga Pass that the Indian maiden Tis-sa-ack took on her way to Yosemite Valley. We'll pass beneath the flanks of Mt. Dana and Fairview Dome, and along the shores of Tenaya Lake.

From there, most ski-tourers drop down steeply into Yosemite Valley on a zigzag hiking trail. Unable to do that, Pagels and I plan to continue skiing another thirty miles to the road head at Crane Flat. The entire trip will cover some sixty miles, and we'll have to push ourselves every foot of the way with our ski poles. We think we can do it in five days—although, after Half Dome, I'm not making any guarantees.

We've decided it would be "cheating" to cache food and fuel along the way. Jeff and I will carry everything we need in sleds we drag behind our sit-skis. To go as light as possible, we're planning to leave behind tents and stoves. We'll depend on Gore-tex bivy bags to keep us warm, and we hope to find snow-melt water to drink along the way. Of course, we'll have to keep a wary eye on the weather. With our safety margins cut to a minimum, a surprise late-season storm could prove serious.

Why do it this way? I've always believed that true adventure involves discovering things about yourself as you edge ever closer toward the boundaries of your personal limits. I learned plenty about myself on El Capitan and Half Dome. But with Mike Corbett along to lead the climb and haul most of our supplies, I don't feel I reached my personal limits.

With no able-bodied person along to help with the hard work or bail us out if things go wrong, Jeff and I will depend entirely on our physical conditioning, our wilderness skills, our savvy and our abilities to make the right decisions. That's what adventure is all about.

Our fate will be in our own hands, and that's the way we want it. Ever since my accident transformed me, that's what my life has been about. I now know that the only limits are the ones inside my head. If my mind is set on a goal, lifeless legs are not a handicap.

There will be plenty of other mountains to climb in years to come—both the rock-and-ice variety and the personal kind. In each case, I know the summit is within reach if I focus my sights on it and take that first step off the ground.

The philosopher Goethe understood this when he wrote: "Whatever you can do, or dream you can, begin it. Boldness has genius, power, and magic in it."

See you on the summit.

GLOSSARY

aid climbing: ascending a rock by the use of pitons and other hardware. Most of the routes on El Capitan and Half Dome consisted of aid climbing.

ascenders: mechanical ascending devices that will slide up a rope but bite hard when a downward pull is applied. Using these, climbers can literally walk up ropes.

belay: paying the rope out in such a way that one can stop a falling partner immediately.

bolts: metal expansion bolts that are drilled directly into blank rock.

carabiners: metal snap-links used to attach ropes, pitons and other items on a climb. (Imagine an overgrown safety pin strong enough to lift an elephant.)

chimney: a cleft in the rock wide enough for a climber to insert his entire body.

étriers: stirrups made out of nylon slings. During direct-aid climbing, a climber attaches these to pitons and stands in them.

exposure: a term that describes the steepness of the rock face and the amount of fresh air beneath the climber's toes.

free climbing: ascending a rock with only one's hands and feet. The ropes, pitons, etc., are used only for safety, like a trapeze artist's safety net.

Friend: the brand name of a spring-loaded camming device that can be inserted into a crack instead of a piton. Also called cams, Camalots.

Gibbs ascender: brand name of the mechanical ascender Wellman used on his climbing harness.

haul bags: large sacks made out of tough canvas or ballistics nylon that hold a big-wall climber's supplies. These are dragged up the rock face behind the climbers.

Jumar: brand name of a mechanical ascending device used by Wellman and Corbett. "Jumaring"—also known as "jugging"—means walking up a rope.

nailing: to hammer a chain of pitons into a crack during direct-aid climbing.

pitch: one rope length of the rock face, roughly one hundred to 140 feet. Many big-wall climbs such as El Capitan and Half Dome are twenty or more pitches in length.

piton: a steel spike that is hammered into small cracks in the rock face.

Portaledge: a cot-like sleeping platform, suspended on a vertical rock face from pitons.

rappel: to slide down a rope using a mechanical friction device.

randonee: form of ski mountaineering gear that allows both cross-country and downhill skiing.

rock chaps: special padded leggings developed to protect Wellman's legs from the rough granite.

roof: an overhanging section of rock that bars upward progress and must sometimes be overcome by spectacular means.

scree: small rock debris found on ledges and at the bottoms of big rock faces.

traverse: to move sideways across a rock face or mountain.

A Note From The Publisher

The focus of WRS Publishing is on contemporary heroes who
have fulfilled impossible dreams. These stories are about individuals who
embody determination and mental toughness and who have overcome
tremendous odds to achieve incredible successes. Americans are yearning for
leadership; we have complained about the negativism of our media for too long.
Let our books turn your attention to role models who can inspire us all.
Call us at 800-299-3366 for questions or suggestions.

W. R. Spence, M.D.
Publisher

Watch for these other titles

Blind Courage
By Bill Irwin and David McCasland
Bill Irwin, with his guide dog Orient, became the only blind
person to thru-hike the 2,100-mile Appalachian Trail.

Young At Heart
By Frederick Lewis and Dick Johnson
The story of Johnny Kelley, Boston's 84-year-old marathon man.

Passing The Baton
By Richard Traum and Michael Celizic
The story of the Achilles Track Club, founded by Traum for disabled runners worldwide.

December Champions
By Bob Darden
Profiles of a wide variety of athletes over age 75 who are still enduring and improving.

I'm Not Dead Yet
By Randy Bird and Ron Westmoreland
Randy Bird survived a disabling accident and is currently the only paraplegic
professional rodeo competitor.

Suicide Is Not Painless
By Harold Elliott and Brad Bailey
The experiences of a police department chaplain, in responding to over 200 suicide cases.

Springtime Is Coming
By Millicent Collinsworth and Jan Winebrenner
Actress Collinsworth's story of her troubled childhood and the accident that
blinded her, yet set her free.

New Horizons
By Harry Cordellos and Janet Wells
Autobiography of Harry Cordellos, often called the world's greatest blind athlete.

Athletes vs. Cancer
By Robert Brody
Profiles outstanding athletes who have survived cancer, and examines the
advantages of the athlete's personality in this respect.

WRS
PUBLISHING

A Division of WRS Group, Inc.
Waco, Texas

"Hey, Tom," asked Corbett, "doesn't David Letterman work in this building?"

Brokaw said yes, then disappeared. He returned a few minutes later and told us to follow him. We rode the elevator up a few floors, went down a couple of hallways and knocked on a door. It opened, and there was the *Late Night* host in shorts and a New York Mets baseball cap. He flashed that familiar gap-toothed smile and invited us inside.

We couldn't help noticing that the ceiling above Letterman's desk had close to five hundred pencils stuck in it. Apparently he flips them up when he's looking for inspiration on a comedy routine, and they stick in the soft ceiling tiles. It looked like a pin cushion.

"You know, you guys are crazy," Letterman told us. "I would never try anything like what you did."

We sat down and he turned to Corbett.

"Aren't you the one who had some problems with your family? How is all that working out?"

Letterman was gracious, earnest and warm, a far cry from the cynical, smart-aleck talk show host he becomes when the cameras are rolling. Corbett asked him for an autograph and he wrote a pleasant little note wishing Mike good luck with his family. As we got up to leave, Letterman invited us to watch the taping of his show later that day.

Brokaw and his staff met us in the NBC commissary for lunch. Craig White and some of the other cameramen were there, and we all had a great time swapping behind-the-scenes stories from the climb. Brokaw loves the mountains and told us about some of his own adventures. I got the impression that he yearned to climb more, but that the top brass at NBC were nervous at the prospect of their star anchorman dangling from his fingertips on some windswept rock face.

Corbett and I watched the Letterman show from the green room, which is where all the guests wait before they go out on stage. Sitting in one corner was Maria Shriver, the *NBC News* anchorwoman. On another couch was actress Andie McDowell, who was there to plug her movie *sex, lies and videoptape*. Also in the room were the Staples Singers. When they heard who we were, Mavis Staples came over and gave me a big old hug and a kiss. I thought she was going to cry.

It would have been fun to go on the air ourselves, but it never happened. These shows are planned weeks in advance, and while they might make room for an unexpected drop-in like Bill Murray, we weren't quite on that level.

Mike Corbett:

When we returned to Yosemite, I went back to my old job of swabbing the floors at the medical clinic for five dollars an hour. Without a doubt, I was the world's most famous janitor.

The rewards from the climb kept rolling in. In September I got a surprise phone call from a figure out of Yosemite's past. It took me a moment to realize whose high-pitched, folksy voice was at the other end.

It was Warren Harding, a living legend to all big-wall climbers and my all-time personal hero. A hard-drinking, tough-as-nails maverick, Harding had been the first man to climb El Capitan. His bold 1958 ascent had been accomplished without camming devices, Portaledges, sticky-soled shoes or any of the other gear we take for granted today. What he had, though, was plenty of boldness and determination. The story of how he stayed up through the last night drilling bolts on the final headwall of the climb is still told around climbers' campfires. In 1970, on his second ascent of El Capitan, by the route called the "Wall of the Early Morning Light," he and his partner spent twenty-seven days straight on the rock—a record that still stands. In its day, the climb attracted as much media hoopla as Mark's and mine had. No doubt about it—I was talking to a living piece of Yosemite history.

"Mike, I followed your climb on TV, and I think what

you did was fantastic," Harding said over the crackly phone line from his home in Utah. "What do you think about you and me doing El Cap together?"

This was too good to be true—imagine if Willie Mays called you to say he wanted to play center field for your softball team I did some quick calculations in my head, and figured out that Harding must be sixty-five years old. He would be the oldest person ever to climb El Capitan—by a considerable margin.

"Great, Warren," I said without reservation. "Come on out here and we'll do it."

"Well, it's not that easy," Harding said. "I'm a little overweight and I'll have to get in shape. I can tell you that if I do come out I will be in the best shape possible."

I knew Harding was a long way from being in fighting shape. But after climbing El Capitan with Mark, I was so confident I knew we could pull it off. I felt honored that Warren had such confidence in me.

We did the climb in November, to coincide with the thirty-first anniversary of Warren's first ascent. My old high-school buddy, Steve Bosque, an excellent big-wall climber in his own right, came along. Warren showed up with a little potbelly, but his mind was in mid-season form. He was as tough and ornery as ever. That's what mattered.

We spent seven days retracing Warren's 1958 route. Every night he'd pour himself a cup of brandy and fill our ears with stories of the old days in Yosemite. He said all of the headwalls and ledges on El Capitan looked so much smaller than he'd remembered. I guess it's like going back to visit the house you lived in when you were a little kid. It always seems tinier than you'd remembered.

The climb went off without a hitch, and it remains one of my fondest memories. It was certainly thrilling to meet the president, but for me the greatest honor was sharing seven days on El Capitan with the man who started it all.

Not long after that, Gwen broke the news that she was leaving Yosemite to study nursing in Ohio. It was the end *for our relationship. Living in Yosemite and hanging out with a climbing bum just wasn't what she envisioned for herself. Gwen's leaving devastated me for a while. To find consolation, I did the only thing I knew. I grabbed a rope and headed for the warm granite walls of Yosemite.*

On September 6, as the Oakland Coliseum announcer called out our names, 25,037 people stood on their feet and roared at the top of their lungs. I wheeled my chair out of the Oakland A's dugout, across the infield toward the pitcher's mound. Mike was right beside me.

I was to throw out the first pitch of the game, and I was so jittery I felt as if I had a swarm of bumblebees in my stomach. When I got the invitation I hadn't tossed a baseball since Little League, and I was afraid I'd blow it in front of the huge crowd. Before we left Yosemite, Mike and I had paced off the proper distance and practiced the throw time and time again.

The roar reverberated around inside the ballpark and seemed to grow louder as we reached the pitcher's mound. Ron Hassey, the A's catcher, came out a few steps in front of home plate and got down in his crouch. I was shaking from nervousness. We were supposed to get a verbal cue, but I couldn't hear a thing. Was I supposed to throw it? I looked up at Mike for help.

"I don't know... what do you think I should do?" I said.

"Hey, just throw it," he answered.

I reared back in my chair and uncorked one of the wildest pitches the A's catcher had ever seen. It hit the infield grass halfway to home plate and took a crazy bounce. Amazingly, Hassey was able to stretch out and smother the ball with his mitt. I would have been mortified if it had gotten past him and rolled all the way to the backstop.

Three days later, Mike and I were in Los Angeles to tape an appearance on a game show called the *Third*